BODY IDIOMS AND MORE
For Learners of English

May Pare

First Edition, April 2005
Second Edition (Revised), November 2005
ISBN 0-9773928-0-5
Printed in Thailand by Ruks Printing

Acknowledgments

I owe many thanks to the following people:

To James Oliver for his editorial input. His contribution was so enormous that his name could have appeared on almost every page of this revised edition. I want to thank him for letting me shine.

To Japhet Ward for his editing. He is so good at spotting things that other people missed.

To Roger Nelson for proofreading. I am so grateful to have had someone of his caliber to do the job.

To Melissa Milburn, Gloria Gomez, Bill Kaplan, and a very dear friend Albert, who wishes to remain anonymous, for their valuable editing of the first edition.

To Theresa R. Yaivijit for designing the cover of both editions

To my sister, Waraporn Savetsomphob, for all her support from the very beginning

Also to Larry Pare and Felipe Higuera for their help transferring the manuscript to CD form

Dedication

To my mother, Pranee Durongbhan, who always wondered why I spent so much time on the computer, never really believing that I was actually writing a book!

To my husband, Larry Pare, for his great patience throughout the course of my endeavor

CONTENTS

ABOUT THE BOOK

A while back I asked a few of my Thai friends who had been living in the United States on the average of fifteen years, what it meant if someone had said to them "*You have such a big head! You just let your success go to your head!*" None of them had any idea what I was talking about. I realized then that there was a need for this kind of book.

Mastering idioms (in any language) requires a great deal of listening, studying, practice and usage. As far as English body idioms are concerned, the best approach, at least from my own experience learning English as a second language, is to put them in groups, either groups of the same root, groups that have the same and/or similar meanings, or groups that may look almost the same but are quite different in meanings. Then *compare* and *contrast*. This is a good way to really understand the real meanings of idioms and expressions in question and to be able to use them correctly. I often follow this same approach throughout the book.

Another approach is to compare idioms in English with idioms in the mother tongue. This can be both an interesting exercise in itself and a means of remembering idioms more effectively. I myself have learned a lot of idioms this way.

My main emphasis is on the usage of idioms and expressions, not on grammar. In real life, people don't follow strict grammatical rules when they talk; for example, many often refer to "someone" as "they" and "them" instead of "he/she" and "him/her"; others will use "but" or "and" at the beginning of the sentence. The sample sentences and the explanations given, therefore, do reflect this reality.

This book is not meant to be a definitive authority on the subject and does not attempt to judge what is right or wrong (in terms of the way the native English speakers use their language). The expressions discussed are mostly American English, unless noted. The origins of certain idioms and some personal language observations are also included when relevant or deemed useful.

Most of the idioms and expressions listed are related to the human body; there are a few that allude to certain animals and/or other things. Some are more appropriate to use in most situations whereas others are considered to be slang terms, the use of which has to be watched out for. This is something I often point out throughout the book. There is no need to try to use all of them but you should learn to recognize them and understand their meanings. This will help to improve your receptive skills - your ability to read in English and to understand day-to-day conversation.

I had quite a few American friends do the editing to ensure that the explanations are less one-sided and the language is up to standard. I do, however, accept full responsibility for any errors, all of which are unintentional.

I have really enjoyed writing this book and have learned so much from it. I hope it will benefit the reader.

May Pare

TERMS AND ABBREVIATIONS

adj. adjective

adj. phr. adjectival phrase

adv. adverb

adv. phr. adverbial phrase

allude to make an indirect reference to someone or something

bad language language that is vulgar and may sound offensive to other people

derogatory describes an expression that insults or mocks someone

euphemism the use (or substitution) of word or phrase that is less offensive than another

hyperbolic describes an expression that is exaggerated to make a point

informal used in an informal situation

interj. interjection

n. noun

n. phr. noun phrase

prep. phr. prepositional phrase

sarcasm sneering or mocking a person, situation or thing. It is often used in a humorous or ironical manner. The remark made often means the opposite of what it says.

Or, as my editor, Japhet Ward, puts it:

It's an attempt to produce a clever reply which would be more polite than saying, "that's fairly obvious, stupid!"

saying an often repeated and familiar expression setting forth wisdom or a truth

slang words or phrases that have not been accepted as standard English even in everyday speech

Teen & College describes an expression that is typically used by teenagers and college students

term of address describe an expression that is used to address someone directly

v. verb

v. phr. verb phrase

ARMS

In Their Words:

"Open your arms to change, but don't let go of your values."
The 14th Dalai Lama (1935-)
Tibetan spiritual and temporal leader

"A place to look for a helping hand is at the end of your own arm."
Author Unknown

Arm in arm (adv. phr.): In a friendly way

These people marched arm in arm to the Capitol, supported each other through five long weeks of the strike, beaten and arrested by the police.

When we first came to America, my sister and I used to walk around arm in arm everywhere we went. I noticed that people were often giving us a real funny look. It didn't dawn on me until much later what might have been on their minds to see two girls acting like that!

Usage note: I've seen both *"arm in arm"* and *"arm-in-arm."*

As long as your arm (adj. phr.): Very extensive, remarkably long

The guy is one of Hollywood's best directors. The credits for his work are as long as your arm.

Usage note: At first, I wasn't even sure whether this phrase was listed in the dictionary or not. I decided to include it because I've heard people use it. I found out later that Cambridge Advancd Learner's Dictionary has it.

Cost (someone) an arm and a leg (v. phr.): To be very expensive

Our house may have cost us an arm and a leg, but we're very happy we bought it.

The underdog's upbeat, relaxed style played well on the debate stage. In states like NY and CA, where campaign advertising cost an arm and a leg, debates would provide him with free access to thousands of potential voters.

Origin: The phrase is of American origin. The story often told was that it derived from the 18th century portrait painters charging extra for each arm and leg appearing in the paintings. However, this story has been discredited by some experts in the field, including www.word-detective.com. According to this website, the phrase was probably an outgrowth or an exaggeration of the older expression *"I'd give my right arm"* (also in this section).

Usage notes:

1. A very common expression

   A funny anecdote:

   With the gasoline prices soaring lately in the U.S., a friend of mine told me he happened to see a cartoon with the following description in a newspaper:

   New Prices: Regular-$3.05
   Plus-$ 3.15
   Premium- an arm and a leg

2. Other terms often used, *"cost a (small) fortune", "cost a bundle"*
3. Some people might say, *"pay an arm and a leg (for something)".*
4. Compare: *"pay through the nose"*; see under **NOSE.**

Give /cut off/ one's right arm (v. phr.): To give something of great value

My only regret is that I didn't spend enough time with my mother when she was still alive. I'd give my right arm to have her back with me now.

"I'd give my right arm to be ambidextrous." (This is simply a funny quote.)
Author Unknown

Usage notes:

1. To give a part of your body for something means you want it badly. Since most people are right-handed, the right arm, therefore, is considered more valuable than the left.
2. Used with the conditional "would"
3. See also *"give one's eyetooth"* under**TEETH.**
4. *"One's right arm"* is a chief assistant, especially an indispensable and trusted one; it means the same as *"one's right- hand man"*:

Special thanks to my wife who has been my right arm and who has always believed in me.

Keep someone/something/ at arm's length (v. phr.): To keep a safe distance away from someone/something; avoid being friendly with someone

If you keep her at arm's length, she wouldn't be able to exploit your weaknesses and take advantage of you.

Local clergy keep gay issues at arm's length, preferring to focus on things that bring people together.

Usage notes:

1. The opposite is *"keep/have/ within arm's reach"*:

   Now I have my finance and accounting textbooks within arm's reach of my desk because I know I'm going to have to use them.

2. You can also *"embrace someone (or something) at arm's length"*, meaning that you reluctantly accept someone's help because you know you need it:

   Embracing Clinton at arm's length, Gore formally begins run for President. (N.Y. Times Headline, June17th, 1999)

   China has tried to embrace the Internet at arm's length. Its government even issued a decree warning that the Internet, while important for the economy and science, threatened to usher in pornography and other 'harmful materials' if not well managed.

Shot in the arm (n. phr.): A sudden help; something that renews your energy or spirits

The superstar's return to the NBA after a four-year retirement was a major shot in the arm for his team.

The city's donation will give the symphony the shot in the arm it needs to promote future concerts.

Usage notes:

1. A very common expression
2. Also, *"a lift"* or *"a moral boost"*

Talk someone's arm off (v. phr.): To talk so much so as to exhaust the listener

He talks my arm off every time he sees me.

Usage notes:

1. It's listed in *The American Heritage Dictionary of Idioms* (Ammer, Christine 1997); most people are probably more familiar with *"talk someone's ear off"*.
2. Also, *"talk someone's head/someone's pants/ off"*

The long arm of the law (n. phr.): The law thought of in terms of its power and extent

They fled to Mexico but the long arm of the law soon caught up with them.

Origin: *"To make a long arm"* is an old way of describing extending your regular reach as far as possible.

There was also *"the strong arm of the law"* which was used widely in the 1800's. *"The long arm of the law"* might have been created as a punning alternative to "*the strong arm of the law*" (www.worldwide words.org)

Usage note: The term is often used as a mildly humorous expression:

"Tom, the money got stuck between the cabinets. You're a cop, you think the long arm of the law can get this out for me?"

Twist someone's arm/twist arms (v. phr.): To persuade, to convince

I had to twist her arm a little bit before she agreed to be in our show.

An outspoken former Army Ranger, he has strong conservative opinions and uses his wealth to twist arms in the Congress.

Usage notes:

1. It can be used humorously:

   Waitress: "Would you like more coffee?"
   Customer: "Ok, since you twisted my arm."
   (Or, *"OK, you talked me into it."*)

2. Also as a noun:

She is very adept at mobilizing the residents in the community to give their support to the Boys Club programs. She does her arm-twisting in a nice way.

My dad used to work as an arm-twister, raising campaign funds for his political party.

(With) open arms (n. phr., adv. phr.): (With) great hospitality

After more than 150 rejections, the two gay pastors finally found open arms at the Congregational Church in Michigan.

I'm going to welcome him with open arms and give him every opportunity to do what he wants to do.

Origin: It alludes to the way one would welcome other people – the "arms" are "open" in order to form an embrace. (Rogers, James 1985)

Usage note: Also, *"to welcome an idea with open arms"*.

"Arms" Bonus

A babe in arms (n. phr.): A baby, a child

A glass arm (n. phr.): Baseball term. A pitcher's arm that is highly prone to injury or strain

A golden arm (n. phr.): Slang. A heroin addict. (from shooting the heroin into one's arm)

A good arm (n. phr.): Sports term. The ability to throw a baseball/football well

Usage note: The opposite is *"no arm"*:

He can hit; he has a good glove. But he has no arm.

Arm candy (n. phr.): U.S. Informal. An extremely beautiful person who accompanies a member of the opposite sex to a party or event but is not necessarily romantically involved with that person.

The actress shielded away from playing just 'the girl' roles – the arm candy because she wanted to be taken seriously.

Full moon and empty arms (expression): A saying of the old west that refers to loneliness and a longing for romance

One-armed bandit (n. phr.): A slot machine for gambling operated by pulling a lever on the side

Put the arm on someone (expression): To ask someone for or demand money (Ammer, Christine 1997)

Usage note: Also, *"to put the bite/touch/squeeze/ on someone"*

Short arms, long pockets (expression): Describing someone of a miserly (cheap) disposition – unwilling to reach for their wallet

Strong-armed (adj.): (A method or a type of behavior) that involves using force or threats to make people do what you demand

The police finally had to resort to strong-armed tactics to disperse the civil rights demonstrators.

Usage notes:

1. Also used as a verb:

   The die-hard fans are hoping to strong-arm 20th Century Fox into launching the film at Grauman's Chinese Theater, where the original 1977 film was first screened.

2. Compare: *"heavy-handed"* under **HANDS.**

Strong in the arm and thick in the head (expression): Strong physically but not mentally (not so bright)

ASS

In Their Words:

"I have never seen an ass who talked like a human being, but I have met many human beings who talked like asses."
Heinrich Heine (1797-1856)
German Romantic poet

"A smart man covers his ass; a wise man leaves his pants on."
Author Unknown

Please note: Some people might find certain parts of the language in this section offensive.

This book would not be complete without talking about expressions involving the word "*ass*", which is quite prevalent and important in everyday communication for certain groups of people. Some call them "folk speech intensifiers" since they are used to show defiance, emphasis or command attention. I simply consider them slang expressions.

Since I don't use this kind of language nor do I feel comfortable when I hear it being used, writing about it is quite a tall order for me. Fortunately, there are quite a few informative websites on the subject, some of which I've relied heavily on.

A few points I want to make here. First, this is not going to be a complete list of *"ass"* expressions; I see no use in that, let alone it being beyond my ability. Second, most of the expressions discussed here are American English as I have heard people use. Most are not appropriate for all audiences. Also, for the English language learners, this section is covered just to help you with your receptive skills-so that you will understand what other people say. You can communicate in English just fine without having to use any such words yourself.

Now, back to "*ass*". There are two basic definitions of *"ass"*: a donkey or that part of your anatomy between your lower back and upper legs. Few of the following expressions involve the donkey; others refer to that part of the anatomy.

According to George Fairbanks in his article *Ass Idioms* (www.groupedia.com/node/view), there are two generative formations for "*ass*" expressions:

1. Adjective + *"ass"* to indicate extreme or excessiveness:

   expensive ass car (very expensive car)
   big ass fish (very big fish)
   strong ass medicine (very strong medicine)
   mean ass dog (very mean dog)
   long ass trip (very long trip)

2. Verb + "*your ass off*" to emphasize, as in "*work your ass off*"' or *"laugh your ass off*"'.

   Usage note: You can always use more polite words in this sense, e.g. *"work your butt off"* (or "*work like a dog"* considered OK in English, but may be not in some other languages), and *"laugh your head off"*.

The following are some selected "*ass*" expressions:

A kick in the ass (n. phr.): Has several meanings:

1. Bad luck or an unfortunate setback, a surprising and dampening rebuff

   His money was stolen while on the trip; it was a kick in the ass especially when he couldn't go on a shopping spree like he had planned to.

   It was a kick in the ass when she turned me down like that.

2. A strong stimulus

   If the new campaign ad doesn't get a kick in the ass, we're dead meat.

   He needs a kick in the ass to get going; he's not a self-starter.

   Usage note: I was told that the term can also be used to mean "funny":

   That's a real kick in the ass! ha! ha! ha!

A pain in the ass (n. phr.): An annoying or troublesome person or thing

I can't stand that guy. He's a real pain in the ass.

Freeway traffic at this time of day is a pain in the ass.

Usage note: Use *"a pain in the neck/butt"* to avoid being offensive.

Bet your (sweet) ass (v. phr.): To assert that something is true; be absolutely sure of something

Don't worry; I'll be there on time. You can bet your ass on it. (You can count on it.)

I'd bet my ass he knew it all this time.

Usage note: More polite version: *"you can bet your bottom dollar/shirt/boots/life".*

Bust (your) ass (v. phr.): To make your best effort, work hard

I've got to bust ass to get this term paper done by Monday.

Usage note: There are many other different ways to express the idea of making one's best effort, for example *"bust one's tail/ butt", "break one's neck"*

Can't find his/her/ ass (with both hands) (expression): He's/she's exceptionally stupid

I wouldn't assign that project to him. He can't even find his ass.

Chew someone's ass (out) (v. phr.): To scold /reprimand someone severely

Dad would chew your ass for taking the car without permission.

The boss chewed her ass out for not being focused enough.

Origin: The term originated in the army, probably referred to some drill sergeant who was chewing on a soldier like a dog chewing on someone.

Usage note: Also, *"to get one's ass chewed"*:

Man! Someone's really gonna get their ass chewed over this one.

Cover your ass (v. phr.): To attempt to escape blame. Also known as CYA

The reporter tried to cover his ass by warning his editor there might be complaints from a certain group of readers about the article he wrote.

The keys to CYA around the workplace are to anticipate trouble, inform the bosses and follow their advice.

Usage note: I would think one really has to be familiar with this kind of language to know what the CYA means.

Don't know your ass from a hole in the ground (expression): You are clueless and have no common sense.

What kind of ignorant answer is that? This moron doesn't know his ass from a hole in the ground.

Usage note: Also, *"don't know your ass from your elbow"*

Drag ass (v. phr.): To go slowly because you've got no energy; be extremely exhausted you can't even move

I was dragging ass after that uphill bike ride.

When we were through we were really dragging ass.

Get off your ass (v. phr.): To get up and do something

Get a life, get off your ass and use your brains!

People on welfare make me mad. Why don't they get off their asses and find a job?

Usage note: Variant: *"get off your butt/ get off your tail"*

Get your ass in gear (v. phr.): To get moving, to get started

After holidays, I'll get my ass in gear and paint the house.

I just can't seem to get my ass in gear today.

Usage note: The less offensive term would be *"get your rear in gear"*.

Half-assed (adj. phr.; adv. phr.): Not well planned or executed; done poorly or incompletely; not well planned or executed

The painter did such a half-assed job I had to redo the whole house again myself.

"If you don't like your job, you don't strike. You just go in everyday and do it really half-assed. That's the American way."
Homer Simpson (A TV cartoon character)

Origin: According to www.rootsweb.com/~genepool/meanings.htm, this term evolved from 'half-adz'-an axe like tool with a curved blade used for shaping wood. If one was wealthy and paid top money for a new fireplace, the mantle would be shaped, using an adz, in the front as well as the back side, which was not visible. However, if one was not wealthy or wanted to save money, one could have only the front visible part of the mantle shaped, a 'half-adz' job.

Have/get/ your ass in a sling (expression): To be in trouble

The candidate's desire to be all things to all people is going to get his ass in a sling if he's not careful.

I just started a new job and I will show up on time so I don't get my ass in a sling.

Haul ass (v. phr.): To hurry up, to move faster

He was late so I called him up and told him to haul ass.

Kick ass (and take names) (v. phr.): To assert one's supremacy or authority with distinct force; to take forceful or hard measures to achieve an objective; to prove one is best

The auditor started to kick ass the minute he walked in our office.

I just cover a lot of territory and I do it aggressively and I do it fairly. I just kick ass. That's what they pay me to do.

Yes, it's now an established fact that they suck and we kick ass. I mean, we went on a 21-2 run at the start of the second half.

This band kicks ass! This is the only band I would recommend.

Usage notes:

1. Also used as an adj.:

   Get ready for a kick ass show! (impressive, cool)

   You're a kick ass dude!

2. It's better to use *"kick butt and take names"*.

Kick some ass/get your ass kicked (v. phr.): To beat the opposition/ to be beaten badly

"We kicked a little ass last night."
George H.W. Bush (1924-)
The 41st U.S. President (1989-1993)

We got our asses totally kicked in the second half. It sucks.

Kiss my ass! (expression): Screw you!

I don't even care. If the boss doesn't like it, he can kiss my ass!

Kiss someone's ass (v. phr.): To act submissively in order to gain favor, to flatter

Linda is good at kissing the boss' ass. I could never do it like she does.

Usage notes:

1. I'd simply say, *"kiss up to someone"*.
2. Also, *"to brownnose"*; see under **NOSE**

Make an ass of yourself (v. phr.): To behave stupidly and look ridiculous, embarrass yourself

John made an ass of himself after only a few beers.

Usage note: Polite version: *"make a fool of yourself"*.

Sit around on your ass (v. phr.): To be idle, lazy, aimless

Ever since he lost his job, he's been sitting around on his ass collecting unemployment money.

Usage note: If you don't want to sound that offensive, use *"sit around on your butt/sit around on your tail"* instead.

Talk out of your ass (v. phr.): To not know what you are talking about

The guy thinks he knows a lot about stocks and investment, but he's mostly talking out of his ass.

Usage note: A more severe way of saying is *"he has his head up his ass"*; this term is derogatory.

Throw someone out on his/her/ ass (v. phr.): To eject someone, especially violently

I just raised a little question and they threw me out on my ass.

Usage note: Use *"throw someone out on his/her/ ear"* in polite company.

Up to your ass (in alligators/in rattlesnakes) (expression): To have a lot of, in the sense of being overwhelmed, oversupplied

I hope the teacher doesn't give us another quiz today. We've had quizzes up to our ass already.

Usage note: Other alternatives:
Up to your eyeballs/ eyebrows
Up to your ears
Up to your neck/up to here (with hand signal to the neck area)

Your ass is on the line. (expression): You are responsible for an action or decision, be accountable for an error or failure

I decided to send the packages express mail because my ass is on the line if they arrive late.

Usage note: I'd just say *"my job (my welfare, reputation, etc.) is on the line."*

"Ass" Bonus

A dumb ass (n. phr.): An idiot

I'm not going to talk to that dumb ass again!

Usage note: Also, *"a stupid ass", "a jackass"*

A piece of ass (n. phr.): Someone who is attractive and obviously an object of one's sexual attention

Usage note: *"To get a piece of ass"* means to have sex.

A smart ass/a wise ass (n. phr.): A person who tries to be witty.

"Can you pass me the sugar?"
"Yes."
"Don't be such a smart ass! Just pass me the sugar.

"Give a jackass an education and you get a smart ass."
Author Unknown

Usage note: Also used as an adjective:

I don't want to talk to that guy. He always tries to make smart ass remarks.

An ass (n): An unpleasant person

Buzz off, you silly ass!

He was just being an ass.

Usage note: The British word is *"an arse"*- basically it means the same as *"ass"* but is much ruder.

An asshole (n.): An unpleasant person

What an asshole!

"If assholes had wings, this place would be an airport!"
Author Unknown

Usage note: To me, *"an ass"* and *"an asshole"* mean roughly the same, with the latter sounding cruder. I have a friend who, when really mad or annoyed with someone, would simply use the word *"an ass"* to describe the person. She said it doesn't sound as bad. (i.e. it doesn't sound like she was really cursing.)

Suck ass (v. phr.): To be no good

This band sucks ass.

Usage note: Variant of *"to suck"*, another popular slang term

BACK

In Their Words:

"If you cannot lift the load off another's back, do not walk away. Try to lighten it."
Frank Tyger

"The only really decent thing to do behind a person's back is pat it."
Author Unknown

A backbreaker (n): A very hard task that can cause backaches

Lifting that 200-pound-flat grill was a real backbreaker even for two strong men.

Usage notes:
1. See also *"break your back"* in this section.
2. We English learners have often been taught that a word that ends with "*-er*" indicates "a person/a doer". It's not always true, though, as shown in this phrase.

A backslapper (n): Someone who is overly friendly and outgoing

Some stand-up comedians often cast President Bush as a frat-boy backslapper who never has read a book.

He is friendly, and sometimes he can be a bit of a backslapper.

Usage notes:
1. The term has a connotation of being 'insincere'.
2. See also "*a glad-hander*" under **HANDS.**

A monkey on your back (expression): Has two meanings:
1. Slang term for drug addiction

She has had a monkey on her back for several years now.

There's no question I feel much better mentally. Getting that monkey off my back really does enhance my self-esteem.

2. A persistent or annoying problem or burden

That business deal turned out to be a monkey on our back.

Origin: The term probably came from an old Sinbad story about a tormenting ape-like creature that mounts a man's shoulders and won't get off. (www.etymonline.com)

Usage note: Compare: *"an albatross around your neck"*; see under **NECK**.

Be on someone's back (v. phr.): To make constant demands; be a bother or annoyance

The coach has been on my back about missing the game last week.

Most kids don't like it when their parents are on their backs about cleaning their rooms.

Behind someone's back (prep. phr.): Without someone's knowledge

I wouldn't trust her if I were you. She acts friendly but she always goes behind someone's back.

We used to talk normally, but in the last few years, he'd say one thing to my face and another behind my back.

"Your best friends are those who speak well of you behind your back."
Sam Ewing (1920-2001)
American writer, humorist

Usage note: The opposite is "*to someone's face*".

Bend over backward (v. phr.): To go out of your way, to try harder to accommodate someone than you really have to

She's so ungrateful; and after I bent over backward to help her!

The boss bent over backward trying to be fair.

"Bend over backward for the customer. Don't bend forward."
Author Unknown

Break your back (v. phr.): To work very hard, use all your efforts

I've been breaking my back over this project the past few weeks.

Usage note: Compare: *"break your neck"* under **NECK.**

Break someone's back (v. phr.): To overpower, overcome

We got the ball back and made a couple of plays. The play that really broke our backs was that second interception.

Usage note: Also, *" to break the back of":*

Our defense strategy really broke the back of the opposing team.

This term can also mean "to get through the most part, the hardest or the worst part of something":

We're over halfway there; we've broken the back of this trip.

It's listed in the Cambridge Advanced Learner's Dictionary as a British expression.

Flat on your back (expression): To be sick in bed; be in a helpless situation

The flu put my mother flat on her back for over a week.

I wish I could help you out, but paying all these bills has really put me flat on my back.

Usage note: Variant: *"to be in bad shape"*

Get off someone's back/get off someone's case (v. phr.): To stop finding faults or criticizing someone

I wish he'd get off my back and stop asking me when I'm going to look for another job.

Usage notes:

1. Also used as an order
2. The opposite is "*to be on someone's back/case.*"
3. There is also an expression *"to get someone off one's back"*

Get your back up /get your dander up (v. phr.): To become angry or make someone angry, especially in a way to cause one to resist; to lose one's temper or become aroused to some form of action

It really gets her back up when cars tailgate her on the freeway.

The boxer suddenly got his dander up and started charging his opponent with a vengeance.

Don't get your dander up! (Don't get mad!)

Origin: As "back", the expression most likely came from the cat's habit of arching its back when angry.
"*Dander*" is an old word meaning "*anger*"; it may have come from the Dutch "*donder*" meaning "*thunder*".

Give the shirt off your back (expression): To give anything and everything you have

He's the kind of person who'd give the shirt off his back to help you.

Got your back (expression): We are in this together; whatever comes, I am with you.

Don't worry, I got your back. I'll help you out anytime.

By purchasing this CD, you're making a donation to Operation Military Pride. This is your opportunity to say to our troops...I've got your back.

Have your back (up) against the wall/your back to the wall/your back is against the wall. (expression): To be in a desperate situation or to be under heavy attack

The coach had his back against the wall. Either his team had to win next time or he could be fired.

Our home team is famous for squandering big leads. They're a team with their backs to the wall with a 20-point lead.

Bankruptcy is not the best choice, although it can be seen as a way out for families who feel their backs are against the wall.

Pat someone on the back (v. phr.): To praise or congratulate

I'd love to shake your hand and pat you on the back for a job well done.

Usage notes:

1. Also used as a noun:

   The award is a pat on the back, saying you are doing the right thing and keep going at it.

2. I've also seen *"pat oneself on the back"*.

Put your back into something (v. phr.): To make a strenuous effort to do something

You could get rid of all the weeds and dig this plot in one afternoon if you really put your back into it.

If you put your back into that assignment, you'll soon be done.

Origin: It alludes to physical labor involving the strength of one's back (Ammer, Christine 1997).

Scratch someone's back (v. phr.): To do someone a favor

If I scratch her back this time, maybe one day she'll scratch mine.

Usage note: Often used in the expression *"you scratch my back, I'll scratch yours"*, discussed later in this section

Stab someone in the back (v. phr.): To harm someone by treachery or betrayal of trust

He stabbed me in the back by telling lies about me to other people.

This is a man who came back from Vietnam to stab not only his country but also his comrades-in-arms in the back.

Usage notes:
1. The person who does it is *"a backstabber*".
2. Also used as a noun: *"a stab in the back"*

The world on your back (expression): To be very worried by many different problems

He seemed so depressed, blue with the world on his back.

Usage note: Same idea as *"(carry) the world on your shoulders"*; see under **SHOULDERS.**

Turn your back on someone/something (v. phr.): To refuse to help someone, ignore someone or something, stop being involved in something

I needed your help so badly, but you just turned your back on me.

The guy is a loudmouth jerk who turned his back on his country and turned his back on his faith.

America cannot afford to turn its back on the problem of terrorism in the Middle East.

Usage note: Also, *"to turn away from something"*

Watch your back (v. phr.): To be careful of the people around you, making sure they don't do anything to harm you.

You've got to watch your back more at work. Do you realize how many people would love to have your job?

You scratch my back and I'll scratch yours. (expression): You do a favor for me and I'll do a favor for you.

"Can you take me to the airport tomorrow? I'm going to Thailand for a few weeks."
"OK, if you promise you'll bring me back a few things from there."
"Sure, you scratch my back and I'll scratch yours."

"Back" Bonus

Backside (n.): Informal. The part of the body that you sit on

Usage note: A polite way of describing your posterior

(Like) water off a duck's back (expression): Criticisms or warnings that have no apparent effect on the person

The scathing reviews rolled off the actor like water off a duck's back.

Origin: It alludes to the fact that duck feathers shed water.

Piggyback (adj., adv.): Carried atop your shoulders or back

"Daddy, give me a piggyback ride, please!" said the little boy.

She carried her son piggyback while holding her purse in her arm.

That's the straw that broke the camel's back. (saying): There's a limit to everyone's endurance; everyone has his/her breaking point.

My old boss constantly used vulgar language. When he said 'God damn it!...' to me right in front of everybody, that was the straw that broke the camel's back. I quit the next day.

Usage note: Or, *"that was the last straw."*

BELLY

In Their Words:

"It is any day better to stand erect with a broken and bandaged head than to crawl on one's belly, in order to save one's head."
Mohandas Gandhi (1869-1948)
Indian leader

"Fish die belly upward, and rise to the surface. It's their way of falling."
Andre Gide (1869-1951)
French critic, essayist, novelist

"Belly" and "abdomen" are often used to mean more or less the same thing. "Abdomen" is the anatomical name; "belly" is the more familiar name and can refer to the visible front outer part, the stomach. It is also called "the tummy", especially by kids.

(A) fire in your belly (expression): Enthusiasm/driving force/ passion, for what you are doing

Enthusiasm is a powerful force. Whatever you do, do it with all your might. Let your goal put a fire in your belly. Live your life with passion.

Some small business owners gain fire in their bellies by joining a business's support group.

"I never could stand losing. Second place doesn't interest me. I had a fire in my belly."
Ty Cobb (1886-1961)
American baseball player

Bellyache (v.): To whine, complain, especially to do so habitually

Quit bellyaching about the referee! Just do the best you can.

You are constantly bellyaching that there's nothing good on TV.

Origin: It may allude to the idea that someone afflicted with a bellyache might do a lot of complaining.

Go/turn/ belly up (v. phr.): To die, go bankrupt; collapse

I wonder why the cat turned belly up all of a sudden.

With many companies continuing to downsize, merge or go belly up, how come the President repeatedly talks about low unemployment and new jobs?

My computer turned belly up right in the middle of my term paper.

Usage notes:

1. Also, *"to go under"*:

   If the magazine had attracted the attention of many people, it would not have gone under.

2. A completely different meaning of *"belly up"* is found in the expression *"belly up to the bar"* ("sit close to the bar, find a chair at the bar"):

   After work, the cops could always be found belly up to the bar.

3. I've seen it used both ways: *"belly up"* and *"belly-up"*.

Not have the belly for something (expression): Not up to the challenge

The bigger boy wanted to fight my little brother but my brother didn't have the belly for it.

Usage notes:

1. Same as *"not have the stomach for something"*; but more graphic and picturesque
2. Also, *"not have the guts for something"*

"Belly" Bonus

A beer belly (n. phr.): A fat stomach you get from drinking too much beer over a period of time

A belly button (n. phr.): A small hollow in the center of the front of the stomach

A belly flop (n. phr.): A dive in which the stomach hits the surface of the water first; it's usually very painful.

Usage note: Also used as a verb *"to belly flop"*

A belly laugh (n. phr.): A deep, loud laugh as if it comes from the belly

Thanks, I really need a good belly laugh. It's good for the soul.

A potbelly (n. phr.): A fat stomach, like a big round pot

Belly of the beast (expression): The core, the nitty gritty

The trip to Southeast Asia took the President deep into the belly of the terrorism beast.

Have a belly (v. phr.): To be fat around your stomach

I'm not exactly overweight but I do have a belly.

Usage notes:

1. As an English learner myself, I'm sometimes at a loss at expressing something as simple as this. I'm sure it can happen to other learners as well. That's why I include this phrase here.
2. Also, *"to lose your belly"* or *"to lose your gut/ a gut"*

He's lower than a snake's belly. (expression): He's not very honest.

Usage note: It's hyperbolic - an exaggeration to make a point.

Yellow belly (n. phr.): A coward; the term is often heard in western movies.

Usage note: Also as an adjective: *He's such a yellow-bellied coward, always running away from a fight.*

BLOOD

In Their Words:

"Ambition breaks the ties of blood and forgets the obligations of gratitude."
Sallust (86 BC-34 BC)
Roman historian

"There are no true friends in politics. We are all sharks circling, and waiting, for traces of blood to appear in the water."
Alan Clark (1952-)
British politician

Some blood idioms point to group identity; others indicate our temperament..

(Almost) burst a blood vessel (expression): To become angry

She almost burst a blood vessel when I told her what happened.

He's going to burst a blood vessel if he doesn't get to talk to the boss soon about the problem.

Usage note: Often used humorously

Be after someone's blood/be out for someone's blood (v. phr.): To be very angry with someone and threaten to harm or punish him/her

Try to stay out of her way for now. She's really after your blood.

Be (only) flesh and blood (expression): To have normal human needs and limits

What's wrong with looking at pretty girls? I'm only flesh and blood.

Bad blood (n. phr.): Longstanding resentment due to past problems, either between two people or between the people on two sides of an issue

There has been bad blood between them since their business deals went astray years ago.

Origin: Blood was once considered the seat of the emotions, and bad blood meant anger. (Rogers, James 1985)

Blood is thicker than water. (saying): Family ties are stronger bonds than other relationships.

Whenever his best friend and his brother got into a fight, he usually took his brother's side. No wonder they say that blood is thicker than water.

Blood will tell. (expression): One's true nature eventually will always show or prevail; what is inherited cannot be hidden - it will come to the surface sooner or later.

Underlying Harry Potter's world is the 'ancien regime' message that "blood will tell" – Harry is the hidden prince, right down to his effortless grace at games and his enormous powers.

Bloody but unbowed (adj. phr.): Wounded in body or spirit but not defeated or deterred by the circumstances

"Our heads are bloody but unbowed", runs a popular student slogan against their government's suppression of educational freedoms.

They continued to fight on, bloody but unbowed.

Origin: The phrase came from a popular poem called "*Invictus*" ("Unconquered"), written by William Ernest Henley (1849-1903). In the poem, the speaker proclaims his strength in the face of adversity:

My head is bloody but unbowed
I am the master of my fate
I am the captain of my soul.

Blue blood (n phr.): Member of high society, someone of noble birth

Both Bush and Kerry are, by American standards, blue bloods with roots in old-money aristocracy.

Origin: Blood veins seen through fair skin usually look blue. Some Spanish people took pride in their fair skin, which indicated that they possessed no Moorish blood. They therefore came to be referred to as "*sangre azul*" (a Spanish term for "*blue blood*"), to differentiate them from the Moors, or those Spaniards who had intermarried with the Moors. The term caught on in Britain in the early 19th century and probably arrived in America shortly thereafter.

Draw blood (v. phr.): To injure someone physically or emotionally

He drew blood on his first hit.

I have a feeling her caustic remarks were intended to draw blood.

Origin: The term alludes to drawing blood for diagnostic purposes.

Draw first blood (v. phr.): To gain the first point or advantage in a contest

The Lakers drew first blood in the series, winning game one 96- 78.

The champ drew first blood in the boxing match but eventually was defeated by his opponent.

Flesh and blood (n. phr.): See under **Flesh**.

Have (someone's) blood on your hand (expression): To be responsible for someone's death

Some people strongly believe that this movie has been used as a recruitment film by terrorist groups and many of its lies have motivated some of the very people shooting at our troops right now. Anyone who paid to see this movie, therefore, practically has blood on their hands.

In cold blood (adv. phr.): Without compassion or mercy, usually associated with ruthless murder

The man was convicted of murdering his own wife in cold blood.

Usage note: Also used as an adj. *"a cold-blooded murder"*

In one's blood (expression): A trait or talent that one seems to have naturally

He has baseball in his blood. He's a star baseball player at his high school.

The writer was born with ink in his blood.

Usage note: It could be a talent that is present in the person's family; hence, the expression "*run in the family*" or "*run in the blood*". (I've also heard "*run in one's veins*".)

Make your blood boil (v. phr.): To make you very angry

Seeing how he mistreated his own mother really made my blood boil.

It made my blood boil when I found out that my co-worker took all the credit for the work I had done.

Usage note: Also, "*burn you up*", "*have steam coming out of your ears*", "*blow off some steam*", "*be steamed-up*" and "*be steaming mad*"

Make your blood curdle/curdle your blood (v. phr.): To fill you with great fear

Once in a very great while this owl gives a shriek to make one's blood curdle.

The stories that were told of the inhuman tortures these recruits were subjected to were enough to make one's blood curdle.

Usage notes:

1. Also used as an adj., "*blood-curdling*" (scream, story, etc.)
2. Roughly, the same idea as "*to make your blood run cold*" (see the next expression); people often use them interchangeably.

Make your blood run cold (v. phr.): To be chilled from fright or horror

The scene of that freeway big crash made my blood run cold.

The way she talked about the tragedy made one's blood run cold.

Usage note: Also, "*blood freezes*" and "*blood turns to ice*"; they both indicate an extreme degree of fright.

Out for blood (adj. phr.): Trying to defeat, seeking revenge

The Lakers were out for blood tonight because they lost big time last night.

The defense attorney claimed that the police department was out for blood when it tried to charge his client with capital punishment.

Scream bloody murder (v. phr.): Informal. To angrily protest as strongly and loudly as one possibly can

Homeowners screamed bloody murder when they learned that the county raised property taxes twice in the same year.

The girl screamed bloody murder when her brother took away her teddy bear.

Smell blood (in the water) (v. phr.): To sense victory, be aware of an opponent's weakness

Many people think that he entered the Senate race now because he smelled blood in the water.

Bankruptcy lawyers smell blood. They expect their business to boom because they think there will be a significant surge in corporate bankruptcy in the coming months.

Origin: The phrase alludes to sharks and their well-developed sense of smell. They are capable of recognizing even very small concentrations of scents, such as blood of their victims, in their immediate environment.

Sporting blood (n. phr.): Willingness to take risks

The girl's sporting blood tempted her to try to ride the wild horse.

Usage note: Rarely used in the U.S.; possibly a British expression

Sweat blood (over something) (v. phr.): To do agonizing physical work or worry agonizingly over a situation

He always believed in the documentary project and he sweat blood over

filming it.

The car engine stopped right in the middle of the freeway. I sweat blood as I put on emergency signal and tried to call 911 on my cell phone.

Origin: The term refers to the agony of Jesus on the Mount of Olives.

Too rich for my blood (expression): Something or some involvement is more expensive or more risky than I can afford.

Most everything I found listed in their catalogue was too rich for my blood.

Usage note: You hear it often in poker games when the betting gets too high to prudently stay in the game.

You can't get blood out of a stone/a turnip. (expression): It's useless to try to get something or to get help from some people or sources.

The bill collector simply couldn't get her to pay because she had no money. You just can't get blood out of a stone.

Don't expect to get any help from him. It's like getting blood out of a stone.

Usage note: I've also heard a variant of this expression:

You could get blood out of a stone before you got the money from him!

Your blood is up. (expression): You are excited or angry, ready to fight.

He's usually friendly, but he can be dangerous when his blood is up.

Usage note: I've also heard *"one's blood pressure is up/is rising."*

"Blood" Bonus

A bloodbath (n.): Any large- scale destruction of people or animals, especially in situations of war

He was raised to power by the dictator for the specific purpose of setting up a bloodbath.

A blood brother (n. phr.): Either an actual birth brother or two friends who are extremely close (possibly one vowing to treat another as his own brother in an arranged ceremony)

Blood and guts (adj. phr.): Marked by great zeal or violence; giving it all one has inside oneself

The General gave a blood and guts speech to get his men ready for battle.

Blood and thunder (n. phr., adj. phr.): The violence and bloodshed of stories with the concentration on fast action rather than understanding of characters.

Most westerns usually have lots of blood and thunder.

I never can stand watching blood-and-thunder movies.

Blood money (n. phr.): Money paid to the victim's family; or money earned in a way that caused someone's blood to be shed

Bloodshot (adj.): Red and irritated

Blood sports (n. phr.): Sports that involve animals being killed or hurt to excite the people watching or taking part

Bloodsuckers (n.): People who take as much money as they can from others, for example, moneylenders or pimps

Bloody (adj., adv.): British slang. Very, extremely

She must think I'm a bloody fool.

He's done bloody good to make it to the finals.

Usage note: Often used to emphasize in a slightly rude way

Bloody-minded (adj.): British. Purposely being irritating or obstructive 'for the sake of it'

I find your attitude bloody-minded and immature.

Blood, sweat and tears (expression): Exertion of great effort to achieve a goal

Though I've poured my blood, sweat and tears into this project, I don't think it's up to the standards I've set for myself.

Usage note: Whereas *"heart and soul"* emphasizes the passion, *"blood, sweat and tears,"* emphasizes both the physical effort and the passion.

New/fresh/ blood (n. phr.): New people in an organization; someone with new ideas

Since the post-election Cabinet shuffle is inevitable, wouldn't it be a good time to bring in some new blood?

Shed blood (v. phr.): To take life, especially with violence

"A man who is good enough to shed his blood for the country is good enough to be given a square deal afterwards."

Theodore Roosevelt (1858-1919)
The 26th U.S. President (1901-1909)

Usage note: Also used as a noun: *"a bloodshed"*

Young blood (n. phr.): Young people with energy and enthusiasm

Young blood has infused new life into the marketing staff.

BONES

In Their Words:

"Success depends on your backbone, not your wishbone."
Author Unknown

"Man is an animal that makes bargains; no other animal does this—no dog exchanges bones with another."
Adam Smith (1723-1790)
Scottish economist

Backbone, to have the (v. phr.): To have courage, integrity, strength of character

He seems like a good guy, but I don't believe he has much of a backbone.

You have to ask yourself which candidate has the vision, the will power and the backbone to best protect your family.

Usage note: Fairly common

Barebones (adj., n.): Only the necessary things; basic elements

Sound Records is a barebones operation. Its office – a spare bedroom – contains a computer and a fax machine. Its main assets – some 500 compact discs – are in boxes under the kitchen table.

This is someone who doesn't want to fuss; a totally no frills, barebones guy.

I'll outline the barebones of the proposal first, and will get into details later.

Usage note: Always with the "–s" ending

Bone dry (adj. phr.): Very dry, as dry as an old bone

After that long discussion, my throat is bone dry. Can I please have a glass of water?

Someone must have drained the pool. It looks so *<u>bone dry.</u>*

The fish was cooked too long and looked *<u>bone dry.</u>*

Bone of contention (n. phr.): An issue that causes tension and arguments, a reason for quarrels or subject for a fight

The main <u>bone of contention</u> at the company's general meeting was the amount of employees' Christmas bonus that was cut down last year.

Origin: The term alludes to the idea that a meaty bone thrown to a group of dogs will cause intense rivalry and dispute.

Bone up on (v. phr.): To try to learn a lot about something in a short time

Ann <u>boned up on</u> her Spanish to be ready for her trip to Mexico.

Usage note: Also, "to brush up on", but "bone up on" seems more informal.

Close to the bone/near the bone (adj. phr.): Something that may be offensive because it's too vulgar, too personal or too painful

This topic is <u>too close to the bone</u> to be discussed in front of the children.

The lyrics kind of struck me as a little <u>too close to the bone</u> –like depressing or distressing somehow.

Usage note: Also, *"near the knuckle"* under **KNUCKLES.**

Don't let it rattle your bones! (old expression): Don't let it bother you!

Come on; <u>don't let it rattle your bones!</u> It's not worth it.

Usage note: Variants: *"don't let it get to you!" "don't let it keep you down!", " take it easy!*

Feel/know/ (it) in your bones (expression): To feel sure, to have a premonition or intuition about something

These are characters that stay with you; the kind of people you know in your bones.

Things are going to be better. I can feel it in my bones.

Have a bone to pick (with someone) (expression): To have something to disagree or argue about with someone

If you really have a bone to pick with someone, wait until you've had time to think it over, and then approach the person directly.

I have a bone to pick with you, God. How could you let my wife die in the 9/11 tragedy? How could you leave me like this?

Origin: The term probably comes from the way a person picks every bit of meat from a bone.

Usage note: Similar to *"to pick a fight with someone"* but without a threatening tone

Make no bones about something (expression): To not mince words; speak directly and plainly

He made no bones about wanting to be president of the club.

They made no bones about their dislike for each other.

Origin: The expression may have originally arisen as a metaphor referring to someone who did not make a fuss if bones turned up in their soup or stew. Or it may be based on "bone" being a very old slang term for "dice". Someone who "made no bones" would be a player who simply cast the dice when his turn came, omitting all the mystical little rituals gamblers often developed to conjure up good luck in a game.

Not have a lazy (prejudiced, etc.) bone in one's body/ there's not a lazy (prejudiced, etc.) bone in his/her body. (expression): He/she is not a lazy (prejudiced, etc.) person.

My cousin doesn't have a lazy bone in his body. He's always on the go, doing

something.

He never had a prejudiced bone in his body. He did more for blacks and Latinos than anyone I've seen.

She was socially gifted and there wasn't an arrogant bone in her body.

Usage note: I'm not sure how common this expression is; I've heard people use it from time to time.

Put flesh on the bone (of something) (expression): See under **FLESH.**

Skin and bones (expression): Extremely thin (a person or animal)

She's a real beanpole, nothing but skin and bones.

Origin: From the Bible
Job 19:19-20 All my intimate friends detest me; those I love have turned against me. I am *nothing but skin and bones.*

Usage notes:
1. I've also seen *"a bag of bones"*
2. *"Skin and bones"* implies "not healthy looking"
   "Skinny", on the other hand, is a synonym for "thin".

Sticks and stones may break my bones, but words/names/ will never hurt me. (saying): People (with the right attitude) cannot be hurt by unpleasant things that are said to or about them.

If you live your life the way you see fit, you shouldn't be worried about those rumors. Just remember this age-old advice: 'Sticks and stones may break my bones, but words will never hurt me.'

Usage note: This is a saying often taught to children. 'Names' is used in the expression "to call someone names".

Tickle your funny bones (v. phr.): To make you laugh

Our website offers clean jokes that will tickle your funny bones.

Origin: The "funny bone" is not a bone; it is the ulnar nerve that runs through the elbow and upper arm. The bone in the upper arm is called the "humerus" in Latin. Because it sounds like "humorous", people began calling it "the funny bone".

To the bone (adv. phr.): To the maximum; thoroughly

I was chilled to the bone.

I was shocked to the bone to find out that my closest friend was spreading a rumor about me that wasn't true.

Because of the budget and staff cuts, the city's animal shelters have been cut to the bone.

What's bred in the bone will come out in the flesh. (saying): When a trait goes very deep in someone, it's always going to be there and it cannot be repressed.

As they say, what's bred in the bone will come out in the flesh. Soon Sundance was found bragging about his former robberies at drunken parties.

Usage notes:

1. Other ways of expressing the same idea:
   "You can't change a leopard's spots".
   "A wolf's pup will grow into a wolf even though it is raised among men".
   "Training cannot change heredity".

2. I've also seen: *"What's bred in the bone will never come out of the flesh".*
   (We inherit certain characteristics from our ancestors and pass them onto our descendents.)

Work your fingers to the bone (v. phr.): To work so hard that you are worn out

She has been working her fingers to the bone doing all the chores while her husband is always out partying and having a good time.

"Bones" Bonus

Bone-idle (adj.): British. Extremely lazy by nature

I don't like working with John; he's bone-idle.

Usage note: I've also heard *"bone- lazy"*.

Get to the bone of the matter (expression): To get down to business

Lazy bones (n. phr.): A lazy person. Also used with animals

Don't be such a lazy bones! Get up and help me clean the house.

Our cat has lazy bones. She always sleeps all day.

"Lazy bones take all day to get started."
German Saying

Usage note: Always in the plural form

Not enough meat on her bone! (expression): She's too skinny!

Pull a boner (expression): To make a blunder

I pulled an awful boner when I asked her about her ex-boy friend.

Origin: It comes from the noun "bonehead" – a stupid person.

Usage note: "Boner" is also slang (although a bit old-fashioned) for an erection.

Roll the bones (expression): To cast dice, especially in craps.

BRAIN

In Their Words:

"The human brain starts working the moment you are born and never stops until you stand up to speak in public."
Author Unknown

"Many complain of their looks, but none of their brains."
Yiddish Proverb

"When God endowed human beings with brains, He did not intend to guarantee them."
Author Unknown

Our brain is often associated with our intellect, rational thought (or lack thereof). Surprisingly, ancient Egyptians believed it was the heart that was the center of intelligence (and also of emotions). They thought so little of the brain that during mummification, they removed the brain entirely from bodies.

"Brains" vs. "brain"
The plural usually refers to cleverness, intelligence (e.g. *My brother's got brains but too lazy to use them.*) whereas the singular refers to the physical organ in your head. There are some exceptions however (e.g. *May I pick your brain?*).

A brain (n.): Informal. An intelligent person

What a brain! She got an A again in Calculus.

Usage note: "The brains", on the other hand, means the cleverest person in the group, usually it's the person who does the thinking and planning:

The brains of this project is the boss' wife.

The brains behind the success of President Bush's reelection was his political chief advisor, Karl Rove.

Beat your brains out (v. phr.): To tire yourself out by thinking, expend great mental effort

John beat his brains out getting ready for the test, but he flunked it any way.

Can you help me with this math problem? I've been beating my brains out with it but I just couldn't solve it.

Usage note: Compare: *"to beat someone's brains out"* (to hit someone very hard especially on the head)

Brain drain (n. phr.): Has two meanings:

1. The loss of the leading intellectuals to other countries where conditions are better

   Many Asian nations risk a brain drain as parents trying to improve children's lives send many of their brightest youths to study abroad.

   At the end of World War II, there was a brain drain from Germany to the United States.

2. A difficult mental task resulting in fatigue and exhaustion

   A marathon chess tournament can be a real brain drain.

Brainstorm (v.): To collectively try to come up with a new idea or find a solution to a particular problem

Researchers are still brainstorming about how to solve global warming.

Brain trust (n. phr.): A group of experts who serve as unofficial but vital advisors

The candidate's brain trust met first thing in the morning and planned at least one other session before taking their recommendations to him.

The physician gathered a brain trust around himself at the college he worked.

Origin: The term was closely associated with President Franklin Roosevelt's advisors on domestic and foreign policy in the late 1930's.

Usage note: The British would use *"brains trust."* (http://dictionary.cambridge.org)

Brain wave (n. phr.): A sudden, useful and clever idea

I had thought for days on how to write the proposal. Then wham, a brain wave struck.

Left brain vs. ***right brain*** (n. phr., adj. phr.): Logical, reality-based way of thinking as opposed to intuitive, fantasy-based way

The artist created fantastic images with his right brain but had trouble using his left brain to figure out his family budget.

Most people associate business careers with the logical left-brain way of operating, but she has found a way to add some right-brain creativity.

Origin: These terms came into the English language in the late 1960's. According to the American psychobiologist Roger W. Sperry, the human brain has two very different ways of thinking. The right brain is visual and nonverbal and processes information in an intuitive and simultaneous way, looking first at the whole picture then the details. The left-brain is verbal and processes information in a linear, sequential and logical way, looking first at the pieces then putting them together to get the whole. (http://painting.about.com/library/blpaint/blrightbrain.htm)

No-brainer (n. phr.): An easy decision; a task which is not intellectually challenging

The actor said that his co-star's future stardom is "pretty well a no-brainer. He has it, it's literally that simple."

When I really sat down and considered the opportunities here, the decision to become the Waves' basketball coach was a no-brainer.

Usage note: Your 'brain' is what you use to think, and some questions or tasks are so easy that you don't even have to think to get the right answer or to get the job done. 'No brain' is required.

Pick someone's brain/pick someone's brains (v. phr.): To get ideas from someone, draw on someone's experience

I spent as much time as possible with my teacher in order to pick his brain.

Music fans will get to pick the singer's brain about the music industry prior to the concert.

Rack your brain (v. phr.): To think hard, search your memory

I racked my brain trying to remember where I put my glasses, but still I couldn't.

Origin: It refers to a medieval instrument of torture, the rack, on which people were stretched until-in some cases -their limbs were pulled off. Sometimes we seem to do that to our brain to get it to function as we want it to.

Usage note: Another older expression used is *"cudgel one's brains"*

Wrap your brain around something (expression): To figure it out, to comprehend

It takes a little while to wrap one's brain around how this works.

I still can't find the strength to wrap my brain around the fact that he's gone.

Usage note: Also, *"wrap your head/mind/around something"*

"Brain" Bonus

A brainchild (n.): An original idea or invention regarded as the product of someone's mental effort

The concept of evolution by natural selection is sometimes referred to as Charles Darwin's brainchild. Some people argue, however, that he got the idea from many of his predecessors.

A brain teaser (n. phr.): A mentally challenging problem or puzzle

Brain teasers are an excellent way to help increase students' critical thinking skills.

A brainiac (n.): Teen & College. A smart, studious person

We all agreed that Paul was pretty cool, even though he was a brainiac.

A few ounces light on the brain scale (expression): In a diminished mental state

In Bonanza, Michael Landon plays Little Joe – a happy-go-lucky, easy to laugh kind of guy with a few ounces light on the brain scale.

A lamebrain (n.): A stupid person

A pea brain (n. phr.): A stupid person

A scatterbrain (n.): A forgetful person; someone who is mentally disorganized

Usage note: Also used as an adjective *"scatterbrained"*:

According to some experts, it's not unusual for teenagers to seem scatterbrained and forgetful.

Brain-dead (adj.): Doltish, stupid

You must be brain-dead if you couldn't figure out what he wanted from you.

Have something on the brain (expression): To not be able to stop thinking or talking about one particular thing

My cousin has had gambling on the brain after a trip to Las Vegas. That's all he wants to talk about.

Your brain is fried. (expression): The brain is tired or ruined by drug abuse.

BREATH

In Their Words:

"There are two types of mints you never turn down in life: breath mints and compliments. Either way, someone is trying to tell you something".
Author Unknown

"The clever cat eats cheese and breathes down rat holes with baited breath."
W.C. Fields (1880-1946)
American comic and actor

We English learners may have not realized this, but the "breath" idioms are pretty common in everyday language.

A breath of fresh air (n. phr.): A nice change, a new presence

This brilliant pianist brings a breath of fresh air to these wonderful old pieces, many of which are recorded here for the first time.

This movie is totally original and a breath of fresh air for the film industry.

Usage note: *"A breath of air"*, on the other hand, means "a small amount of wind"; it is used literally:

There wasn't a breath of air in the room.

Breathe a sigh of relief (v. phr.): To feel relieved after a time of worrying or tension

We breathed a sigh of relief when we found out that the children were safe.

Usage note: Also "*to breathe easy*".

Breathe new life (v. phr.): To energize

Remodeling can breathe new life into your home.

This class will teach you how to use the power of the Internet to breathe new life into your existing business.

Catch your breath (v. phr.): To stop to rest and regain your normal pace of life

After working sixteen days in a row, he felt the need for a few days off to catch his breath.

Plan a little break – a weekend away. This will give you time to catch your breath.

Don't hold your breath. (expression): You shouldn't have high expectations about something; something is not going to happen soon, so be prepared to wait.

I know you gave that girl your phone number, but if I were you I wouldn't hold my breath. She might not call.

Yes, it's possible that they may raise the minimum wage, but don't hold your breath.

Usage note: A very common expression

Hold your breath (v. phr.): To stop breathing for a moment when you are excited or nervous; to endure great nervousness, anxiety or excitement

The basketball player made his last shot just as the final buzzer sounded. Everyone held their breath to see if the shot would go in.

My son held his breath for weeks before he found out that the college he chose had accepted him.

Usage note: Used figuratively in the second sentence

In the same breath (adv. phr.): At or almost at the same time

It's funny to hear him talk about how much he loved his wife and in the same breath mentioned another woman he was attracted to.

For politicians to demand immigration controls and argue against racism in the same breath is a deep contradiction.

Usage note: There's also an expression *"In one breath……….and in the next breath":*

In one breath he said that he was not competitive, yet in the next he admitted that he couldn't stand to lose.

Save your breath (v. phr.): To save yourself energy and/or time

He wouldn't listen to you any way; might as well save your breath.

Usage notes:

1. You can also say "*don't waste your breath*"

   If I were you, I wouldn't waste my breath on him.

2. There's also an expression: *"it's a waste of breath".*

Take you breath away (v. phr.): To surprise, to overwhelm, to put you into the state of awe or shock

Many have said that Yosemite's natural beauty has the power to take your breath away.

The book is intellectually brilliant; some of its insights virtually take your breath away.

"Life is not measured by the number of breaths we take, but by the moments that take our breath away."

Author Unknown

Usage notes:

1. The adj. is *"breathtaking".*
2. You can also use *"breathless":*
   "You leave me breathless."
   A song by Jerry Lee Lewis

Under your breath (adv. phr.): Spoken in a whisper, usually to yourself

"I guess it looks good if you've never eaten the real stuff," my girlfriend commented under her breath as we scanned the menu.

With bated breath (adv. phr.): With worry and tension, with suspense

With bated breath, they waited for the news of the people who were trapped under the building after the earthquake.

Origin: *"Bated"* comes from *"abated"* which means *"to slow down, to restrain"*. People often hold their breath when in anticipation (Hence, another expression *"hold one's breath"*) perhaps so as not to be distracted by breathing.
"Bated" was once a very common word. It appears a number of times in Shakespeare. It is now used only in this one set expression. As a result, many people don't know what *"bated"* means, and change it to *"baited"* by the process of folk etymology—the unclear *"bated"* is altered to associate it with the common *"baited"*.
(http://www.randomhouse.com/wotd/index.pperl?date=19970806)

"Breath" Bonus

Bad breath (n. phr.): Breath that smells unpleasant when it comes out of the mouth

Morning breath (n. phr.): Unpleasant smell from the mouth that some people have when they first wake up in the morning

Short of breath (adj. phr.): Unable to breathe very well

The guy was always very short of breath and often had to pant before he could even finish a sentence.

Usage note: Also, *"out of breath"* and *"breathless"*:

After climbing the four flights of stairs, the old man was quite breathless.

Take a (deep) breath (expression): To relax, slow down, not get so worked up

BUTT (& CO.)

In Their Words:

"No matter how you twist and turn, your butt is always in the back."
Swedish Saying

"I can't hit a ball more than 200 yards. I have no butt. You need a butt if you are going to hit a golf ball."
Dennis Quaid (1954-)
American actor

"Butt" is short for *"buttocks"*.

If you have to, use *"butt"* instead of *"ass"* as it is less crude and is often accepted in reasonably polite conversation.

Even more acceptable would be *"fanny", "tush"* (also *"tushy"* or *"tushie"*) and *"backside* ; *"backside"* seems to be the least offensive one in my opinion. (I was told that in England, the polite or common word is *"bum"*.)

Other terms sometimes used for *"butt"* are *"rear-end", "buns"* and *"tail"*. Unless you know people you are talking to well enough, try not to use such words.

Butt-related conversation can be literal, referring accurately to that part of the anatomy, for example, "*My butt is gonna get wider if I eat more donuts!" "That woman has a significant butt!"* or *"I have no butt."* (See the second quote above.)

Be aware that *"butt-related"* references are completely acceptable in some social contexts, and unacceptable in others.

A pain in the butt (n. phr.): A bother, a lot of trouble; a person who causes problems

Doing all this typing is a pain in the butt.

The guy kept interrupting me at the meeting. He was such a pain in the butt.

Usage note: Variants: *"a pain in the neck"* or *"a pain in the ass"* (bad language)

Beat someone's butt (v. phr.): To get a significant win

I want to stay here with the Clippers until we beat the Lakers' butts on a regular basis.

Butt heads (with someone) (v. phr.): To oppose someone; to argue with someone

I'm sure there are ways you can butt heads with your boss without putting your job at risk.

In the old TV sitcom, "All in the Family", the main character, Archie Bunker, always ends up butting heads with his son-in-law about all kinds of social issues.

Butt in (v. phr.): To intrude, interrupt or interfere

Next time, please don't butt in our conversation like that.

I don't approve of folks butting into other people's business.

Usage note: Use *"butt in"* when one interrupts a conversation; use either *"butt in"* or *"stick your nose into"* when talking about interfering with other people's business.

Butt naked/buck naked (expression): Slang. Completely naked

He was so drunk he took all his clothes off and danced butt naked on the pool table.

The homeless man was lying down on the sidewalk butt naked, tightly holding his bottle of whiskey.

Origin: No one knows for sure which is the standard expression or which is the original expression. Some think that the original is *"butt naked"* and that *"buck naked"* is either a euphemism or a mishearing. Others (the British wordsmith Michael Quinion and "The Mavens' Word of the Day" at Random House, for example) argue that the "buck" in *"buck naked"* refers to the color of "buckskin", along the lines of "buff" (from "buffalo leather"), as in the expression "to be in the buff" or naked.

Butt out (v. phr.): To tend to your own concerns

I think stadium development should be done strictly with private money. The city should butt out totally.

Butt out! It's none of your business.

Usage note: There is an expression *"Don't be a buttinski"*- a humorous way to ask someone to butt out.

Butt ugly (expression): Slang. Extremely unattractive, very ugly

I was thinking about going on a blind date with my sister's girl friend, but I changed my mind after I saw her picture. She's so butt ugly.

My brother's new dog is so butt ugly it scares everybody away.

Chase your tail (v. phr.): To go in circles not knowing what you are doing, never getting anywhere; signifying a futile act

He's a hard worker, but not efficient. Yesterday, he was chasing his tail all day, trying to find some old reports on something.

Origin: It refers to the actual practice of the dog going in circles chasing his tail.

Usage note: This is uniquely American. Compare a person to a dog (often called "the man's best friend") is simply considered being totally silly and light; this same expression might sound insulting in some other cultures.

Cover your butt (v. phr.): To protect yourself, assembling evidence so you won't be blamed

I wrote a letter telling them the machine should be repaired. I wanted to cover my butt in case it broke and someone was hurt.

Usage note: Less crude than saying *"cover your ass"*

Get off your butt (v. phr.): To get busy, start working

Why don't you get off your butt and get a job so you can help me pay the bills?

Usage notes:

1. Compare: *"get off your ass"*.
2. The opposite would be *"to sit on your butt"*:

   "Baseball is a very simple game. All you have to do is sit on your butt, spit tobacco and nod at the stupid things your manager says."
   Bill "the Spaceman" Lee (1946-)
   A retired baseball pitcher

Kick someone's butt/have your butt kicked (v. phr.): To beat someone/to be beaten

They beat us last time. Let's kick their butt tonight.

I just had my butt kicked out there in the real world.

Usage note: The term is used figuratively in the above sentences; it can also be used literally as well.

Kiss someone's butt (v. phr.): To flatter someone for your own benefits

I hate this guy. You can't believe the length people go to kiss his butt.

Usage note: Also used as a noun:

I don't play the game with the media. I don't play that kiss-butt, suck-up.

He's nothing but a butt kisser. (Same idea as *"a brownnoser"*)

Light a fire under your butt (expression): To motivate you, to inspire you

That's a flattering compliment. Every time I hear it, it lights a fire under my

butt to keep learning and getting better.

She sure knows how to light a fire under people's butts and get them moving.

Put your tail between your legs (v. phr.): See under **LEGS.**

The butt of someone's jokes (expression): The person who comes out ridiculed when a story is told; the target of the joke

I hate it when my son uses me as the butt of his jokes.

The President is often the butt of the jokes on late night talk shows.

Usage notes:

1. It's slightly humorous and derogatory.
2. Most people think it refers to a body part; I was told it actually comes from the Middle English word (butte) meaning "target".

Work your butt off (v. phr.): To work your hardest

I'm not happy working my butt off for so little money. What else can I do?

Usage note: Also, *"work your fanny/ass/behind/ off"* and *"bust your butt"*

"Butt" Bonus

A butt-head (n.): Vulgar slang. A person regarded as stupid or inept

I'm freezing my butt off! (expression): I'm/feel/ really cold!

Usage note: Also, *"I'm freezing my ass/my tail/off." and "It's so cold you could freeze your butt."*

Turn tail and run (expression): To run away

She scared that little boy so much he turned tail and ran.

CHEEKS

In Their Words:

"The best blush to use is laughter. It puts roses in your cheeks and in your soul."

Linda Knight

" If you dip your nose into the water, your cheeks will also get wet."

Turkey Saying

(A reference to greed)

Cheek by jowl (adv. phr.): Side by side, very close together

They were walking down the stairs cheek by jowl when the alarm sounded.

Living cheek by jowl with North Korea, the South Koreans are wary of the kind of tensions that can trigger war.

Origin: A "*jowl*" is a cheek. (Rogers, James 1985)

Usage note: *"Cheek by cheek"* is more commonly used in the U.S.

Put the roses (back) into your cheeks (expression): It makes you look healthier, better.

Get out of the house! Cold air and the sun will help put the roses back into your cheeks.

Usage notes:

1. I think whoever came up with this expression probably had a woman or a child in mind. I would feel funny using it with a man.
2. Variant: *"to put color into your face/cheeks"*

Tongue in cheek (n. phr., adj. phr., adv. phr.): See under **TONGUE.**

Turn the other cheek (expression): To go out of your way to avoid a nasty confrontation.

When John realized the guy was trying to pick a fight with him, he decided to <u>turn the other cheek</u> and walked away.

We all know that the <u>turning-the-other-cheek</u> mentality is not going to work as far as the terrorists are concerned.

Origin: The phrase is taken from the New Testament, Matthew 5:39-40, when Jesus says:
"But I tell you, do not resist an evil person. If someone strikes you on the right cheek, *turn to him the other also."*

Usage note: The Chinese have a similar saying:
If anyone spits in your face, let it drip dry.

"Cheeks" Bonus

Cheek (n., v.): British. Rudeness; to be rude

I can't believe you had the <u>cheek</u> to insult your hosts like that!

Don't <u>cheek</u> me! You rascal!

Cheeky (adj.): British. Be a little bit of a smart aleck; slightly rude, often in a funny way

What's he up to? He's got such a <u>cheeky</u> grin.

Dance cheek- to- cheek (expression): To dance while holding each other closely, so close that the cheeks touch

<u>Dancing cheek- to- cheek</u> is an excellent workout.

Fuzzy cheeks (expression): Used to refer to a young boy (pre-shaving) implying lack of experience, being unworldly

(Lower) cheeks (n.): Slang. The two halves of your buttocks

CHEST

In Their Words:

"There are thousands of causes for stress, and one antidote to stress is self-expression. That's what happens to me everyday. My thoughts get off my chest, down my sleeves and onto my pad."

Garson Kanin (1912-1999)
American writer, actor, film director

"For every dark night, there's a bright day after that. So no matter how hard it gets, keep your head up, stick your chest out and handle it."

Author Unknown

Get something off your chest/something to come off your chest (v. phr.): To tell someone about something that has been bothering or worrying you

I've got to get this off my chest before I explode.

I think a lot has to come off everybody's chest before this project can go on.

Usage note: Or, "*to get something out of your system*"

Play your cards/play it/ close to your chest (v. phr.): To be extremely secretive or cautious about your intentions or strategies

To be a good businessman, you need to learn to play your cards close to your chest when negotiating with another company.

Origin: From holding your cards close to you in card playing so that your opponents will not see them

Usage note: Also, "*play it close to the vest*"

That'll put hairs/hair/ on your chest! (expression): See under **HAIR**.

CHIN

In Their Words:

"I get whatever placidity I have from my father. But my mother taught me how to take it on the chin."

Norma Shearer (1900-1983)
American actress

"In a fight for survival, you don't lead with your chin."

Gord Kelly

Keep your chin up (v. phr.): To keep a positive attitude, to remain cheerful in a difficult situation

In spite of her many disappointments, she managed to keep her chin up and carry on with dignity.

The President was trying to keep his chin up and was doing his job while the Senate was trying to impeach him.

Try to keep your chin up. I'm sure you'll get a new job soon.

Usage notes:

1. You can also say *"hang in there"*, or *"grin and bear it"* in a more casual, informal situation.
2. Sometimes it can be shortened to *"to chin up"*
3. Bear with me; this is going to be a long one:

   I was led to believe, after having read all these so called 'idiom websites', that the expression *"to keep your pecker up"* is the British way of saying *"to keep your chin up"*. I already had this in my draft version. One of my editors spotted it and started laughing and would not stop. Too embarrassed to tell me in front of other people, he had to write it down what that phrase would mean to the Americans:

   The literal meaning of *"keep your pecker up"* is to maintain a penile erection (*"pecker"* is a U.S. slang term, meaning "penis", the male sex organ). Its metaphorical meaning is to maintain one's readiness.

Reluctant to believe what he said, I double checked with a few more people and came up with the same answer. I finally went back to the Internet again and got this explanation from www.english2american.com:

The phrase *"keep your pecker up"* is derived from a time when *"pecker"* was simply a reference to a bird's beak; if it is held up, so is the head. The whole phrase was, therefore, used to encourage one to hold one's head up and not let it droop in despair. The word became a euphemism for "penis" after the poet Catullus used it to refer to his love's pet sparrow in a rather suggestive poem that drew some fairly obvious parallels.

I have to admit – I will never forget the meanings of *"keep your pecker up"* again! And I probably wouldn't try to use it in its original sense for fear of causing either misunderstanding or laughter.

Take it on the chin (v. phr.): To be soundly defeated; to take a blow; to accept a difficulty or misfortune bravely without complaining

The home team took it on the chin badly in the last period.

She took it on the chin today when she got fired from her job.

My friend's criticism was quite justified. I took it on the chin and apologized.

Origin: This is a boxing term. A well-delivered punch to the chin can result in a knockout. *"Taking it on the chin"*, therefore, is a major event in a boxing context. It's the ultimate blow.

"Chin" Bonus

A chin-up (n. phr.): An exercise where one hangs from a bar and then pulls one's body up to the bar, touching the bar with one's chin

A chin-wag (n. phr.): British. A chat; a light informal conversation for social occasions

I'd go for a good chin-wag over a cup of coffee anytime!

Origin: From the movement of the chin when one is talking

A chinless wonder (expression): British. A foolish person, typically of high social class

Origin: It is believed that members of the upper classes often have receding chins.
http://www.phrases.org.uk/meanings/92000.html

A glass chin (expression): A boxing term referring to one's vulnerability, i.e. one who cannot take a punch to the chin

EARS

In Their Words:

"Be a good listener. Your ears will never get you in trouble."
Frank Tyger

"A politician is an animal that can sit on a fence and yet keep both ears to the ground."
H. L. Mencken (1880-1956)
American writer

A good ear (n. phr.): Has a few meanings:

1. Musically good with one's ears:

   Talented musicians have a good ear, whether by natural talent or deliberate training.

   The key to being a good improviser is to have a good ear.

2. A good listener

   We all need someone with a good ear from time to time.

   He is perfect for the job as a grief counselor. He has a good ear and empathy for people.

3. The ear that hears well

   He has such a good ear. I didn't think he'd hear what we were talking about. But he did! (Or, "*he has such good hearing*".)

   Speak into his good ear! (As opposed to *"That's his bad ear"*.)

A flea in your ear (expression): Informal. An annoying hint, a stinging rebuke, an idea or answer that is not welcome

I put a flea in her ear about the article deadline she had missed.

He had a flea in his ear about their relationship.

Origin: The phrase probably comes from the discomfort experienced by animals, such as dogs and cats, scratching themselves to relieve the irritation caused by fleas biting or moving inside their ears.

Usage note: Possibly British

An ear to listen (to) (expression): Someone to listen to

I think she just needed an ear to listen to her to help her feel that perhaps there was a way she could climb out of the debt hole.

I don't want a pity party; but just a little support and an ear to listen once in a while would sure be nice.

Be all ears (v. phr.): To listen attentively and with great interest

The lecture was so fascinating the audience was all ears for the entire evening.

Everybody was all ears when the subject of promotion came up.

Be out on your ear (v. phr.): To be forced to leave a job or place because you have done something wrong

Son, if you don't straighten up and help around the house more, you'll be out on your ear in no time!

Usage note: Also, *"to be kicked/thrown out/ on your ear"*

Be up to your ears (in/with something) (v. phr.): To be deeply involved in or occupied with (something), be extremely busy

The editor was up to his ears in complaints from readers about the way the story was handled.

I can't go to the movie with you this Saturday. I'm up to my ears with chores and errands.

Usage note: Also, *"be up to your ears in debt"*

Bend someone's ear (v. phr.): To talk to someone about a problem, thought or idea, and maybe get his/her advice or sympathy

Can I bend your ear? I want an opinion about my research project.

Tomorrow is our "Chatter Night". You'll get to bend someone's ear about the things you've done or would like to do. It may be just the occasion to raise a question that will help you get over a problem.

With a little arm-twisting and ear-bending, we hope to be able to raise quite a lot of money for the earthquake victims.

Can't believe one's ears (v. phr.): To not believe what one hears

I couldn't believe my ears when I heard that my niece got pregnant again! It seemed like she just had her first baby not long ago.

Usage notes:

1. Also, *"I heard/have heard/ it with my own ears"*
2. See also *"can't believe one's eyes"* under **EYES.**

Chew someone's ear off (v. phr.): To talk to someone for a long time in a boring and bothering way, especially to complain or to discuss a problem

My sister can easily chew your ear off once she starts talking about her kids.

It has been my observation that any animal owner can chew your ear off with stories about animals that appear to be just as emotional as humans.

Ear-to-ear (adj.): Broadly – used to describe a smile or a grin

His smile was ear-to-ear.

She broke into an ear-to-ear grin.

The coach was grinning from ear to ear when his team won the World Series.

Fall on deaf ears (v. phr.): (Said of advice, remark) to be ignored

Her doctor told her if she continued to drink, her habit would kill her. His advice fell on deaf ears.

My wife often spends money frivolously instead of trying to pay off our debts. I've asked her repeatedly to curb her spending, but it falls on deaf ears.

Feel your ears burning/ Your ears are burning. (expression): A tingling or burning sensation in the ears supposedly means that you are being talked about by others.

Your ears must have been burning because we were just talking about you.

Origin: This belief goes back to the Roman times. The idea that the left signifies evil and the right good applies here also: if a person's right ear burns then he/she is being praised, but a burning left ear indicates that he/she is the subject of evil intent. English literature, from Chaucer to Dickens, is full of references to burning ears. (users.tinyonline.co.uk/gswithenbank/sayings.htm)

From your lips to God's ears (expression): See under **LIPS**.

Get an earful (v. phr.): Informal. To hear more (of usually unwelcome news) than one expects or wishes to hear

Whenever I go see my dentist, I always get an earful of on how to take care of my teeth and gums.

The mayor got an earful from the protestors because of the rape allegations he was facing.

The referee got an earful of boos from the local fans for not calling the foul play by the visiting team.

Go in one ear and out the other (v. phr.): Listened to but immediately disregarded; make no impact

For many voters, most of the campaign rhetoric of both presidential candidates went in one ear and out the other.

His mind is already made up. My argument is never going to work. Whatever I say would just go in one ear and out the other.

Usage note: Also, *"go in at one ear and out at the other"*

Have an ear for (v. phr.): To have an aptitude for

Mike has an uncanny ear for music and easily memorizes tunes.

Alex has an ear for foreign languages. Not only can he say a foreign word perfectly the first time he hears it, he remembers it well too.

Once I started reading this book, I could tell right away the writer has a good ear for dialogue.

Have itching ears (v. phr.): To enjoy gossip

We all agree that she has itching ears.

Have someone's ear (v. phr.): To have access to and influence with someone, to have them willing to listen or pay attention

The President seemed to waver between the two positions on North Korea, depending on who last had his ear.

Dick Morris used to have former President Clinton's ear before he was forced to resign because of the prostitute scandal. He was, as a matter of fact, Clinton's political advisor for most of his two-term presidency.

Have something coming out of your ears (expression): To have excessive amount of something, have too much or too many

Many people brought meat loaf to the potluck party last night. Now we have leftover meat loaf coming out of our ears.

My nephew is only five years old, but he's got musical talent coming out of his ears.

Keep your ear to the ground (v. phr.): To pay close attention to the way things are going, or to the way people feel and think

Something important is about to happen. Be sure to keep your ear to the ground.

I'll keep my ear to the ground for any job openings at my work and I'll let you know as soon as possible.

Origin: From the American Indian practice, though it could be an invention of Hollywood westerns, of putting one's ear to the ground in order to detect the vibration of approaching hooves before they can actually be heard.

Lend an ear (v. phr.): To listen attentively, pay close attention

A true friend should always be there to lend an ear.

I have my faults, just like anybody else, but I feel that overall I'm a very compassionate person with a huge heart, and I'm always willing to lend a sympathetic ear.

Usage note: This is quite an old expression. To say *"lend me your ear"* ("please listen to me, hear me out.") is a polite way of asking for a person's full attention to listen to what you have to say. Shakespeare used it in the play *Julius Caesar*:

"Friends, Romans, countrymen, lend me your ear," says Mark Anthony.

Listen with half an ear (v. phr.): Not to give your full attention

Many people only listen to advertisements with half an ear.

When she's busy, she tends to listen to her kids with half an ear.

Little pitchers have big ears. (old saying): Children hear and understand more than you think they do.

Many children have learned how to disrespect parents from simply hearing

the conversation at the dinner table. Like they say, little pitchers have big ears.

Origin: The handles of pitchers are shaped like human ears. Also an old term for "*handles*" is "*ears*".

Usage note: The implication of this saying is that adults must be careful about what they say within the hearing of children.

Music to your ear (expression): Something you want to hear, good news or information

Did you say you'd pay for the meal? That's really music to my ear.

The President's pledge to make hydrogen-powered cars commonplace was very encouraging and music to many people's ear.

On one's ear (expression): In a state of amazement, excitement or uproar

'Fahrenheit 9-11' is a controversial movie that set the film industry on its ear.

Play it by ear (v. phr.): To act without a fixed plan, handle situations spontaneously as they arise; to go with the flow, just let things happen

"What are you going to do when you get to Bangkok?"
"I'm not sure yet. I'll just play it by ear.

Paul hasn't decided how long he's going to keep working. He's told his family he'll play it by ear.

Origin: It comes from *"to play music by ear"* meaning, to be able to accurately reproduce a melody one has heard, without needing written music.

Steam is coming out of your ears. /have (see, hear) steam coming out of your (someone's) ears (expression): To become very angry

She was so furious it's like steam was coming out of her ears.

Whereas some were able to discuss this topic calmly and thoughtfully, you could almost hear the steam coming out of others' ears.

Usage notes:

1. The term is used figuratively.
2. Notice the difference between *"have steam coming out of your ears"* and *"have something coming out of your ears"*.

Talk someone's ear off (v. phr.): To talk too much

I hate to run into Joe. He would talk my ear off the entire evening.

When you're on a date with her, don't try to talk her ear off. Try to listen to what she is saying and respond along the same line of thought.

Usage note: I've also heard *"talk the ears off a brass monkey", "talk the leg off an iron pot", "talk the hind legs off a donkey" and " talk someone's head/arm/pants/ off".*

Turn a deaf ear to someone/something (v. phr.): To refuse to listen

To turn a deaf ear to the needs of the seniors in our community would be unconscionable.

Californian politicians, from both parties, often turn a deaf ear to the problem of illegal immigration because they don't want to hurt their minority base.

Walls have ears, (the) (saying): This is a warning to watch what you say or what secrets you divulge, wherever you are, because someone might be listening.

"She and I were alone when we discussed this. How did you know what we were talking about?"
"Well, walls have ears, don't you know that?"

Origin: During the reign of Catherine de Medici (1519-1589), certain rooms in the Louvre Palace were constructed to conceal a network of listening tubes so that what was said in one room could be clearly heard in another. This was how the suspicious queen discovered state secrets and plots.

The legend of Dionysus'ear may also have been the inspiration for this saying. Dionysus was a tyrant of Syracuse (431-367 BC). His so-called 'ear' was a large ear-shaped underground cave cut in a rock that was connected to another chamber in such a way that he could overhear the conversation of his prisoners. (http/;//users.tinyonline.co.uk/gswithenbank/sayingsw.htm)

Famous Use: One of the war slogans in Britain during World War II was *"Careless Talk Costs Lives: Don't forget that walls have ears."*

Usage note: This kind of saying is common in most languages:
Thai and Japanese - *"The walls have ears; the doors have eyes."*
Chinese – *"Behind the wall, there are ears."*
Hungarian - *"Even the walls have ears."*

Wet behind the ears (expression): Inexperienced or naive

I was looked upon as the leader of the team in my second year, even though I was still wet behind the ears.

Don't give him a management position yet. He just joined the company and is still wet behind the ears.

Origin: The term alludes to baby farm animals. The last part of a newborn horse or cow to dry out after birth is usually the area behind the ears. Thus to say that someone is *"wet behind the ears"* is a folksy way of saying that they lack the experience or savvy necessary to complete a task.

Usage notes:

1. The opposite is *"dry behind the ears"* usually used in the negative sentences:

   My sister just started working at her new job, and was not dry behind the ears yet.

2. Or, you can say *"know one's way around"*.

Within earshot (expression): Close enough to hear

My mother has become increasingly more physically dependent to the point of needing me to be within earshot at all times.

Sunday's attack, which killed 25 people in a compound within earshot of Saudi royal palaces, came despite a tough six-month government campaign against Islamic fighters.

"Ears" Bonus

A cauliflower ear (n. phr.): A swollen, badly shaped ear caused by repeated hitting

A glue ear (n. phr.): A medical condition that is commonly found in children, where the middle part of the ear becomes filled with a liquid, and this prevents them from hearing correctly.

A swimmer's ear (n. phr.): Problem caused by water getting inside the ears while swimming (or bathing)

A tin ear (n. phr.): A lack of sensitivity to noise; a lack of musical ability, a state of being tone-deaf

The noise from the airplane didn't bother him; he has a tin ear.

People with a tin ear should not try to join a choir group.

Box someone's ear (v. phr.): To hit someone on the ear

Ear candy (n. phr.): Music that is pleasant; beautiful music

The theme song in this movie is ear candy.

Usage note: The term leans toward "insipid", without substance.

Ears like Dumbo (expression): Informal. Someone with big ears

Origin: Dumbo is Walt Disney's cartoon elephant who was born with hugh ears. He later discovers through the help of his faithful mouse friend that he can use his oversized-ears to fly.

Get the wax out of your ears! (expression): An old way of saying "pay attention!", "listen!"

Give someone a thick ear (expression): To slap someone on the ear, as a punishment

Have a word in someone's ear (v. phr.): To give someone a piece of advice or information secretly

Perk/prick/ up your ears (v. phr.): To take notice; to become alert. Many animals do it when they hear a sound or see an action.

She perked up her ears at the magical sound of a large jackpot coming out of the slot machine she had been playing.

Pin someone's ears back (v. phr.): Slang. To beat; to scold

After winning five games in a row, the Lakers finally had their ears pinned back by the Celtics.

The teacher pinned John's ears back for not studying hard enough.

Poke your big ears into someone's business (expression): To eavesdrop; to listen, uninvited, on a private conversation

Van Gogh's ear for music n. phr.): Tone deaf. A reference to Van Gogh's well-known ear that was cut off.

ELBOWS

In Their Words:

"No man lives without jostling and being jostled; in all ways he has to elbow himself through the world, giving and receiving offence."
Thomas Carlyle (1795-1881)
Scottish historian and essayist

"It's going to be the year of the sharp elbow and the quick tongue."
George W. Bush (1946-)
The 43 rd U.S. President (2000-2008)

At your elbow (expression): Immediately beside or behind someone

The interpreter was at the visiting President's elbow ready to do his job.

My new trainee was at my elbow all day.

Usage note: Someone who stays that close to you could be ready to give you help or could also be a nuisance; you can use it in either sense.

Bend the elbow/bend an elbow/bend your elbow (expression): 1. To drink beer or alcohol, usually frequently and heavily 2. To have a drink

We cautioned him that he was bending the elbow a little too often.

Your eyes look red. Bend your elbow last night?

Most tourists bend an elbow at this pub.

Origin: It alludes to the motion of lifting a drink to one's lips, which involves bending the elbow.

Usage notes:

1. This expression is used in an informal setting, e.g. a pub, tavern, bar, beer bar.
2. Some dictionaries also list "*crook/tip/ one's elbow.*"

Elbow grease (n. phr.): A lot of hard, physical work

The pot is so dirty that no amount of elbow grease will get it clean.

Let's get the job done here. Common, guys, let's use a little bit of elbow grease.

John is a citizen crime fighter who would use up his elbow grease and risk life and limb to wipe out graffiti.

Origin: The term is proverbially referred to as the best way to polish furniture (i.e. vigorous rubbing). Hence, allusively, energetic labor of any kind.

Elbow in (v. phr.): To force yourself into a situation where you are not invited

The uninvited guest elbowed her way in to get to the dining table first.

Elbow yourself/someone/ out (v. phr.): To force yourself/someone out

The bus was so crowded that, in order to get off in time, we had to quickly elbow our way out to the exit door.

The warlord complained that the U.S. ambassador had been trying to elbow him out of the presidential race in Afghanistan.

The government spokesperson decided to resign before he was elbowed out.

Elbow room (n. phr.): Has two meanings:

1. Space to move around in

   When their third child was born, they didn't just need more bedrooms, but more elbow room all around.

   I think they invited too many people to this party. There is no elbow room at all!

2. Freedom to do what one wants (similar idea to *"a free hand"*; see under **HANDS**.)

   The owner agreed to give the new manager plenty of elbow room.

Elbow to elbow (adv. phr.): Side by side

Elbow to elbow, they spent hours wading through snow up to their waists.

The party was filled elbow-to-elbow with people from all walks of life.

Usage note: Same idea as *"shoulder to shoulder";* see under **SHOULDERS.**

Rub elbows with (v. phr.): To interact socially with

The convention was a good chance for all of us to gain knowledge and rub elbows with people in our profession.

Usage note: Same idea as *"rub shoulders with"*; see under **SHOULDERS.**

"Elbows" Bonus

All elbows and knees (expression): Used to describe someone who is all angles, thin and long

Flying elbows (expression): Used to describe a fight. Also, in such sports like basketball, some players have a hectic, thrashing style and inadvertently their elbows are flying all over the place

No more Karl Malone means no more flying elbows. At least there won't be any more players getting knocked senseless by those large arms of his.

In basketball, injuries occur more from flying elbows or fingers than from the ball itself.

I had to go around my elbow to get to my thumb! (expression): Used when one is forced to do something that is simple, the hard way (www.deepsouth.ms11.net/southmouth)

More power to your elbow! (expression): British. Good luck! I hope your venture succeeds.

Usage note: The Americans would say *"More power to you!"*

Out at the elbows (old expression): Poorly dressed, lacking money

"I met in the street a very poor young man who was in love. His hat was old, his coat worn, his cloak was out at the elbows, the water passed through his shoes—and the stars through his soul."

Victor Hugo (1802-1885)
French Romantic author

Tennis elbow (n. phr.): A painful elbow disorder. The pain comes from injured or damaged tendons near the elbow. The term is misleading because most people who have it didn't get it from playing tennis.

EYES

In Their Words:

"If the eyes do not want to see, neither light nor glasses will help."
German Proverb

"Keep your eyes wide open before marriage, half shut afterwards."
Ben Franklin (1706-1790)
American author, inventor, scientist

"To find a friend one must close one eye – to keep him, two."
Norman Douglas (1868-1952)
British novelist and essayist

A black eye (n. phr.): Has two meanings:

1. The result of a hit or a punch to the eye

   When we saw him the next day we knew he had been in a fight because of his black eye.

   Usage note: Also called *"a shiner"* (a black and blue eye)

2. An adverse and damaging public image; a bad reputation

   The record number of Cal State freshmen unprepared for college-level math and English has increasingly become an academic black eye.

   The news that some automakers have been selling lemon cars is the latest black eye to the U.S. auto industry.

A sight for sore eyes (expression): A person or thing one is pleased to see, usually because one is beleaguered in some way and relieved by the sight

It was a sight for sore eyes to see my grandfather reunited with a friend he last saw badly wounded during World War II.

That girl is a sight for sore eyes!

Usage note: At a glance, it's easy to get *"a sight for sore eyes"* mixed up with *"an eyesore"*. The two have completely opposite meanings. One would not want to welcome *"an eyesore"* ("an unpleasant or ugly sight in a public place"):

Those discarded broken-down appliances were an eyesore that spoiled the otherwise impeccable scenery.

(All) eyes are on someone/something. (expression): All the attention is on someone/something; everyone is watching (someone/something) carefully.

In the business world, all eyes are on China, Taiwan and Hong Kong. The trio now takes center stage as economic and political fortunes shift in the region.

Usage notes:

1. *"To be all eyes"* is to be watching with a lot of interest.
2. See also *"to be all ears"* under **EARS**.

An eye for an eye, a tooth for a tooth (saying): Equal punishment for the crime; making the punishment fit the crime

In America, the death penalty is legal in most states. Supporters say it's a simple case of 'an eye for an eye, a tooth for a tooth', a phrase that comes from the Bible.

"An eye for an eye will only make the whole world blind"

Mohandas "Mahatma" Gandhi (1869-1948)
Indian leader

Usage notes:

1. It's common for people to just say *"an eye for an eye"*; others know what they mean.
2. This is an old command in the Bible. It states that when you pay back a person, you should not hurt him more than he hurt you. The phrase is often misused today. In its original context in the Bible, the phrase is not a quote from a personal vendetta. It's not for individuals to do the works of revenge. The quote is found in a legal system where a judge is at work.

An eyeful (n.): An attractive or satisfying sight that is worth looking at, especially an attractive girl or woman

That nude picture is quite an eyeful!

Those who thought that the quarterback's skills would rust after he turned 35 got an eyeful Sunday. He completed 13 of 23 passes for 257 yards and three touchdowns as his team defeated the opponent 36-27.

Apple of your eye (expression): An admired or desired person or thing; most beloved

Their lost child was the apple of their eye. They were obviously heart-broken when he died in a car accident.

She is the apple of his eye, but she hardly knows he exists.

That sports car in the show room is the apple of my eye.

Origin: In Old English the pupil of the eye was called "*the apple*". The pupil was thought to be spherical and solid and was the crucial part of the eye.

From the Bible:
Proverbs 7:2 Keep my commandments, and live; and my law as *the apple of thine eye.*

Psalm 17:8 Keep me as *the apple of your eye*; hide me in the shadow of your wings.

Usage notes:

1. Usually with verb "to be" and always with the definite article "the"
2. Since this is an expression, we simply say *"their eye"* and not *"their eyes"*.

Beauty is in the eye of the beholder. (saying): Different people have different opinions about what is good, beautiful or valuable.

People often think of supermodels as being beautiful. To me, they look so anorexic and unhealthy. Like they say, beauty is in the eye of the beholder.

The Americans can't stand the idea of eating fish heads, let alone looking at them. But beauty is in the eye of the beholder. People in some other countries love them and eat them all the time.

Usage note: Other expressions you can also use:
"Each to their own"
"To each his own"
"Different strokes for different folks"

Bright-eyed and bushy-tailed (adj. phr.): Lively, cheerful and outgoing; alert and ready to do something

I'm glad to see a much more cheerful you. You look bright-eyed and bushy-tailed after a good night's sleep.

To her credit, the actress acknowledged that her coming across as bright-eyed and bushy tailed does turn some people off.

Origin: Some people think that the bushy tail is a reference to cats that fluff their tails when excited; most others think it refers more to squirrels.

Bring a fresh eye (v. phr.): To bring new ideas

The candidate vowed he would bring a fresh eye and his accounting background to what he said was excessive spending at the state level.

As one of the most accomplished and prolific choreographers of her generation, she continues to bring a fresh eye to an ancient art of Chinese dance.

Usage note: Notice the indefinite article and the singular use of 'eye' in this expression.

Can't believe one's eyes (v. phr.): To not believe what one sees

I couldn't believe my eyes when I saw what my husband gave me for my birthday – a brand new BMW!

Usage note: Another related expression is *"I saw someone/something/ with my own eyes."*

Catch someone's eye (v. phr.): To attract someone's attention

What a bright red sweater! It really catches my eye.

Try to catch the waitress' eye and tell her I need more coffee, please!

Usage notes:

1. Notice that we use 'eye' - the singular form
2. Also used as adj. "*eye-catching*":

   What an eye-catching bright red sweater!

3. *"An eye-catcher"* is someone or something that strongly attracts the eye.

Cry your eyes out (v. phr.): To cry uncontrollably

She cried her eyes out after leaving her four little girls behind in Cambodia in order to come to America in the hope of finding a better life for them all.

Easy on the eyes (adj. phr.): Pleasant to look at

I don't want to sound superficial, but I wouldn't mind having a boyfriend who's easy on the eyes - someone who takes good care of himself, hygienically and physically.

Most people would agree that the candidate's running mate is easier on the eyes than the candidate himself.

Eyeball to eyeball (adj. phr.): Accepting or initiating a challenge; face-to-face with each other in a bad-tempered or quarrelsome way; dealing with matters frankly and firmly

The anchorman has always considered himself a reporter first and foremost. He loves to be in the field, to be eyeball to eyeball – to see it, feel it, hear it.

Difficult negotiations are often described as eyeball to eyeball.

Eyes and ears (n. phr.): Someone who works on someone else's behalf in order to help out

Officers said residents are their eyes and ears in the neighborhoods who help them prevent and solve crimes.

Usage note: Notice the word order. In such languages as Thai and Spanish, one would say *"ears and eyes"*.

Get some shut-eye (v. phr.): To get some sleep

You need to get some shut-eye; you have an early meeting tomorrow.

Usage note: An old-fashioned term that is still in use

Give someone the eye (v. phr.): To look at someone in an insinuating seductive way

I think you have an admirer. The guy at that table keeps giving you the eye.

Usage note: "*Give someone the eye*" can also mean "to look at someone with a critical eye":

The storeowner gave the homeless woman the eye when she walked into the store.

Give someone the hairy eyeball (v. phr.): To give someone a nasty look, especially with your eyelids partially lowered

The priest gave me the hairy eyeball when I inadvertently yawned during the sermon.

Usage note: Possibly a British expression

Have an eye for/have a keen (good/ great) eye for (v. phr.): To have a well-developed visual sense or aptitude

"I think he has a lot of promise," said the principal of the Art Gallery. "He has an eye for color and form."

She has a keen eye for discovering the hidden value in all sorts of things – especially children.

Have an eye to/with an eye to (v. phr.): To pay attention to; to plan for

Have an eye to spelling in these term papers.

My sister is going to college with an eye to being a doctor.

Have eyes in the back of your head (expression): To have the ability to see or notice everything around, to know what happens even when your back is turned

Mothers are famous for having the eyes in the back of their heads. They usually know right away when their kids are doing something wrong.

Have one eye on something (and the other on something else) (expression): To divide your attention to two different things

The front-runner had one eye focused on Michigan, as he campaigned in Missouri.

The President, with one eye on education and the other on fundraising, arrived in St. Louis today to promote 'No Child Left Behind Initiative' campaign.

Have your eye on (v. phr.): To have as your objective

She has her eye on an early retirement.

Usage note: Also, *"to set your sights on"*

Here's mud in your eye! (expression): Informal. A cheering exclamation when people drink, much like "*cheers!*"; to your good health and success

Bon appetit, here's to you. Here's mud in your eye!

So here's mud in your eye! Cheers to a good show!

Origin: The toast was originally made either in the muddy trenches of World War II, or in the cafes where the soldiers spent their leaves trying to forget about the war scenes. The implication was that it would be good fortune only to get mud from the trenches in your eye, since all the very real possibilities, such as artillery shrapnel, were absolutely horrific.

www.one-six one;fifthinfantrydivision.com/mudeye

Another theory is that the term originally expressed the wish that farmers would find soft earth easily turned by a plow.

Usage note: Often used as a silly, humorous incongruous toast (who would want mud in their eye?}

Hit you between the eyes (expression): To have a sudden impact on you

Some of the stories in this book will hit you between the eyes.

It was a relief to get the diagnosis; but it hit me between the eyes when I realized I was losing my health.

In the blink of an eye (expression): Extremely quick

Through the Internet, you can find anything you want, anywhere in the world, in the blink of an eye.

Everyone with grown children says the same thing: "Enjoy your kids while they're young, because in the blink of an eye, they'll be grown."

Origin: It refers to the time it takes to wink an eye.

Usage notes:

1. Some people might say "*in the twinkling of an eye*"(the term is from the Bible) or "*in the wink of an eye*".
2. Other terms also used: *"in a split second", "in a flash"*

In the country of the blind, the one-eyed man is king. (saying): A person of even limited ability is at a great advantage in the company of those less able.

In many villages in Kabul, those with even the slightest medical knowledge are revered. "In the country of the blind, the one-eyed man is king."

Origin: The saying is attributed to Desiderius Erasmus (1466 – 1536), a Dutch humanist

Usage note: The idea behind this saying seems to be universal. A similar kind of expression can be found in such languages as French, German, Spanish, Portuguese and Arabic (and I'm sure in other languages as well).

In your eyes (prep. phr.): In your opinion, in your estimation

In my eyes, fathers are the unsung heroes of their sons' lives.

My husband always makes excuses for our daughter. In his eyes, she can do no wrong.

In your mind's eye (expression): In your imagination, in your photographic memory

The painter, before beginning the painting, will see what he plans to paint in his mind's eye.

When you look back at that day in your mind's eye, what could have been done to have prevented the 9-11 tragedy?

Usage note: *"The mind's eye"* is sometimes called "the third eye".

It's all fun and games until someone loses an eye. (expression): It's fun until someone gets hurt.

It's all fun and games until someone loses an eye. This is one of those lines that everyone's mother seems to have used one time or another.

Origin: From Ancient Rome- the only rule during wrestling matches was "no eye gouging"; everything else was allowed. The only way to be disqualified was to poke someone's eye out.

Jaundiced eye (n. phr.): A prejudiced view

Strangers often looked at me with a jaundiced eye when they first met my family. Because I'm light-skinned compared to my other siblings, they all assumed that I was adopted.

To his jaundiced eye, the visitor could see only ugly buildings and could hear

only ugly sound.

Origin: Jaundice is a condition brought on by a disease that would turn various parts of the body, including the eyes, yellow ("*Jaune*" is French for "yellow").

It was believed that the person looking through such eyes saw everything as yellow. By extension, the jaundiced eye came to mean a prejudiced view, usually negative or critical (Rogers, James 1985).

Keep an eye on someone/something (v. phr.): To check regularly

The doctor told him to keep an eye on his blood pressure; it has been high lately.

The police have been warning residents to keep a close eye on their pets after dogs were killed recently in the community.

Keep an eye out for (v. phr.): To watch for

Keep an eye out for Kay at the school reunion; she should be there.

Keep your eyes peeled /skinned (v. phr.): To be watchful and observant

"It's very hot out tonight, so keep your eyes peeled for the police," said the drug dealer to his people.

Keep your eyes peeled for a gas station; we're about to run out of gas.

Origin: It alludes to the eyelids not covering the eyes.

Usage note: Same idea as *"keep an eye out for"*, only more dramatic and graphic

Keep your eye on the ball (v. phr.): To focus on the task at hand

If my daughter can keep her eye on the ball during law school, she's sure to become a fine lawyer.

According to some senators, the President did not keep his eye on the ball about the war on terror when he diverted his attention to Iraq and started the

war there.

Origin: In baseball, in order to hit a ball that is pitched toward you and to make contact with your bat you have to keep your eye on the ball.

Keep your eyes (and ears) open (v. phr.): To be alert, watchful and observant

Parents have to keep their eyes and ears, as well as their doors, open so their children are encouraged to talk when they have problems.

He decided to go back to school full time and kept his eyes and ears open to different career opportunities.

Usage note: Same as *"keep your eyes peeled/skinned"*.

Look at someone cross-eyed (v. phr.): To give someone a dirty look

In pro basketball, the referee could hand out double technicals to players who look at each other cross-eyed.

Why do we look at others cross-eyed when they don't fit our standard of living?

Heather looked at me cross-eyed after I told her she couldn't buy the watch.

Look someone in the eye(s)/in the face (v. phr.): To look at someone directly so as to convince them you are telling the truth or you have nothing to hide

My coworker made a pass at me at a company party. I was uncomfortable, got my coat and left. After that incident, she couldn't look me in the eye.

He is so embarrassed. He has not looked his daughter in the eye since last June, when he passed out while standing beside her at her wedding.

It took a very big man to look you in the eye and admit that he did something wrong.

Usage note: I've seen it used both ways: *'eye'* or *'eyes'*.

Make eyes at someone (v. phr.): To flirt

Everybody noticed that Mary and Bill were always making eyes at each other at work.

Make /give/ eye contact (v. phr.): To try to get someone's attention by keeping looking at them

I was trying to make eye contact with the man sitting at the table next to me; he was so attractive.

Not bat an eye (v. phr.): To show no sign of shock or surprise, nervousness or worry; to show no emotion; to do something without thinking about it

He didn't bat an eye when she walked out on him.

She spent $5000 shopping without batting an eye.

He jumped into the water to save the boy without batting an eye.

Usage notes:

1. Almost always used in the negative and with 'an'
2. Also, "*not bat an eyelid*", "*not bat an eyelash*" and "*not turn a hair*" (British); see under **HAIR**.
3. However, if a girl "*is batting her eyes*" it means she is blinking her eyes in a sexy way (as when she wants to get a guy's attention).

Only have eyes for (v. phr.): To want nothing but

Of all the Christmas gifts he got this year, my 5-year-old son only had eyes for Thermo Man.

Sometimes I think you only have eyes for her.

Open someone's/some/ eyes (v. phr.): To make someone realize the truth about something

His coach's illness opened his eyes to what can happen in life.

All I can do is pitch well, open some eyes, and assure them if they do give me

the position, I can do the job.

Tiger Woods has opened a lot of eyes that the game of golf should be open to anybody, regardless of their age or racial background.

Usage notes:

1. The adj. form is "*eye-opening*":

   We've had many eye-opening discussions since he gambled away the rent and food money, and we've worked through a lot of problems.

2. And a noun: "*an eye-opener*":

   Listening to him talk about his trip to Cambodia was an eye-opener for me.

   "Love may be blind but marriage is a real eye-opener."
   Author Unknown

Pull the wool over someone's eyes (v. phr.): To fool someone

I'd thought Lee was such a good person until the police arrested him for shoplifting. I guessed he just pulled the wool over my eyes.

It's not like we are trying to pull the wool over someone's eyes or ramrod this thing through without proper public debate or input.

Origin: It goes back to the days when gentlemen wore powdered wigs. The word 'wool' was then a popular, joking term for hair. The expression came from the practice of tilting a man's wig over his eyes, so that he would not be able to see what was going on.

Another theory was that the wool in question was originally part of the wigs worn by judges to enhance their dignity. Unfortunately, the wigs often slipped around and sometimes slid down over their face. It's hard to look dignified that way. The expression was probably generated by the lawyers to signal that they had outwitted the judges.

Run your eyes over (v. phr.): To look quickly at the whole of something

Let me have a copy of your article to run my eyes over before you send it to the newspaper.

See eye to eye (v. phr.): To agree on something/view something the same way

My wife and I saw eye to eye on this issue.

I know we don't always see eye to eye, but at least we're learning how to discuss our differences without always making it a confrontation.

Usage note: Very common expression

See (something) with half an eye (v. phr.): To notice the obvious, tell at a glance, see or understand something very clearly or easily

I could see with half an eye that the guy slept the whole time I was giving the speech.

The teacher saw with half an eye his students' lack of attention.

Origin: This is a hyperbolic expression. Presumably it alludes to an eye that is only half-open. (Ammer, Christine 1997)

The scales have fallen from my eyes. (expression): I finally understand.

We used to think of him as almost superhuman, but now the scales have fallen from our eyes, we see him as he is.

Now that the scales have fallen from our eyes (so to speak), I find myself wondering how I could have even missed the most important point of the book.

Usage note: Used figuratively, often as an exaggerated description of one's feelings.

There's more (to someone/something) than meets the eye. (expression): There is more to understand than just what's obvious on the surface; something is more complex than it looks.

This glamorous actress has bewitched us all - with her cool beauty and amazing talent; but there's more to this stunner than meets the eye.

I'm pretty sure there's more to this story than meets the eye. You don't know what goes on behind closed door.

Usage note: I once heard the flip side of this expression – "*There is less to this than meets the eye*" which I think pretty creative:

There is less to this than meets the eye here. The candidate's Convention speech sounded bold, but there's not much substance to it.

Throw dust in someone's eyes (v. phr.): To mislead, deceive

This article explains in details how certain groups of people are trying to throw dust in our eyes about some dangerous situations in the world.

Origin: The term alludes to throwing dust or sand in the air to confuse a pursuing enemy.

Usage note: I personally have never heard of this expression. I've checked with a lot of American friends, most of whom confessed not having heard of it either. It seems to convey the same idea as "*pull the wool over someone's eyes*", which most people are more familiar with.

Turn a blind eye (v. phr.): To pretend not to see something you know is wrong

USA Track and Field should be applauded for its effort to cleanse its sport of drug users instead of turning a blind eye to the problem.

Usage notes:

1. Often used with *"to"* or *"toward"*.
1. You can also say "*look the other way*", "*close (shut) one's eyes to*".

With your eyes open/with open eyes (expression): Fully aware of the possibilities or risks involved

Well, she went into this relationship with her eyes open; so I don't feel sorry for her all that much.

Your eyes are bigger than your stomach. (expression): You take more food than you will eat, thinking you are hungrier than you are.

Our eyes are often bigger than our stomachs. Try to take only what you'll be able to eat; when you are full, stop eating.

The experience taught him a valuable lesson: it is dangerous to let your eyes be bigger than your stomach.

Usage notes:

1. The term is not limited to talking about food. It is often used to describe a person who wants more than is good for him/her.
2. You can also say "*bite off more than you can chew*".

Your eyes pop out. (expression): Informal. You are very much surprised.

Lynn's eyes popped out when she saw her ex-boyfriend's car passing by with a blonde sitting very close to him.

When he found a 100-dollar-bill under the Christmas tree, his eyes popped out.

Usage note: Used with a possessive noun or pronoun

"Eyes" Bonus

A pink eye (n. phr.): A common eye infection – redness or irritation of the membranes on the inner part of the eyelids and the membranes covering the whites of the eyes.

A private eye (n. phr.): A private investigator

A red-eye (n.): Mainly U.S. A late-night, coast-to-coast flight

He took the red-eye from New York and got to L.A. right on time for the meeting.

Usage note: It can also refer to whiskey of an inferior quality. It's a term of the old west that is still in use.

All my eye (and Betty Martin)! (old expression): That's nonsense/rubbish!; Baloney!; In no way!

Origin: According to www.worldwidewords.org, it was found in British

English from the eighteenth century on, but is hardly known today. No one really knows where the saying came from, but the most often cited source was that it was a corruption of 'o mihi beate Martine' (O grant me, blessed Martin) from the words of a Latin prayer to St. Martin.

Usage note: The British often shorten it to *"All my eye!"*; the Americans *"My eye!"*.

Better than a poke in the eye (with a sharp stick) (expression): Used to minimize something extremely negative. It means "not really that bad".

"How was the food at the restaurant you ate last night?"
"It was probably better than a poke in the eye!"

Usage note: Variant:
Better than a slap across the belly with a wet fish
http://www.phrases.org.uk/bulletinboard/8/messages/519.html

Eagle eye (n. phr.): A person who has a sharp vision like that of an eagle; the ability to notice everything, even tiniest details or errors

This referee has an eagle eye for even tiny fouls on the court.

The students started the test under the eagle eye of the professor.

Usage notes:
1. Usually used in a singular form
2. Also as an adj.:

My eagle-eyed mother knew right away I had been crying.

Eye candy (n. phr.): Someone or something that is visually attractive or pleasing to look at.

The billionaire's new wife is not merely eye candy; she does have a good head on her pretty shoulders.

I met your brother at the party last night. He's pure eye candy.

The pictures in this illustrated Encyclopedia are well-chosen and wonderful

eye candy.

Usage note: The implication is that it is something that will occupy your time, but it doesn't necessarily have a lot of substance.

Hand-eye coordination (n. phr.): Ability to execute with the hand what the eyes desire

Tiger Woods is one of those rare exceptional athletes with amazing hand-eye coordination.

(Have) a discerning eye (v. phr.): To be particularly good at judging the quality of something

These two body art designs may look the same to a lay person, but a discerning eye can spot the difference between them.

Have (keep) your eye on the clock/be watching the clock (expression): To be looking to see what the time is, either because you're bored or eager to leave

I had to get to the bank before it closed, so I kept my eye on the clock all through the meeting.

Hawk eyed (adj. phr.)/***Hawk eye*** (n. phr.): Having extremely good eyesight/ the ability to see small things from a great distance

In a pig's eye! (expression): Never!

In the public eye (expression): Widely known, much in the news

Even though he was a big movie star, he never felt comfortable being in the public eye.

Usage note: The opposite is *"out of the public eye"*:

Keep your eye on the prize (expression): To not lose sight of your goal

If you want to reach your goal, you should first define it – in specific measurable terms – and write it down. Having it written down allows you to stay focused and to keep your eye on the prize.

Raccoon eyes (n. phr.): Someone with darkness under the eyes

Roadmap eyes (n. phr.): Tired and overworked eyes causing blood vessels to look like the lines in the road map

Usage note: Also, *"bloodshot eyes"*

The eye of the tiger (expression): An undefeatable will and focus to get to the goal/prize

There wasn't a dry eye in the house. (expression): Everybody (at that particular place) felt very emotional about what they had seen and many of them were crying.

There wasn't a dry eye in the house during the ceremony, especially during the lighting of the candles in memory of our fallen soldiers.

When someone was a (mere) twinkle in their father's eye (expression): Humorous. At a time before someone was born

FACE

In Their Words:

"A face is like the outside of a house, and most faces, like most houses, give us an idea of what we can expect to find inside."
Loretta Young (1913-2000)
American actress

"Take care that the face that looks out from the mirror in the morning is a pleasant face. You may not see it again during the day, but others will."
Author Unknown

The face is the representation of one's reputation or good name - it has to do with respect and dignity. It could be an indicator of one's emotions as well.

A slap in the face (n. phr.): A shocking insult

Seeing his wife kissing another man was a slap in the face for him.

Usage note: Contrast: *"a slap on the wrist"*. See under **MISCELLANEOUS.**

Be another face in the crowd (expression): To be ordinary, be an average person

Some people are content to be just another face in the crowd.

We often think that people who color their hair pink or wear black lipstick are hungry for attention; but it could be that they don't want to be just another face in the crowd.

Usage note: The opposite is *"to stand out from the crowd"*.

Be laughing on the other side of your face (British)***/Laugh out of the other side of your mouth*** (American) (expression): Used to tell someone that although they are pleased now, they'll not be pleased later when things don't turn out as they expected or planned (http://dictionary.cambridge.org)

He's so happy now about the big raise he's just got, but he'll be laughing on the other side of his face when he sees all the extra work that goes with it.

Do an about face (v. phr.): To turn around and face the opposite direction; to drastically reverse one's opinion or course of action

We got to a point on the mountain hike when we felt it was too dangerous and did an about face.

We all thought he would vote against the issue, but he did an about face at the last minute.

Origin: It alludes to the army command to turn around.

Usage note: Variants: *"to do a one-eighty"* or *"to make a 180-degree turn (on the issue)"*

Also, *"to do a flip-flop"* or *"to flip-flop"*

People who follow American politics may recall that this is the term used widely (and negatively) by the Bush campaigns to attack his challenger, John Kerry, in the 2004 Presidential election.

Do something until you are blue in the face (v. phr.): To do something as hard and as long as you possibly can (until you are able to do no more), but without success

I could talk until I'm blue in the face about the dangers of smoking, and still you wouldn't quit.

He can ask, beg, and plead until he's blue in the face, but I'm not going out on a date with him!

You can work out until you're blue in the face and not see results if you're eating improperly.

You can watch me write computer programs until you're blue in the face, but you won't learn until you do it yourself.

Usage note: This term is usually associated with "talking" (and other such verbs as "ask, argue, beg, plead, scream, discuss, debate") until you're out of breath, hence "you're blue in the face". I've sometimes seen it used with other verbs, as in the last two sentences, although not as often.

Face someone down (v. phr.): To get the upper hand over someone by behaving forcefully

The challenger obviously faced his opponent down in the first presidential debate.

They decided to face their business competitors down and got right back on track.

Face the music (v. phr.): To suffer the unpleasant consequences, especially of one's own actions, to face punishment and criticism

It's time to face the music because of the way we acted in school.

He's going to have to face the music sooner or later.

Origin: There are two theories. The first is that it's a musical theater term with the pit orchestra that the performers must face while on stage. The term alludes to their dogged determination to go on with the show in spite of stage fright.

The other theory comes from the military, possibly a ceremony stripping a soldier of his rank. The 'music' may have been a reference either to the gunfire of battle or the loud reprimands by officers, either of which would be difficult to face. (www.word-detective.com/093098.html)

Usage note: Another expression used in this sense is "*to take your own medicine*".

Face to face (adv. phr., adj. phr.): Directly in each other's presence

The two superstars didn't come face to face despite being in the same room for a news conference.

I think you should meet her face to face and tell her exactly why you want nothing to do with her any more.

A face-to-face meeting might be good for both of you to clear the air.

Face up to someone/something (v. phr.): To bravely confront a person or a challenge; to admit, to confess to have done something

I never can face up to my father-in-law. He always wins every argument we have.

Why don't you just face up to the problem and deal with it head-on?

The new teller finally had to face up having stolen the money from the bank.

Fall (flat) on your face (v. phr.): To fail completely, embarrass yourself

We know what people are thinking. They're waiting for us to fall flat on our face because of this whole thing.

"Every once in a while we may fall on our face, but we insist on doing what we wanna do."

Cliff Burton (1962-1986)
Bassist for the band *Metallica*

Get in your face (expression): To confront someone very directly, to be in someone's presence, especially in a provocative way

The coach can get in your face, but he's never laid a hand on anyone.

In professional sports today, it has become cool to get in someone's face, taunting and telling the guy you're guarding that his game is no good.

Origin: It originated in the 1970's in the U.S. sports journalism.

Usage note: Its adj. form "*in your face*" is also widely used in the U.S.:

Some sports, like American football and basketball, are more in your face than the others.

The play is more of an in-your-face realism because it deals with real issues – teen suicide, abortion, sexual abuse and alcoholism.

Some of the television commercials nowadays are pretty loud and in your face.

Get out of someone's face (v. phr.): To not bother someone

He was so annoying I finally had to tell him to get out of my face.

Get out of my face! Try finding something to do with your life!

Usage notes:

1. Often used as an order and in anger
2. Variants: *"take a hike!", "go fly a kite!", "go climb a tree!", "go jump in a lake!", "go fry an egg!"*

Have/get/ egg on your face (v. phr.): To be left looking embarrassed or foolish

He ended up with egg on his face when he couldn't fix my car like he said he could.

"We don't just have egg on our face - we have an omelet"
Tom Brokaw (1940-), former NBC News anchorman, commenting on the news debacle in 2000 in which the news media predicted the Presidential winner way too soon

Origin: It is an American expression, probably from the 1950's. It could have come from the image of a sloppy eater who got embarrassed because he had food on his face; or it might have come from the custom of rude audiences in the old days throwing raw eggs at performers they did not like. Another source (www.worldwidewords.org/qa/qa-egg-egg2.htm) suggests that working farm dogs sometimes develop the bad habit of taking eggs from the nests and eating them, so the expression might be a figurative extension from that of a dog found with egg around its muzzle.

Usage note: Not only does this expression often imply that one has made a serious mistake, it strictly indicates that something one has done or some turn of events has left one looking extremely embarrassed or foolish.

In the face of something (expression): Despite having to deal with a difficult situation or problem

She married the guy in the face of strong opposition from her parents.

Keep a straight face (v. phr.): To hold back from laughing or smiling

He made us laugh the whole time, so it was actually quite difficult to keep a straight face and concentrate on the scene we were doing.

The more I tried to act serious the less I could keep a straight face.

Usage note: There's also another expression: "*to lie with a straight face*".

Laugh in someone's face (v. phr.): To show disrespect to someone, not to obey someone openly

She asked her husband not to drink too much at the party. He just laughed in her face and ordered more beer.

It's hard not to laugh in someone's face when they say something stupid like that.

Let's face it. (expression): To accept reality

Let's face it! We can't afford to go on vacation this year. We don't have any money!

Usage note: Used when stating a fact or making a comment about something unpleasant or something one doesn't really want to admit.

Look someone in the face (v. phr.): See "*look someone in the eye*" under **EYES**.

Lose face (v. phr.): To lose your reputation or dignity

Getting fired from the job made Lisa feel she'd lost face among her co-workers.

He was scared to ask her out because if she turned him down he would lose face with his friends.

Usage notes:

1. Also used as a noun:

   The Oakland Raiders suffered a loss of face when they didn't play well in the SuperBowl.

   The general manager quit for loss of face.

2. The opposite of "*lose face*" is "*save face*":

   "The easiest way to save face is to keep the lower half shut!"
   Author Unknown

3. The "*face*" here is figuratively the aspect that one presents to the world. "*Saving face*" and "*losing face*" are said to be of immense importance to the Asian people. As a matter of fact, "*to lose face*" is a translation of the Chinese "*tiu lien*". –www.wordorigins.org. I'm pretty sure it's equally practiced in other parts of the world.

Make/pull a face (at someone) (v. phr.): To grimace, scowl, frown

Don't make a face! The medicine is bitter but it'll help you.

Being a strict vegetarian, she can't help but making a face every time she sees her husband eat a steak.

Not just another pretty face (expression): Phrase used to imply substance as well as physical attractiveness

It took a long time before she could convince her boss and her co-workers that she was a genuine financial expert, not just another pretty face.

Usage note: It can also be used with men, but with slight sarcasm.

On the face of it (expression): From appearances alone, at first glance

On the face of it, the problem seemed minor to all of us.

On the face of it, the business might be able to break even in about six months, but we have to wait and see.*

Put a good/brave/ face on something (v. phr.): To try to hide disappointment or fear concerning something

The candidate sought to put a good face on the fallout, telling a crowd of several hundred that voters would see through his faults.

The challenger claimed that the President just tried to put the best face on a policy in Iraq that has gone wrong.

Put a smile on someone's face (v. phr.): To make someone smile

That compliment put a smile on her face.

Usage note: Other useful 'smile' expressions:
This puts a smile back on my face.
The videotape will bring a smile to your face.
My mom has taught me how to meet and conquer all of life's challenges – all the while keeping a smile on my face.
He can't keep the smile off his face.
Wipe that smile off your face!

Say something to someone's face (v. phr.): To tell someone something in person, directly

If you've got something to say, say it to my face. Don't be a little coward and talk to the media. I'm tired of that.

Usage note: The opposite is *"to say something behind someone's back"*; see under **BACK**.

Show your face (v. phr.): To appear somewhere when you are not expected to because you have done something bad.

Don't you ever show your face again on my property!

How dare he show his face at your work again after all the terrible things he'd done to you?

Usage note: Often used in negative sentences and questions

Stare you in the face (v. phr.): To be plainly visible or obvious, forcing itself on your attention; to be imminent or unavoidable

The money on the table was staring me in the face.

The explanation had been staring him in the face all along.

Bankruptcy now stares us in the face.

Take something at face value (expression): To believe something is what it looks like without questioning

It's hard to take at face value her response to the question of whether she's considering a run for Mayor in the upcoming year.

Two-faced (adj.): Insincere, deceitful, disloyal

What a two-faced liar!

Origin: From Roman mythology – Janus was the two-faced god, the god of polarities, one looking to the future and one to the past.

Written all over your face (expression): It's clear what you are feeling by the look on your face.

I'm absolutely sure the man is guilty. It's written all over his face.

Usage note: Or *"I can tell/see/ by the look on his/her face.*

"Face" Bonus

A baby face (n. phr.): Someone who looks a lot younger than his/her age

A barefaced liar/a boldfaced liar (n. phr.): Someone who displays no shame about lying even if they are exposed

A face like thunder (n. phr.): Someone who is clearly very angry or upset about something

A face only his mother could love (n. phr.): An unattractive child except to his mother

A horse face (n. phr.): An elongated face, resembling a horse

A long face (n. phr.): A sad, unhappy face

A poker face (n. phr.): A face with no expression (done in the game of poker, so that nobody knows if you have good cards or not)

A stone face (n. phr.): Like stone, i.e. without expression, cold, granite like, hard, immobile

Dog face (expression): Slang term for the U.S. Army infantry in W.W. II (the 'dog face' soldier also wore 'dog tags')

Facelift (n. phr.): The procedure through plastic surgery to bring youth to the face

Have a face as long as a fiddle (expression): To have a sad, unhappy face

Hound dog/Basset/ face (expression): A face with a lot of lines and creases, wrinkled deeply.

What's his/her/ face? (expression): Informal. What's his/her/ name? I can't remember his/her/ name now.

Did what's his face pay you back the money yet?

Usage note: I've heard it used quite often.

FEET

In Their Words:

"I had the blues because I had no shoes until upon the street, I met a man who had no feet."

Persian Saying

"The foolish man seeks happiness in the distance; the wise grows it under his feet."

James Oppenheim (1882-1932)
American poet

"Only a fool tests the water with both feet."

African Proverb

Feet represent the foundation – the base of support for the whole body. So they show up in a lot of expressions having to do with our independence and freedom, or lack thereof.
Our feet also symbolize the will of man. You can't go anywhere without your feet taking you there. Thus, we have such idioms as "*drag your feet*" and "*vote with your feet*".

(Be) on your feet (v. phr.): To be standing

The crowd was on its feet cheering for their home team in the final seconds of the game.

Usage note: Compare: *"to your feet"* (to a standing position):

When he saw the bus coming, he jumped to his feet and ran out.

Be/get/ back on your feet (v. phr.): To return to good physical or financial health

The doctor told him he would be back on his feet in a few days.

I'll pay you as soon as I can get back on my feet.

He decided to stay as long as it took to get the orchestra back on its feet.

Caught flat-footed (v. phr.): To be caught unprepared, unable to react quickly

He was caught flat-footed by his brother-in-law's cheap shot.

Could the world leaders be caught flat-footed again if faced with similar crimes against humanity as in Rwanda?

Origin: It was an American slang term from early 20th century, and was used at first in horse racing. A horse that was slow out of the barrier was said to be "flat-footed".

Usage notes:

1. The term is now used figuratively to describe someone who's asleep at the switch, or caught by surprise.
2. It's the opposite of being *"on your toes"*; see **TOES**.

Cut the ground from under someone's feet (v. phr.): To upset someone's plan; spoil the argument for someone in advance

Bill wanted to be the captain of the team but we cut the ground from under his feet by saying that Bob was the best player and therefore, was more qualified.

Several high- ranking city officials applied for the retiring Police Chief's job but the city cut the ground from under their feet by hiring someone from out of state.

Usage note: Or simply, "*cut the ground from under them*".

Drag your feet/drag your heels (v. phr.): To intentionally delay; take longer than necessary to do something

He should have finished the project weeks ago. Why is he dragging his feet?

The two countries have been blaming each other for dragging their feet in the peace process.

Feet of clay (n. phr.): A hidden fault or weakness in an esteemed person

When the coach was arrested for drunk driving, the players were shocked to find out that their hero had feet of clay.

We all tend to worship our idols unreasonably and then are disappointed to discover their feet of clay.

Origin: The reference is to a biblical story of King Nebuchadnuzzar (604-561 BC) who had dreamt of a huge statue with a golden head, silver arm and chest, brass midriff and thighs, iron legs, feet partly of iron and partly of clay. Called in to explain this dream-image, Daniel interpreted that just as iron and clay don't mix, so some future kingdom descending from Nebuchadnuzzar's will be divided and just as clay is easily broken the kingdom too will crumble.

Usage notes:

1. Today, the term simply means "a small weakness relative to the strong whole".
2. Compare: *"Achilles' heel";* see under **HEELS**.

Find your feet (v. phr.): To become more self-confident in a new situation; become familiar with a new place; get used to something

The team needs two or three weeks to find its feet.

You can't just walk in and do it. It's a different kind of work in a different kind of place. It's going to take a while to find your feet.

Origin: The term probably alludes to the baby that starts to stand and walk on its own.

Usage notes:

1. I'm not sure whether this term is in common use in the U.S. or not. I saw it on an Australian website.
2. Other expressions used in this sense: "*to learn the ropes*" or *"to get the hang of (something)*"

Footloose and fancy-free (adj. phr.): Uncommitted, not tied down

He stays so footloose and fancy-free that he never establishes a solid base on which to stand.

As a mother of four young children, there isn't much time to be footloose and

fancy- free.

Developers say their target buyer is someone who has had property and is looking to lead a footloose and fancy- free life.

Origin: According to Rogers (1985), "*footloose*" is a word of 19th-century American origin, meaning "unhampered and ready to move". "*Fancy*" here is used in its now largely forgotten sense of being in love. Shakespeare has it in his *A Midsummer Night's Dream.*

Foot-in-mouth disease (expression): A tendency to say a wrong or inappropriate thing

When it comes to foot-in-mouth disease, the President holds his own.

Foot-in-mouth disease is a highly contagious disease that spreads from one politician to another on the Capitol Hill.

Origin: The term is a play on the foot-and-mouth disease of livestock and on the saying about putting your foot in your mouth (discussed later in this section).

Have a foot in both camps (expression): To be connected with both of two opposite parties.

He was a trained classical composer and pianist who had a foot in both classical and jazz music camps.

We used to think of academics as living in ivory towers and being cut off from the real world. However, many academics now have a foot in both camps – writing best- sellers, appearing on TV, as well as teaching in the institutions that employ them.

Usage note: The key word here is 'opposite'.

Have /keep/ a foot in both worlds (expression): To be connected with two different groups of people, or cultures or ways of life

Unlike the generations of immigrants before them, young Latinos today are happy to have a foot in both worlds. Speaking Spanish is no longer a shame, while speaking English is deemed a necessity.

Embracing someone else's culture doesn't mean you have to discard your own. It's not always easy to keep a foot in both worlds but it's done by millions of people from different ethnic groups in America every day.

Have one foot in the grave (v. phr.): To be very old or very ill

There must be something wrong with her. She's not even sixty, but she looks like she has one foot in the grave.

According to The Small Business Administration, thousands of small businesses have "one foot in the grave" over high insurance costs.

Usage note: I've sometimes heard people say "*have one foot in the grave and the other on a banana peel.*" It's probably used more in a humorous sense:

She wants to marry that old man because he's rich and she feels that he has one foot in the grave and the other on a banana peel.

Have the world at your feet/The world is at your feet. (expression): To be extremely successful and admired by a lot of people; have everything that would make you happy

The actress seemed to have the world at her feet even though she had been in the show business for only a few years.

When you're young, life seems endless, and the world is at your feet. You're invincible and health concerns are just about the last thing on your mind.

Usage note: There is a difference between *"to have the world at your feet"* and *"to be on top of the world"* - the former implies "conquering or achieving something"; the latter "feeling of happiness".

Have two left feet (expression): To be very awkward /clumsy; fall over easily

When you go to this folk music festival, you'll get off your chair and dance even if you're deaf or have two left feet.

Usage notes:

1. The term is often used lightheartedly to describe someone who is a

poor dancer.

After a quick check on the Internet, I found out that a lot of dance and music groups often use this term as part of their names.

2. Contrast: *"twinkling toes"*; see under **TOES**.
3. You can also use this expression in other situations:

She played tennis like she *had two left feet.*

That soccer player had *two left feet.*

I must *have two left feet.* *Why am I failing the obstacle course in the Training Mission? Is it because I'm not doing it correctly or because I'm one heck of a klutz?*

Hold someone's feet to the fire (v. phr.): To crucify, punish publicly; hold someone accountable for a commitment, make good on a promise

Some senior senators announced they *would hold the President's feet to the fire* *if they found out he took part in the scandal.*

Before we let him go, we'll *hold his feet to the fire* *for making that mistake.*

Origin: The term came from the torture used during the Crusades to extract confession for heresy: the accused were positioned in a manner that allowed the inquisitor to apply flames to their feet. This was done until they confessed or died.

Get /have/ cold feet (v. phr.): To back out because of loss of courage or confidence, especially just before doing something that has been planned

She *got cold feet* *at the last minute and refused to sign the contract.*

He told himself that this time he was really going to demand a pay raise from his boss. But as soon as he walked right in the office he *got cold feet.*

Origin: The most convincing theory seems to be that card players would sometimes use their cold feet as an excuse to back out of a game when things were going badly.

Get itchy feet (v. phr.): To want to travel

Bob can't stay in one place for long. Every now and then he gets itchy feet and starts going on a trip again.

Usage note: As a noun: *an itching foot* – a craving to travel.

Get the lead out (of your feet) v. phr.): To move faster, pep it up

The coach told his players to get the lead out and get ready for the big game.

Origin: Literally to have the weight of lead in your feet would slow your movement. This expression probably started figuratively, with someone getting impatient by another's slow pace (Rogers, James 1985).

Usage note: Often used as an imperative

Get your foot in the door (v. phr.): To get started with a career opportunity; start working for a company at a low level with the hope that one day will have a better job there (or somewhere else)

I took the job because I saw it as the opportunity to get my foot in the door.

Temporary jobs are a good way to get your foot in the door. They offer a chance to gain experience and maybe qualify for full time jobs.

Usage notes:

1. Very common expression
2. You can also use it as a noun:

   I look at it more like a stepping- stone. Any foot in the door is good for me.

Get off /start off/on the right/wrong/ foot (v. phr.): To make a good or bad start to a project or relationship

By writing a business plan, you're starting on the right foot.

I knew I started off on the wrong foot because I was two hours late for our first date!

Somehow he has the knack of always getting off on the wrong foot

with people.

Origin: It used to be considered unlucky to put your left foot on the floor first when getting out of bed (i.e. *"to start off on the wrong foot"* or, as one would say *"to get out of bed on the wrong side"*).

Get your feet wet (v. phr.): To become familiar with something, to get involved, to try something

"It feels good to get out there and <u>get my feet wet</u> a little bit", the rookie said. "I've learned more about NBA basketball."

The best way to <u>get your feet wet</u> when you learn ice-skating is to get a partner. That way you'll have someone to hang on to when you're about to fall.

Jump in with both feet (v. phr.): Has two meanings:

1. To commit wholeheartedly

   Congratulations on your graduation! <u>Jump into life with both feet</u> and give it all you got.

   As a substitute teacher, I don't have to interact with parents or do the paperwork. I just get to <u>jump in with both feet</u> and enjoy being with the kids.

2. To become totally involved in a situation too quickly without thinking about it first; act without thinking about the consequences

   That's just like my sister- always <u>jumping in with both feet</u> in a business deal without studying all the facts first.

Origin: The term alludes to jumping into water all at once.

Usage notes:

1. Variant: *"to take a plunge"*
2. The opposite would be *"look before you leap"* or *" dip your toe"* (see under **TOES**).

Keep /have/your feet on the ground (v. phr.): To continue to act in a sensible and practical way, even after you have become successful

Don't try to be a big shot. Keep your feet on the ground. You're not as cool as you look.

My old friend has kept his feet on the ground while his political status has soared.

Land on your feet (v. phr.): To come out of a bad situation successfully; maintain your life after a misfortune; to be successful or lucky, especially after a period of not having success or luck

If my boyfriend and I break up, so be it. I've broken up with guys before and managed to land on my feet.

My life is filled with ups and downs. Luckily, I've always been able to land on my feet.

My brother has really landed on his feet with that consulting job.

Origin: The term comes from the idea that the cat always falls on its feet unharmed.

Let no grass grow under your feet (expression): You always make the most of the time or opportunity.

John made his million before he turned 30. Ever since high school, he has let no grass grow under his feet.

Usage notes:

1. The opposite: *"to let the grass grow under your feet"*:

   The boss let the grass grow under his feet. As a result, the project was not finished on time.

2. Also used in the expression *"don't let the grass grow under your feet"*:

   You can't let the grass grow under your feet. You've got a lot of money invested in this project.

3. Another expression that's pretty close in meaning is *"keep your feet moving"*:

One of the things they talk about in hockey, as well as in life in general, is that you need to <u>keep your feet moving</u>. If you don't, you're not going to make anything happen.

Pull the rug from under someone's feet (v. phr.): To suddenly take away help or support from someone, or to suddenly do something that causes many problems for them

These countries may not be our enemies per se, but they're also not our friends. They're losers who're bitter and envious of our success. It's time to <u>pull the rug from under their feet.</u>

Eventually his supporters will <u>pull the rug from under his feet</u> and there will be a spectacular fall.

Origin: The image is a rug being pulled out from under someone's feet.

Usage note: You can also say "*pull the rug out from under someone or something*":

She <u>pulled the rug out from under our plan</u> to open a branch office in San Francisco.

Put one foot in front of the other (expression): To go slow and keep trying

Sometimes something happens to us, and we think we can't go on. But we do go on. We <u>put one foot in front of the other</u> and go on with our life, difficult as it may be.

The presumptive Democratic presidential candidate's simple mantra of his revived campaign was "we're going to keep <u>putting one foot in front of the other.</u>"

Usage note: This expression is not usually mentioned in most idiom books or idiom websites, but people do use it.

Put your best foot forward (v. phr.): To make a good impression by showing your strength

I don't know whether we'll get that business deal or not, but we've got to <u>put</u>

our best foot forward and be optimistic.

If you really want to get this job, you need to put your best foot forward at the job interview.

Origin: There are two theories. The first is that if one's trousers, stockings or shoes were a bit shabby, one would tend to stand (or sit) with the best one forward. Another theory is in such activities as jumping and dancing, one is likely to do better with one leg than the other (the expression "best leg" was also used.) The expression is ancient, dating from around 1500 (Rogers, James 1985).

Usage note: In Portuguese, it would be *"go in there with the right foot"* (Thanks to Rosana Grillo for this.) This goes to show that English is not the only language that considers the right (foot) to be better than the left (foot).

Put your foot down (v. phr.): To say no and be firm about it.

I tried hard to get along with my stepdaughter, but she took advantage of me. I finally put my foot down, and now I'm the 'wicked old witch'.

She should put her foot down and tell her husband that he can't go to this bachelor party at a strip club.

Origin: The term alludes to the placing of the foot (or feet) when one intends to stand firm rather than move (Rogers, James 1985)

Put your foot in your mouth /put your foot in it (expression): To blunder; commit a faux pas, a social gaffe

I certainly put my foot in my mouth when I asked him how his wife was doing. Somehow I'd forgotten she had died a few months ago.

To avoid putting your foot in your mouth, think carefully before you speak.

"If you keep your mouth shut, you will never put your foot in it."
Austin O'Malley (1858-1932)
American physicist

Origin: The 18th century Irish Parliamentarian Sir Boyle Roche, who was famous for committing faux-pas, once said, *"Half the lies our opponents tell about me are not true*!" To this, someone with a much firmer grasp of the English language remarked, "*Every time he opens his mouth, he puts his foot in it*". And a phrase was born! (From Mental Floss Magazine, Vol. 2, Issue 2, 2003, cited in www.phrases.shu.ac.uk/bulletin board).

Usage note: This is an expression people use all the time. As a matter of fact, it's one of the first ones that came out of my friends' mouth (just about every one of them) when they tried to help me with the list of idioms for this book.

Put your feet up (v. phr.): British. To relax, take it easy

Now I watch my health, put my feet up when I want to and enjoy myself more.

Hey, it's time to put your feet up and avoid trying to do too much. This is Spring break.

Shoot yourself in the foot (v. phr.): To foolishly harm, damage your own causes or chances by mistake; to inadvertently make a situation worse for yourself

He really shot himself in the foot when he told his future boss he liked to skip work on Fridays to do his errands.

If you use cheap materials to make your products, you are going to end up shooting yourself in the foot. People are going to find out sooner or later and stop buying from you.

Origin: The term alludes to an accidental shooting. The image is of someone holding a gun pointed down or possibly with it still in a cowboy holster and accidentally firing and hitting him/herself.

Usage note: Same idea as *"cut your own throat"*; see under **THROAT**.

Stand on your own (two) feet (v. phr.): To be independent, take care of your own life

Sooner or later you're going to have to learn to stand on your own two feet.

These are not people who can rise up against their government; they can

hardly stand on their own feet.

Sweep someone off his/her/ feet (v. phr.): To be overwhelmed by the impact of something; to greatly impress

Nobody has ever swept her off her feet like this guy does.

Since the term paper was a major part of his grade, he knew that it was going to have to sweep the teacher off her feet.

Origin: The image is an ocean wave sweeping someone off his/her feet.

Usage note: This is a term that is often, although not exclusively, used in the romantic sense.

Take a load off your feet (expression): To sit (or lie down) and relax

Why don't you come sit down and take a load off your feet? You've been working hard all day at the restaurant.

This is a place to relax with your kids, take a load off your feet, and be a kid again for a while.

Usage note: The idea behind this expression is to rest your feet, as in "sit down and thereby take the weight (load) off your feet". It's an informal way to welcome someone.

The shoe/boot/ is on the other foot. (expression): The situation is now the opposite of what it was.

She used to work part time as my secretary while she was going to law school. Now the shoe is on the other foot; she's a partner in a law firm and I'm working for her.

Origin: In the 18th century, there was a major change in the method of making footwear; for the first time, right and left sides could be made. Before that they were the same for both feet and if one boot/shoe was uncomfortable on one foot, it could be tried on the other.

Usage note: This term is usually used when one's situation changes from good to bad, for example from being rich to poor, or from being a leader to being a follower.

Think on your feet (v. phr.): To be able to think and talk at the same time, without help or preparation

I was impressed with the way you got yourself out of that situation. We like people who think on their feet here at our company.

Good debaters need to be able to think on their feet.

Usage note: I've also heard *"to be quick on your feet"*.

Under your feet (expression): Phrase used when someone's presence prevents you from doing what you want to be doing

The kids were under her feet all day so she couldn't get anything done.

Usage note: Compare *"have someone hanging around your neck"*; see **NECK**.

Vote with your feet (v. phr.): To leave a place or a situation you don't like; become a refugee or emigrant; show you don't like something by not buying it or not using it anymore

It must have been nice for you to be able to vote with your feet and come here after the fall of Saigon. A lot of people weren't in the position to do that.

Some people voted with their feet and refused to buy the Dixie Chicks' records after one of them had made a negative comment about The President's policy on the Iraq war.

Origin: Voting with one's feet is an old practice. Joseph's brothers went to Egypt during the famine in Palestine to get food. They were hungry and were voting with their feet.

It is probably the flow of refugees from political oppression since World War II that gives rise to this term. (Rogers, James 1985)

"Feet" Bonus

Athlete's foot (n. phr.): The fungal disease that occurs between the toes of feet encased in rarely washed socks

Be dead on your feet (expression): To be very tired

Bigfoot (n.): The common name for the mythological Sasquatch – the manlike hairy creature of the Pacific Northwest

Crow's feet (n. phr.): Narrow lines around the outside corners of your eyes, which appear when you get older

Feet don't fail me now! (expression): American. A comedic way of saying "I got to get running out of here!"

Flatfoot (n.): Slang for a policeman, probably due to 'walking the beat' in the early days

Lead foot (expression): One who pushes the gas pedal to the floor board and keeps it there (a love for speed)

Usage note: "Lead" in this expression is pronounced "led".

Play footsie with someone (expression): Literally, to touch or feel someone clandestinely often under a table with the foot or feet; figuratively, to engage in any sort of collaboration (usually dishonest or corrupt), especially in a political situation

The congressman was suspected of playing footsie with a big-name newspaper columnist regarding this issue.

Pussyfoot around (expression): To proceed with caution, subtlety and delicacy; not to have the courage to say what you think, to be a wimp

I'm not polishing it up. I don't pussyfoot around the issue. I call a spade a spade.

America will no longer pussyfoot around with its enemies. Someone hits us, we hit back tenfold.

Origin: The term comes from the image of a cat's careful tread.

Rush/run/ someone off their feet (v. phr.): To cause someone to be very busy

She's been rushed off her feet all morning at work.

Usage note: Also, *"to run off your feet"*:

This is a good time to kick off bad habits like drinking or eating too much candy. You simply won't have time as you'll be running off your feet.

Tenderfoot (expression): Someone who is new to the outdoors, not yet hardened to rougher life

Usage note: Also called *"a greenhorn"*

Wrong-foot (v.): British. To trick an opponent into losing their balance; to perturb or upset unexpectedly, to catch off guard

This soccer player has the quickness to wrong-foot the opposing team's defense.

The news anchor wrong-footed the listeners with a mixture of slang terms and pompous English in the same breath.

FINGERS

In Their Words:

"When a man points a finger at someone else, he should remember that four of his fingers are pointing at himself."

Louis Nizer (1902-1994)
British-born American lawyer

"He has an oar in every man's boat and a finger in every pie."

Miguel de Cervantes (1547-1616)
Spanish dramatist and novelist

In case you didn't already know the names of the different fingers in English, here they are: the thumb, the index, the middle finger, the ring finger and the little finger (informally known as 'the pinkie').

At your fingertips (expression): Instantly available

With the advance in computer technology, the world is literally <u>at your fingertips.</u>

I usually have at least two to three dictionaries <u>at my fingertips</u> when I write.

He knows this documentary project so well that he has all the details <u>at his fingertips.</u>

Usage note: Compare: *"at your elbow"*

Burn your fingers/get your fingers burned (v. phr.): To suffer unpleasant results of an action, especially loss of money, so you don't want to do the same thing

I'm not going to invest in the stock market any more; I've <u>burned my fingers</u> often enough.

Nothing important was ever done without the risk of <u>getting one's fingers burned.</u>

Butterfingers (expression): Unable to catch or control small objects

I must have butterfingers; this pen keeps slipping out of my hand.

When he dropped the ball again for the fourth time, his brother lost his patience and said, "butterfingers!"

Usage note: Compare: *"all thumbs"*; see under **THUMBS**.

Can/could/count something on the fingers of your hand (expression): It happens very rarely or exists in very small numbers.

We could count on the fingers of our hand the number of times he bought us drinks.

Cross your fingers/keep your fingers crossed (v. phr.): To hope for the best, for a successful or advantageous outcome

There's nothing one can do right now. One can only cross one's fingers at this point.

We've heard that more rain is coming. But let us keep our fingers crossed that the worst is over.

Origin: Crossing one's fingers for good luck started as a way of simulating a cross –a symbol which was believed to ward off evils.

Usage notes:
1. This is a very common expression.
2. Some people just say the words; others cross their middle finger over their index finger while saying it.
3. Sometimes when people make promises they don't intend to keep, they cross their fingers (behind their back, so that the other person, or other people, wouldn't see it); this way it doesn't count. Others, especially children, when being forced to tell a white lie, will cross their fingers (behind their back). This way they've got themselves covered.
4. In Czech, one would say *"to hold one's thumbs for someone"*.

Give someone the finger (v. phr.): To show someone in an offensive way that you're angry with them by turning the back of your hand toward them and pulling your middle finger up; specifically, it means "fuck you!"(bad language)

I think it's pretty rude to give a slow driver the finger. Either you have to try to be more patient or move to the next lane.

She claimed that her right to give me the finger is protected under the First Amendment.

Origin: There's a theory floating on the Internet that the British originated this term after their major upset victory over the French in the 15th century. This theory has been discounted by www.takeourword.com. According to this website, the raised-middle finger-gesture is essentially American. It was largely unknown in Britain until it began appearing in Hollywood movies in the 1960's and 1970's (its first appearance was in *Easy Rider*).

Usage notes:

1. It's also known as "*give someone the bird*" or "*give someone a one- fingered salute*".
2. One of my editors said that he had heard of this expression in the 1950's.
3. A lot of nations have different ways of performing an insulting gesture. In the UK, for example, if the hand is held out, palm towards the person performing the gesture (a peace sign reversed), this is considered to be highly insulting. However, in recent years, its use has declined in favor of the one-fingered salute due to American influence. (en.wikipedia.org/wiki/v-sign)

Have a finger in every pie (expression): To be involved in lots of different things, often to the annoyance of others, and often with the implication that the person is overactive to the point of being a busy body

The new boss irritated some of his employees because he seemed to want to have a finger in every pie.

Being such a successful man, he's involved in many activities, even if the public opinion doesn't like it that he has a finger in every pie.

Origin: This old saying presumably originated with kitchen visitors who couldn't resist testing the food by sticking a finger in it and then licking their finger.

Usage note: Also, *"to have a finger in the pie"* means "to be involved in something, often when your involvement is not wanted".

Have someone wrapped around your little finger (expression): To dominate utterly and effortlessly

She <u>has him wrapped around her little finger.</u> He'll do anything she tells him to do.

Usage note: Same idea as *"under someone's thumb"*; see under **THUMBS**.

Keep/have/ your finger on the pulse of something (v. phr.): To stay familiar with the most recent changes or improvements

The Sports Daily has become an invaluable tool for <u>keeping one's finger on the pulse of sports world.</u>

To really do his job right, the President must <u>keep his finger on the pulse of public and military opinions</u>, without becoming a prisoner of polling data.

Origin: It probably alludes to the way a doctor (or nurse) would check a patient's condition.

Lay a finger on someone (v. phr.): To harm someone even slightly

He has been warned by her lawyer never to <u>lay a finger on her</u> again.

Usage note: Compare: *"lay a hand on someone"*; see under **HANDS**.

Let (something/someone) slip through your fingers (expression): To lose an opportunity or a chance to catch someone or something

You really can't afford to <u>let this opportunity slip through your fingers!</u> So, what are you waiting for?

Don't <u>let this one slip through your fingers!</u> She really is a good catch.

Not lift/raise/ a finger (v. phr.): To do nothing at all

He saw me coming in the door with a heavy bag in my hand but he didn't lift a finger to help me.

John was out partying again, and Julie didn't lift a finger to stop him.

Usage note: Always used in negative sentences

Point a finger/point fingers (at someone) (v. phr.): To point out that someone is guilty

If you didn't do it, fine; but don't point a finger at me.

I'm not one to point fingers. It was our whole team. We came out flat. We couldn't make a jump shot. That's why we didn't have a chance to win.

"It's easy to point a finger, but much harder to point the way."
Duane Alan Hahn

Usage notes:
1. A very common expression
2. Also used as a noun:

   As the challenger's campaign disintegrates into oblivion, the finger pointing in his political party has already begun.

Put your finger in the air to see which way the wind is blowing (expression): To do what's popular, follow the crowd

He keeps changing his positions on issues; he's the kind of politician who puts his finger in the air to see which way the wind is blowing.

Origin: This expression probably alludes to the practice of American Indians before they decide on taking an action.

Put your finger on something (v. phr.): To be able to identify exactly, to discover the exact reason why a situation is the way it is, especially when something is wrong

There's something odd about this guy but I can't quite put my finger on it.

It reminds me of something, but I can't put my finger on it.

Usage notes:
1. Very common expression
2. Often used in the negative sentences

Sticky fingers (n. phr.): A tendency to steal or borrow without permission

How could you trust her with money? Don't you know she has sticky fingers?

Usage notes:
1. This metaphor makes it seem as if valuables adhered naturally to a thief's fingers. (Ammer, Christine 1997)
2. Another term in the same family is *"light-fingered"* (i.e. so light that when one steals something, nobody notices it)

Work your fingers to the bone (v. phr.): See under **BONES**.

Your finger itches. (old expression): You have great desire to do something.

My finger itches. Time to go to the range and work on the gun!

"Fingers" Bonus

High fives (v. phr., n. phr.): The slapping of hands above the head which two people do to celebrate. The five is the five fingers.

The players highfived each other after the big win.

Give me five!

Origin: The term began in the U.S. basketball circuit in the late 1980's.

Usage note: Some people do the "low fives" right after the "high fives".

Finger food (n. phr.): In its original meaning, the term refers to specific types of food, i.e. hors d'oeuvre, canapé, etc. (what the Italians call 'antipasto') that is eaten with the finger.

Nowadays, it's often used for food that you can eat without using forks, knives or spoons.

Finger lickin' good (n. phr.): Slang. Excellent, delicious food

Origin: From an advertising slogan of the Kentucky Fried Chicken, a fast food company

Five finger discount (n. phr.): Taking without paying, stealing. A common slang term for "shoplifting" in America, Britain and Australia (http://en.wikipedia.org)

Did you know she got that purse on a five finger discount?

Usage note: Variant: *"It fell off the back of a lorry."* (British) or *It fell off the back of the truck."* (American)

The fickle finger of fate (expression): The way life changes unpredictably

Usage note: It was made very popular in the 1960's when every week it was used on the TV show- Rowan and Martin's *Laugh-In*

The moving finger writes. (expression): Time is passing; the record of your life is accumulating (Rogers, James 1985).

Origin: It is from the verses in *Rubaiyat,* written by Omar Khayyam in the 12th century and translated by Edward Fitzgerald in the 19th century

To finger someone (v. phr.): To give up the 'guilty' party

The American ex-hostages fingered the newly elected Iranian President as one of their captors during the 1979 hostage crisis in Iran.

Usage note: Used in detective fiction, movies and television

FISTS

In Their Words:

"You cannot shake hands with a clenched fist."
Golda Meir (1898-1978)
Israel's third Prime Minister
(Note: Some credited this quote to Indira Gandhi.)

"The right to swing my fist ends where the other man's nose begins."
Oliver W. Holmes, Jr. (1841-1935)
American jurist

An iron fist (n. phr.): An autocratic rule

Mr. Williams ruled with an iron fist. He never went to a board meeting without knowing what was going to transpire and regularly fired off letters to analysts who said anything negative about the company and its stocks.

Usage note: Also used as an adjective:

The Israeli leaders have adopted an iron-fist policy against Palestinian terror.

An iron hand/iron fist/ in a velvet glove (expression): See under **HANDS**.

Fists fly. (expression): Phrase used to describe a physical fight

Don't get angry and let your fists fly in that situation.

Fists fly nonstop in this action-packed movie.

Usage note: Other related expressions: *"get into a fistfight"* and *"it doesn't take long for fists to fly."*
Also *"flying elbows"*; see under **"Elbows" Bonus.**

Hand over fist (expression): See under **HANDS**.

Tight-fisted (adj.): Not willing to spend money

Don't expect John to buy you a drink. He's very <u>tight-fisted.</u>

The consumers had remained <u>tight-fisted</u> most of the year up until the holiday season.

Usage notes:

1. The term has a negative sense.
2. Variants: *"to be tight", "a tight wad"*
   Also, *"a miser", "a penny-pincher"*

"Fists" Bonus

Give someone a bunch of fives (expression): British. To hit someone hard with your hand closed (i.e. with your fist); to punch someone

Usage note: See also *"give someone a knuckle sandwich"* under **KNUCKLES**.

Mailed fist (n. phr.): The term for armed force or superior might

Threats and <u>mailed fist</u> don't solve anything; negotiations will.

Make a fist (v. phr.): Literally, to fold your fingers into your palm real tight

The first thing you have to learn in boxing training is how to <u>make a fist</u> with your hand.

Two fisted (old expression): Manly, macho, someone who may be quick to fight

Although John Wayne was actually an actor, most Americans think of him as a <u>two-fisted</u> cowboy.

In Their Words:

"Consciousness is more than the thorn; it is the dagger in the flesh."
Emile M. Cioran (1911-1995)
French writer and philosopher

"Thou seest I have more flesh than another man, and therefore more frailty."
William Shakespeare (1564-1616)
English poet and playwright

A pound of flesh (n. phr.): Exactly what is due; a debt whose payment is harshly insisted on; revenge, a retribution for something

The supermarket employees insisted on their pound of flesh when they unrelentingly pressed their demand.

Why is it so hard for some people to forgive the damage done to them? What is it that drives them to vindictively exact a pound of flesh from those who have done them wrong?

Origin: It is the payment demanded by the moneylender Shylock in Shakspeare's *The Merchant of Venice*. When the time for the pay-off debt comes, he is told he may have that pound of flesh but without an ounce of blood because blood was not promised. Since it would clearly be impossible to take his exact due of flesh alone, Shylock's case collapses.

A thorn in the flesh/a thorn in the side expression): A constant source of irritation, a persistent difficulty or annoyance

My mother often compares me to my sister; that's really a thorn in my flesh.

This senator, a fellow Republican, has continued to be a pesky thorn in the President's side, always critical of many of his policies.

Origin: From the Bible
2 Co 12:7 To keep me from becoming conceited because of these

surprisingly great revelations, there was given me *a thorn in my flesh,* a messenger of Satan, to torment me.

Usage note: *"A thorn in the side"* is probably more common.

Flesh and blood (n. phr.): Your family and relatives

How could you give up your son – your own flesh and blood – to a total stranger?

Origin: The phrase comes from Shakespeare's *Hamlet.*

In the flesh (expression): In person

There she is –in the flesh – standing right behind you.

These fans are great. They seem to understand me in some way even though they don't know me in the flesh.

Usage note: Sometimes used loosely to mean being in the presence of the real thing. An example: the difference between viewing an actual painting and/or only seeing it in photographs – the first is 'in the flesh'.

Make your flesh creep (v. phr.): To cause you to shudder with disgust/ fear

The sight of that cockroach was enough to make my flesh creep; it really turned off my appetite.

The persecutions in that country are so bad that one could hardly mention them, as they are enough to make one's flesh creep.

Origin: It alludes to an unpleasant sensation of having something crawling over one's body or skin.

Usage note: Also, *" give someone the creeps", " make someone's skin crawl"* and *" gross someone out"*

Press the flesh (expression): To shake hands and mingle with many people especially while campaigning for public office.

The author is scheduled to press the flesh with fans at four different book-signing sessions within the next two weeks.

Most university presidents work long hours. They flit from city to city pressing the flesh for cash or else they're bogged down in administrative drudgery.

Usage note: Also known as *"to glad hand"*; see under **HANDS**.

Put flesh on the bone (of something) (expression): To add more details to a plan, idea, argument, etc. to make it better or more complete

Hormel is the company that puts flesh on the bone of the canned-meat market.

It will be up to the negotiators, board members and others involved to work together to put flesh on the bone of this merger.

The spirit is willing but the flesh is weak. (expression): One would love to do something but doesn't have the energy or strength to do so.

Another set of tennis? I don't think so. The spirit is willing but the flesh is weak.

Origin: This idiom was first recorded in the New Testament (Matthew 26:41) when Jesus tells his disciples: "Watch and pray, that ye enter not into temptation: *the spirit indeed is willing, but the flesh is weak.*"

Usage notes:

1. Today it is often used ruefully or humorously to admit one's physical weaknesses; an equivalent of "*I would if I could but I can't.*" (Ammer, Christine 1997)
2. There is a story that a computer was asked to translate "*The spirit is willing but the flesh is weak.*" into Russian and then back into English. The computer came up with *"The vodka is good but the meat is rotten."* in both versions!

"Flesh" Bonus

Flesh films (n. phr.): Pornography. Also *"blue films"*

Flesh market (n. phr.): Prostitution

(It's) more than flesh and blood can bear. (old expression): It's more than anybody can take.

Living with the mentally ill is often more than flesh and blood can bear.

Way of all flesh (old expression): Death; a common path through life

Origin: From the Bible

GUT

In Their Words:

"Guts win more games than ability."
Bob Zuppke (1879-1957)
German-American football coach

"I have always believed that anybody with a little guts and the desire to apply himself can make it, can make anything he wants to make of himself."
Willie Shoemaker (1931-2003)
American jockey

"Gut" idioms are used to describe deeply felt feelings, or internal strength.

Bust/burst/a gut (v. phr.): Has two meanings:

1. To exert oneself to the utmost

   Who would want to bust a gut if they're forced to work for nothing?

   I'm going to win the race, even if I have to bust a gut to do it.

2. To explode with strong feeling, especially laughter or anger

   Some people wouldn't find the joke funny; others would bust a gut.

   The boss will burst a gut when he finds out that the copying machine hasn't been fixed yet.

   Origin: The term alludes to hurting one's mid-section through physical straining. (Ammer, Christine 1997)

Have the guts (v. phr.): To have the courage

No, quite frankly, I don't have the guts to do it myself, and I'm not going to ask someone else to do it.

The basketball star had the guts to go public about his HIV-positive status.

Usage notes:

1. There's a saying *"no guts, no glory"*. It's similar to another saying *"no pain, no gain"*.
2. A more sophisticated expression for *"have the guts"* is *"intestinal fortitude"* (n. phr.)

Hate someone's guts (v. phr.): To strongly dislike, to detest their essence or personality

I hate that guy's guts. So don't even mention his name in our conversation.

Gut/gut feeling/ gut reaction (n, n. phr.): An immediate and instinctive response

My heart was telling me to stay with this team, but my gut was saying it was best to move on. I don't know, it was just a gut feeling.

He seems nice, well dressed and educated; but my gut reaction tells me to be careful.

Gut instincts (n. phr.): Your basic feelings about what is right for you.

Baseball is a sport where gut instincts rule.

Gut it out (v. phr.): To show perseverance in dealing with a difficult period or situation

The tennis player tried to gut it out, but she was clearly out of gas.

I was a little nervous when I realized our relationship was getting serious, but I had to gut it out because she could be the one.

Usage note: Similar to *"to tough it out"* but a little stronger

Gut-wrenching (adj. phr.): Agonizing

For the coach, it was another gut-wrenching loss.

Court battles are costly, time-consuming and often gut-wrenching.

Usage note: Similar to *"stomach- churning"*; see under **STOMACH**

Gutsy (adj.): Courageous

On the whole, I think this was a gutsy win for us.

Spill your guts (v. phr.): To tell your secrets and deep feelings

When the three suspects were separated and offered a deal by the prosecutor, they were quick to spill their guts.

It's your first date; so don't spill your guts too early. It might scare her off.

Work/sweat/slave/ your guts out (v. phr.): To work extremely hard

I've worked my guts out to help the company, but nobody notices.

Usage note: Also, *"work your fingers to the bone"*, *"work your butt off"* and *"bust your ass"* (bad language)

"Gut" Bonus

A gut check (expression): Having enough nerve to do something

The candidate asked the Americans to look into their hearts for a gut check.

A gut course (n. phr.): A course in college considered easy

A gutless wonder (expression): Said of someone in a flippant derisive manner

Usage note: Other ways of saying: *"coward", "chicken", "chicken hearted"* and *"lily-livered"*

Gut (n.): Slang. A paunchy stomach, similar to *"breadbasket", "spare tire"* and *"beer belly"*

HAIR

In Their Words:

"There is only one cure for gray hair. It was invented by a French man. It is called the guillotine."

P.G. Wodehouse (1881-1975)
English writer

"Inflation is when you pay fifteen dollars for a ten-dollar haircut you used to get for five dollars when you had hair."

Sam Ewing (1920-2001)
American writer, humorist

How one wears one's hair can be a personal expression of one's beliefs and/or lifestyle, for example, *punk hair, skin head, afro, long hair, crew cut, military hair, dreds, Mohawk, buzz cut.*

The "hair" idioms and expressions discussed here include the hair on the head (or lack thereof) as well as the hair on other parts of the body.

A bad hair day (expression): Has two meanings:

1. A day when one's appearance, especially one's hair, does not look so good

   She's upset because she's having a bad hair day, and it happens on the day she's supposed to give that important speech!

2. That particular day is not going well; things are going badly, out of sync

   Come on! You're not the first one with a bad hair day. Everybody has it from time to time.

Usage note: Other expressions also used: "*not my day*", "*it's one of those days*" and "*(have) a bad day*":

It's just not my day. Nothing seems to go my way.

It's one of those days for me. Problems all day!

I'm just having a real bad day today.

By a hair (adv. phr.): Very narrowly

Our school missed the top spot for scholastic award by a hair.

He came so close to winning he missed it by a fine hair.

Usage note: Also, "*by a hair's breath*" (i.e. the thickness of a hair), "*by a whisker*" and "*by the skin of your teeth*".

Get/be/ in someone's hair (v. phr.): To constantly annoy/hinder someone

I tried to ignore him and go about my business, but he was really getting in my hair.

I'm sorry to keep interrupting you. I promise I'll be out of your hair in a minute.

Get gray hair from something (v. phr.): To be worried or upset by something

Sooner or later I'd get gray hair from my husband's driving.

Origin: It alludes to the belief that extreme anxiety or worry can cause hair to turn gray.

Give someone gray hair (v. phr.): To worry someone

This new business is giving me gray hair; if it's not one thing, it's another.

Have/get/ someone by the short hairs (expression): Informal. To have someone under complete control; to have someone where you want them

The IRS (the Internal Revenue Service) has definitely have John by the short hairs. There's no way he can avoid paying taxes.

The city employees Union had the city by the short hairs before they even sat down to bargain.

Usage notes:

1. This is a euphemism for "*have someone by the balls*" (male genitals). The "*short hairs* "are pubic hairs.
2. Variant: *"by the short and curlies"* (possibly British)

In the crosshairs (n. phr.): A center of interest

The war on terrorism puts many countries in the Middle East <u>in the crosshairs.</u>

This automaker remains singularly <u>in the crosshairs</u> of some environmental activists because of its lagging fuel economy.

Origin: It's a reference to actual crosshairs -the very fine wire crossed in the eyepiece of optical instruments and on the sight of a firearm.

Keep your hair on! (expression): British. Said to someone to stop being so angry or upset

"Hurry, Jack! We're getting late!"
<u>"Keep your hair on!</u> I'm coming right now."

Usage notes:

1. The Americans would say *"keep your shirt on!"*
2. Used as an order. It's a fixed idiom that can only be said at the time the person you're speaking to is starting to get agitated or impatient.
(Shoebottom, Paul http://www.fis.educ/eslweb/index.htm)

Let your hair down (v. phr.): To relax and behave in a carefree manner

Even a king needs to <u>let his hair down</u> once in a while.

You need to take a break, relax, and <u>let your hair down.</u>

The soldiers coming back from war often want to live life to its fullest, to its wildest. They <u>let their hair all the way down</u> and do everything to excess.

Origin: The term alludes to the old practice of women who took down their pinned-up long hair only in the privacy of the bedrooms. (Ammer, Christine 1997)

Make your hair stand on end (v. phr.): To frighten

The very thought of an earthquake would make my mother's hair stand on end.

Origin: It alludes to goose bumps that appear when one is frightened and cause the hair(s) on the arm and at the back of the neck to stand up. From the Bible: Job 4:15
Then a spirit passed before my face; *the hair of my flesh stood up.*

Usage note: It is also where "*hair-raising*" (adj.) comes from, e.g. "*hair- raising ghost story*", "*hair-raising steps*"

Not turn a hair (v. phr.): British. To not show any emotion when one is told something bad or when something bad happen

She handled the crisis without turning a hair.

He didn't turn a hair when the judge sentenced him to 20 years in jail.

Usage note: The Americans would say "*not bat an eye*"; see under **EYES.**

Split hairs (v. phr.): To be picky about small details, to focus on an insignificant aspect of something

It's hard to work out a business agreement with John. He's too busy splitting hairs.

Quit splitting hairs! (Quit arguing about it!)

Tear your hair/tear your hair out/tear out your hair (v. phr.): To be greatly upset, frustrated or distressed

Errors in baseball are what make the game exciting. They also make us scream and tear our hair out in the stand.

"It is foolish to tear one's hair in grief, as though sorrow would be made less with baldness."

Marcus Tullius Cicero (106-43 BC)
Roman orator and statesman

Usage note: It's generally hyperbolic.

That'll put hairs/hair/ on your chest! (expression): Humorous. Used when someone is going to drink something that is very strongly alcoholic or eat something unusual for them (e.g., something hot and spicy, or something new for the first time)

The term can also be used with anything adventurous; for example, sports that will make you feel like a real man.

Here! Drink this Tequila shot. That'll put hairs on your chest!

At this adventure activity center, you'll be able to try a vast array of sports that'll put hairs on your chest and probably make you hurt quite a lot afterwards – rafting, kayaking, hiking, etc.

Origin: Hairs on a man's chest are often considered to be the symbol of his virility.

Usage notes:

1. My editor said the expression he has heard all his life is *"that'll put hair on your chest"* but Cambridge Advanced Learner's Dictionary lists it as *"that'll put hairs on your chest"*
2. A quote from someone with a hairless chest:
   "Hair doesn't grow on steel!"
   (Contributed by Mandel Matheson to www.wordsmith.org/awad/awadmail148.html)

"Hair" Bonus

A hair trigger temper (n. phr.): A tendency to become angry very easily

This woman is incapable of controlling her hair trigger temper.

Origin: It's a reference to the actual hair trigger on a gun – a gun that is set to fire at the slightest touch.

As bald as a billiard ball (expression): Used to describe someone who has a completely bald head

Usage notes:

1. I've also heard *"as bald as a cueball"*.
2. Also, *"As bald as a baby's behind/backside"*
   "As bald as a coot"
   (Note: Coots are not bald; their feature/beak pattern only gives the appearance of baldness.)

3. Other good quotes on 'baldness' that I've come across:

   "A well-traveled path has no grass."
   (Contributed by Chris Crosby-Schmidt to
   www.wordsmith.org/awad/awadmail148.html)

   "I don't care if they call me 'baldie' or 'chrome dome'. God took an eraser and brushed my head clean. I'd rather be bald on top than bald inside."

   Joe Garagiola (1926-)
   Baseball catcher, sportscaster

Big hair (expression): A common expression for the huge hair styles of the 1970's, for example, the Beehive hairdo and the big hair of Priscilla Presley.

Blondes have more fun. (expression): Said to express the common belief that men are more attracted to women with blonde hair

Dumb blonde jokes (expression): Jokes about blonde women who are often thought of being not so smart

Fair-haired boy (n. phr.): A person that gets special favors

If he wins the coming election by a landslide, he'll definitely become his party's fair-haired boy.

Origin: The term alludes to the preference of blond ('fair' or 'golden') hair over dark hair in the late 1800's (Ammer, Christine 1997)

Usage note: Also, *"a golden child"*

Hairball (n.): The disgusting glob that cats cough up

Hair brained (adj. phr.): Something really stupid

Hide or hair/hide nor hair (expression): A trace of someone/something that's gone, lost or missing; usually used in negative or interrogative sentences

I haven't seen hide or hair of him since our argument.

A button fell off my coat and I could find neither hide nor hair of it.

Longhair (expression): A reference to a style that has become more of a political and life style badge

The businessman thought the musician was just another longhair.

Origin: The meaning of this term has changed over time.

According to www.randomhouse.com/wotd/index, in the 19th century, long hair was mostly worn by intellects or artists; thus the term was being used literally.

By the early 20th century, the term became current in the sense 'artistic, intellectual', without referring to the actual length of hair worn by a person thus described.

By the 1930's, a subsense developed that referred to classical music (either a performer or fan). The term was used mainly by jazz musicians and journalists.

A new meaning arose during the 1960's – 'a person wearing long hair, especially a hippie; broadly, a person who's politically liberal'.

My hair looks like a hornet's nest! (expression): I need to comb my hair!

The hair of the dog (that bit you) (expression): An alcoholic drink taken as a cure for a hangover; often used as a way of excusing having a drink early on in the day

Origin: The term comes from the ancient Romans' belief that the bite of a mad dog could only be cured by burning the dog's hair and drinking it with water.

Trichotillomania (n.): Compulsive hair pulling; considered to be a psychiatric disorder

HANDS

In Their Words:

"It takes a steady hand to carry a full cup."
Author Unknown

"Sometimes the best helping hand you can give is a good, firm push."
Author Unknown

"You can wish with one hand and want with the other, but that doesn't mean you'll get what you want."
Heard from a friend

The hands often signify power. We also use them to get things done. These two features can be seen in a wide variety of "hands" idioms.

A bird in the hand is worth two in the bush (saying): It is better to possess something real right now than to count on finding something better in the future.

If I were you, I would take that job. It may not be the best job for you, but a bird in the hand is worth two in the bush, don't you think?

Origin: From Aesop's "Fables". In one tale, a hawk refused to be outwitted by a nightingale it had just caught - the nightingale vainly argued it was a mere mouthful for the hawk and should be let go. "Much good it will do to an empty belly," replied the hawk, "and besides, a little bird that I have is more to me than a great one that has yet to be caught."

A firm hand (n. phr.): A person who will discipline people

Don't you agree that we need a leader with a firm, steady hand?

Some say children need a firm hand. I disagree. I think they need a loving hand.

Usage note: The idiom *"to keep a firm hand on someone/something"* means to control someone/something carefully.

A free hand (n. phr.): Complete authority and freedom to control or handle

The coach came in on a contract fixed for the next six years and was promised a free hand to bring out the best among the players and unearth the new talent.

Having been appointed Chairman of his Communist party, he now has a free hand to push his own agenda.

Usage note: See also *"elbow room"* under **ELBOWS.**

A handful (n.): A lot to handle, to deal with

The baby elephant was only three months old, but at 300-plus pounds, it was quite a handful.

Seven kids are more than a handful for any couple.

An iron hand/iron fist/ in a velvet glove (expression): Apparent gentleness concealing strength or firmness

Some situations can only be negotiated by an iron hand in a velvet glove.

According to this movie director, the attitude to take when working with kids is you have to be like a gentle tyrant. A pure tyrant cannot get the performances out of them. If you're gentle, however, if it's like an iron hand in a velvet glove, it works.

Origin: The iron hand as a symbol of powerful control was found from the early 1700's.
The expression has often been attributed to Napoleon, although it has also been attributed to other, earlier rulers.
(http://users.tinyonline.co.uk/gswithenbank/sayingsi.htm)

Usage note: This expression is somewhat variable; you can also use *"steel fist"* or *"mailed fist"* instead of *"iron fist"* and *"silk glove"* instead of *"velvet glove"*.

Be a dab hand at (something) (expression): British. To be talented or clever at doing something, have a special skill for that particular task

He's a dab hand at decorating.

You're a dab hand at flirting with the ladies.

The guy is a dab hand at illegal ventures.

Usage notes:

1. Also, *"to be a wiz (a wizard) at doing something"*
2. I've asked many, many American people about this expression; none of them knew what it meant.

Be an old hand at (something) (expression): To be an expert at something

My mom is an old hand at looking after children.

Some of the guests invited were old hands at the dating scene.

Usage note: *"To be an old hand at something"* implies that since you've done it before (maybe over a period of time), you should be good at it; be an expert at it.

Bite the hand that feeds you (saying): To be ungrateful, to turn against or hurt a helper or supporter

After the attorney helped clear four men wrongly jailed for a murder they did not commit, one of them tried to blackmail her. She contacted prosecutors and now he's back in jail. It's hard to believe how someone could bite the hand that feeds him like that.

Usage note: Dogs do it literally sometimes; people do it figuratively.

Caught red-handed (expression): To be caught in a forbidden or illegal act; caught in the act of doing something wrong or immediately afterwards with evidence showing

The high-school kids were caught red-handed spray-painting their names in the school restrooms.

The bartender was caught red-handed passing drinks to underage customers.

Origin: This is an old expression, based on the metaphor of murderers being caught with blood still on their hands. It probably dated back to the days even before guns when to kill another person would have involved the use of a direct-contact weapon like a dagger or club. (www.businessballs.com/clicheorigins)

Caught with a/your/ hand in the cookie jar (expression): To be caught in the act of something (often something you are not supposed to do or something dishonest)

The star forward was caught with his hand in the cookie jar when he committed a foul in direct view of the referee and was penalized for it.

The Reverend was caught with his hand in the cookie jar again; this time for paying his mistress $120,000 as an employee of one of his nonprofit groups and failing to declare her on the tax disclosure forms.

Origin: Traditionally, most American homes have a jar of homemade cookies in the kitchen and children are not supposed to touch it before getting permission. More often than not, they cannot resist the temptation.

Usage note: This is probably an American expression, since the British use "biscuit" whereas the Americans mean "cookie". Throughout the course of this book, I've tried hard to find out whether anybody – books or websites – has ever explained the difference in meanings between *"caught with your hand in the cookie jar"* and *"caught red- handed"*; so far I've come up empty-handed.

This is the way I look at it: in a loose sense, *"caught with your hand in the cookie jar"* could sometimes have the same meaning as *"caught red-handed"*, although it is often used more in a humorous way and/or with a less severe offense. Depending upon the gravity of what you get caught doing; the feelings could range from being humiliated, foolish or desperately guilty.

Cold hands, warm heart (saying): A reserved exterior may disguise a kind-hearted person.

"How do you feel?"
"Numb and cool."

"You know what they say "cold hands, warm heart"?
"I don't think that applies when you've spent all morning outside soaking wet in freezing weather!"

Origin: I've heard that this is a saying that originated as a superstition (and so is *"warm hands, cold heart"*-this one is not as common).

Usage note: There's also a new version *"cold hands, warm heart; dirty feet and no sweetheart"*. Somebody might have come up with this just for fun.

Come in handy (v. phr.): To become useful

She is the perfect 'people person'. She never forgets a name and likes shaking hands. That comes in handy in her role as the President's wife.

I always save all my pennies. They come in handy sometimes.

"When ideas fail, words come in very handy."
Johann Goethe (1749-1832)
German author

Usage note: Very common

Get out of hand (v. phr.): To lose control

Your obsession to lose weight has gotten out of hand.

Things just got out of hand in our relationship. I think we should slow down; but I'm afraid to tell her.

These kids are getting out of hand running around the restaurant. Why don't the parents tell them to sit down and behave?

Usage note: Used with people as well, as in the last sentence.

Give someone a hand (v. phr.): Has two meanings:

1. To help someone

Could you give me a hand carrying this box?

2. To applaud someone

Please give a big hand to our guest of honor tonight, Mr. Lee Cheng.

Usage notes:
1. In the first sentence, you can also say, *"lend me a hand"*.
2. Notice this expression is used with the indefinite article "a".
3. If you say *"give me your hand"*, it would be interpreted literally.

Glad-hand (v. phr.): Informal. To greet people superficially, be friendly to people you have never met before as a way of trying to get an advantage

He was not a schmoozer; he didn't glad-hand with people who could help him.

The candidate stopped by the reception, glad-handed for a few minutes, and then left for another rally.

Usage notes:
1. I've seen it used three different ways: *"glad-hand"*, *"glad hand"* and *"gladhand"*.
2. The person doing it is "*a glad-hander.*"
3. This term is used quite a lot in politics.
4. See also "*a backslapper*" under **BACK**.

Go hand in hand (v. phr.): To be part of each other

In America, commercialism and Christmas have always gone hand in hand.

Dieting and deprivation don't have to go hand in hand – you don't have to give up your favorite foods.

Got to hand it to (v. phr.): To give credit to

I never thought you'd get it done. I've got to hand it to you; you did a great job.

We've got to hand it to him the way he turned his business around and became so successful.

Usage note: Another expression often used is *"one's hat is off to someone"* – a more dramatic way of saying the same thing

Hand in glove/hand and glove (expression): On intimate terms or in close association

The two industries are hand in glove with one another.

Banks and law enforcement have traditionally worked hand in glove.

Hand-me-downs (n.): Something previously used, which you are given, especially items of clothing

His parents couldn't buy him skates, so he wore oversized hand-me-downs.

Usage note: Also used as an adjective:

By the time she reached college, she stopped hiding in her brother's hand-me-down jeans and found pants that actually covered her long legs.

Hand/give/ someone something on a plate/ to be handed something on a plate (expression): To allow someone to get or win something very easily without their having to make the least effort

The home team handed the game to the opponents on a plate.

You can't expect to be handed a diploma on a plate without working for it.

Usage note: Also, *"to hand someone something on a silver platter"*

Hand over fist (expression): Taking a lot of something in very rapidly, usually having to do with money

She's making money hand over fist these days with her consulting business.

In the old days, he used to make money hand over fist selling heroin.

Origin: It comes from a naval expression, "*hand over hand"* meaning to travel or progress very quickly, usually from up or down (from the analogy of a sailor climbing a rope or hauling one). The expression extended to grabbing fistfuls of money probably in the late 19th century (Rogers, James 1985).

Usage note: I've heard that although the term is more associated with making money, you can use it to describe losing money as well.

Hands down (adv. phr.): Convincingly, without a doubt, without question

She was voted the prettiest girl in the class, hands down.

John will win the nomination, hands down.

Origin: One version is from horse racing – the jockey doesn't even have to lift his hands to guide his horse if he's way out in front. Another one is from boxing in which the opponent is a pushover and so the winner doesn't even have to raise his hands to protect himself.

Usage note: Often used in the expression *"win hands down"*

Hands off (adj. phr.): Purposely not involved

The conservative mayor wanted his people to take a hands- off approach towards the labor dispute.

Hands on (adj. phr.): Purposely and visibly involved

The city is raising funds for mobile computer labs to give high school students hands-on experience in using computers to design and manufacture things.

The manager's working relationship with the owner had eroded somewhat in recent months as the owner took more of a hands-on role in operating the company.

Have a hand (v. phr.): To play a part in

The candidate's younger sister has had a major hand in all his campaigns and has offered advice on most political matters.

As executive manager of her Chamber of Commerce, she never fails to have a hand in every community event.

He had a hand in my success.

Have a hot hand (v. phr.): To have hot streaks

There's a belief that in basketball and many other sports, a player may occasionally have a hot hand.

Usage note: Often used in gambling or sports

Have your hands full (v. phr.): To be extremely busy

My sister has had her hands full these days with her newborn triplets.

When the primary election season heats up, rival candidates sling mud and the Secret Service has its hands full, protecting all of them from assassins' bullets.

Usage note: Another expression used in this sense is *"have a full plate"*.

Have someone eating out of the palm of your hand/have someone in the palm of your hand (expression): See under **PALM**.

Have/get/ the upper hand (v. phr.): To be in a position of control, to come out the winner in a situation

In hard economic times, employers have the upper hand and can demand that workers in even entry-level positions have years of experience.

The firefighters finally seemed to be able to get the upper hand over the big fire in that area.

Origin: One theory is that during the earlier days of baseball, in order to determine which team would bat first, one player would grasp the baseball bat at the lower end. A player from the opposing team would then place his hand directly above the first player's hand. They would then alternate hands up the bat until the end was reached and one of the players had the 'upper hand'; his team then got to bat first.

Another theory is that the phrase apparently was used long before the age of baseball and probably derives from an English game of chance that has been traced back to the fifteenth century and was played in the same way as the baseball- choosing contest. (From *Encyclopedia of Word and Phrase Origins* by Robert Hendrickson, 1997)

Usage notes:

1. A very common expression
2. Usually used with "*the*"; notice also the spelling- it's two words

Hat in hand (expression): Being humble, deferential

The defense lawyer went back to the penalty phase, hat in hand, to beg the jurors for his client's life.

I'm pretty sure that if she can't find anything better somewhere else, she'll come back to us, hat in hand, asking for her old job.

The tech executives of the Silicon Valley have recently tried an unfamiliar hat-in-hand approach for aid from the state.

Origin: The saying is from the ancient custom of removing the hat as a gesture of respect or salutation. It often alludes to an attitude of servility or humility.

Usage note: Similar idea to *"on bended knee"*; see under **KNEES**.

Idle hands are the devil's playgrounds. (saying): Idleness is the root of mischief; nothing good comes from boredom.

"Idle hands are the devil's playgrounds" may be a cliché, but it holds some truth. Kids rarely misbehave when they are absorbed in enjoyable or challenging activities.

Origin: An old saying dating at least as far as Chaucer in the 12th century who called idle hands the devil's tools. www.phrases.org.uk/bulletin_board/24/messages/1217.html

Usage note: This saying is found in varying forms:

Idle hands do the devil's work.
Satan has some mischief for idle hands to do.
The devil finds work for idle hands (to do).
Idleness is the devil's workshop.
Idleness breeds vice.

In good hands (expression): In the care of an expert or reliable person

Doctor Lee is one of the best internists around. So don't worry, your mother will definitely be in good hands.

After watching the tail end of a recent rehearsal, I have every reason to believe that the show is in very good hands.

Usage note: The phrase *"good hands"* is a sports term, meaning "natural ability to catch a ball".

Know (something) like the back of your hand (v. phr.): To know (something) well

The reporter has lived in Iowa for years. He knows the state like the back of his hand.

I knew the layout of this ship like the back of my hand.

My husband is really good with computers; he knows them like the back of his hand.

Usage note: Often used with a place, but can also be used in other situations as well

Lay a hand on someone (v. phr): To harm someone

After going through rehabilitation, it is hoped he won't lay a hand on his mate again.

Usage note: Compare: *"lay a finger on someone"*; see under **FINGERS**.

Lay/get/put/your hands on someone (v. phr.): To catch someone

I'll kill the guy if I ever lay my hands on him.

Lay/get/put/your hands on something (v. phr.): To obtain something

I can never lay my hands on a stapler or a rubber band in this place!

I know I have that book somewhere in my house, but I can't lay my hands on it right now.

Left-handed compliment/back-handed compliment (expression): A compliment that ends up sounding insulting

My friend said that she was quite impressed that I could write so well about something about which I know nothing. That's the sort of left-handed compliment I've been getting lately.

He gave her a left-handed compliment when he said she was quite competent for a woman.

Origin: The left side has long been associated with wrongness ("sinister" is the Latin word for "left-handed"), a belief shared by many different cultures.

"Back-handed" is often synonymous with "left-handed" and is often used in the sense of being "round-about, indirect, or devious."

Live hand-to-mouth (v. phr.): To survive on little money

In his 20's, he didn't mind living hand-to- mouth or driving a $400 car.

The investment she made didn't pan out, and she's barely scraping by every month, living hand-to-mouth.

Usage note: A newer expression conveying the same idea in this modern-day American context would be *"to live from paycheck to paycheck."*

Many hands make light work. (saying): The more people helping, the faster the task is done.

There is much to be done and if everyone helps in some way then many hands make light work.

Usage note: It seems to contradict another saying: *"Too many cooks spoil the broth."*

Off-hand (adj.): Something said without forethought or preparation;

sometimes it can be surprisingly unpleasant

I don't appreciate an off-hand remark like that!

Origin: It's evolved from the older expression when *"off-hand,"* meant "unprepared"; *"in-hand"*, on the other hand, was used to describe something that was "in preparation" or that something was under control

Usage note: Also used when guessing or estimating something:

Off-hand, I would say about a hundred people were at the event.

One hand washes the other. (expression): The need to help one another; people with different know-how/expertise can very well complement each other.

Media events, such as concerts or Broadway shows, often invite us members of the media to come to their events free of charge. In a sense, one hand washes the other. They benefit by getting free coverage and we benefit in that we get materials to broadcast to our listeners and viewers.

Usage notes:

1. Probably in the same sense as *"You scratch my back, I'll scratch yours."* See under **BACK**.
2. I google-searched and found out that this expression exists in other languages as well; to name a few-Polish, German, Czech, Yiddish, Arabic and Zulu.

Play into someone's hands (v. phr.): To be or do something that another person can use against you, to give someone an advantage

Some people think that the United States is losing the war against terrorism and that the invasion of Iraq has only played into the enemy's hands.

We don't want to be physical with this team. We don't want to appear to bully them, because I think that's playing into their hands.

Usage note: A very common expression

Right-hand man (n. phr.): Chief assistant (of either sex), especially an indispensable and trusted one

The company president's decision to oust his right-hand man and heir apparent, was a puzzle to the industry and Wall Street analysts.

Origin: The right hand is usually the stronger of the two. It has therefore traditionally been thought of as a symbol of friendship and trust. The right-hand side is also the position of honor. These ideas come together in this old expression.

Usage note: I've also sometimes heard *"a right-hand woman"*.

Take matters into your (own) hands (v. phr.): To deal with a problem yourself because people who should have dealt with it have failed to do so

The families of the 9-11 victims took matters into their own hands and lobbied Congress to come up with new laws to better protect the homeland security.

Usage notes:

1 There is also an expression, *"to take the law into your hands"* (to do something illegal and often violent in order to punish someone since you know the law won't take care of it)

2. *"To take your life in your own hands"* is to do something that's very dangerous, especially where you risk death.

The hand that rocks the cradle rules the world. (saying): Used to emphasize that women have a strong influence on events through their children.

It is the mother who cares, nourishes and loves us. Yes, the hand that rocks the cradle rules the world, and makes a human being of you and me.

Origin: This saying comes from William Stewart Ross' poem *"Woman: Her Glory, her Shame, and her God"* (1894)

The right hand doesn't know what the left is doing. (expression): One is not fully aware of what one is doing; in a group, one person on a project is unaware of the action of others.

I don't think the candidate's right hand knows what his left hand is doing, judging from the way he discussed his proposed foreign policy if he got elected.

I'm not surprised that both managers scheduled two waitresses to come to work the same shift. It seems like the right hand doesn't know what the left is doing around here.

These developers are not talking to each other. When the right hand doesn't know what the left is doing, the entire project can be derailed.

Origin: From the Bible-Mathew 6:3-4:
But when you give to the needy, *don't let your left hand know what your right hand is doing,* so that your giving may be in secret. Then your Father, who sees what is done in secret, will reward you.

Usage notes:

1. The term is now used to describe the idea of being unproductive due to lack of corporation or coordination.
2. I've also seen *"the left hand doesn't know what the right is doing."*

Try your hand at something (v. phr.): To make an inexperienced attempt at something unfamiliar

I thought I would try my hand at skating, although I had never skated before.

Dave would like to try his hand at scuba diving one of these days if he can afford it.

Wait on someone hand and foot (v. phr.): To attend to someone's every need to the point of excess

Did you see how she waited on him hand and foot?

I remember that when I was pregnant, my husband waited on me hand and foot. No more of that now!

Wash your hands of something (v. phr.): To refuse to deal with a person, a problem or situation any longer, not accept responsibility

I think consumer product companies, the McDonald's and Sprites of the world, have really washed their hands of this basketball superstar at this point. They probably will look for someone else to endorse their products.

I'm getting tired of wasting time giving you advice and you never listening. I'm washing my hands of all of this!

Origin: From the Bible
Pontius Pilate literally washed his hands when he yielded to the people and condemned Jesus even though he found Jesus guiltless.

With one hand tied behind your back (expression): Very easily

He knows his job so well that he could do it with one hand tied behind his back.

Your hands are tied. (expression): You are unable to act because others are in control.

I don't believe that the President's hands were tied. He could have done something about it if he really wanted to. We're talking about the laws being broken here!

"Hands" Bonus

A dead man's hand (expression): Aces and eights in poker game (when dealt a full hand)

Origin: A reference to a poker hand held by Wild Bill Hickok (a U.S. town marshal famous for his lethal gun skills and his professional gambling) when he was shot dead in a saloon in Deadwood, Dakota Territory (1876)

A safe pair of hands (n. phr.): A person who can be trusted to do something without causing any trouble

Change hands (v. phr.): To go from one owner to another

The food is not as good as it used to be since the restaurant changed hands.

Evenhanded (adj.): Without partiality, fair

We should try harder to pursue evenhanded policy on refugees.

Usage note: I've seen it used three different ways: *"evenhanded"*, *"even-handed"* and *"even handed"*

Give someone the back of the hand (expression): To show contempt. It can be used as a warning that you are about to strike someone (with the back of your hand).

Usage note: I was told that this expression is pretty popular among Irish people. When they get mad at someone, they often say, *"the back of the hand to you!"*

Golden handcuffs (n. phr.): Business term. A package of perks and benefits offered by a company to talented employees or executives to keep them locked into their jobs for a certain period of time

Employee stock options, a company car and a promised sabbatical after seven years are some examples of golden handcuffs.

Golden handshakes (n. phr.): Business term. Special payments to employees who agree to take early retirement without fuss or complaints

Sometimes when employers are downsizing, they lay people off by offering golden handshakes.

Handpicked (adj.): Has been carefully chosen for a special job/purpose

Heavy-handed (adj.): Harsh or cruel in making someone obey; likely to hit or punish hard

Nixon was heavy-handed in sending National Guardsmen against 'flower' children protesting the Vietnam War.

In a quest to convict higher-ups, the prosecutors sometimes put intense pressure on minor figures thought to have some knowledge of the crime. It's scary, and it's heavy-handed, but it's common prosecutorial tactics.

Usage note: Whereas *"strong-armed"* means using direct force, *"heavy-handed"* implies using blunt force, with a hint of insensitivity or dumbness, and brutality.

Overplay your hand (expression): A card game term. To spoil your chance of success by saying or doing too much

Play the hand that is dealt you (expression): In life as in cards you can only work with what you have.

Talk to the hand (expression): "I'm tired of listening to you." (i.e. My ears are getting tired from having to listen to you; why don't you talk to my hand for a change?)

Usage note: A rather rude way to tell someone to shut up.

The hand is quicker than the eye. (expression): I was told that this is the expression often used relating to magicians' abilities.

Throw hands (expression): To fight.

Usage note: See also *"flying elbows"* under **"Elbows" Bonus** and *"fists fly"* under **FISTS**.

Throw up your hands (expression): To give up trying, admit you cannot succeed

She threw up her hands when she saw a pile of dishes in the kitchen sink.

Underhanded (adj.): Not legal, not according to rules

The defense attorney claimed the police employed underhanded tactics by wiretapping his client while refusing to name him a suspect.

"Do you think the boss fired Paul so quickly in order to hire his friend?"
"It's possible, but that would be so underhanded and so unethical!"

HEAD

In Their Words:

"Heads that are filled with wisdom have little space left for conceit."

Author Unknown

"I think there is only one quality worse than hardness of heart and that is softness of head."

Theodore Roosevelt (1858-1919)
The 26th U.S. President (1901-1909)

The head is like the engine of an automobile, that driving force that moves the car down the road. It is thought of as the location of one's intellect. With both the brain and the mind inside, the head is "the thinker". No wonder there are so many "head" idioms dealing with our wisdom, our way of thinking and reasoning.

A good head on your shoulders (expression): Having good common sense

You certainly <u>have a good head on those 19-year-old shoulders.</u>

I was a very overprotective sister. I guess I felt like he needed to be protected. But he really didn't. He always had such <u>a good head on his shoulders</u>, even as a little boy.

A headache (n. phr.): A person or thing that is a nuisance or gives trouble

That customer is a good tipper, but he can be such a <u>headache</u> sometimes.

I think I'm going to get rid of my car; it's been giving me <u>a real headache</u> lately.

Usage note: Also, *"a pain in the neck"*, *"a pain in the butt"* or *" a pain in the ass"* (bad language)

A hothead (n. phr.): A person who gets angry easily and often; a hot- tempered person

Don't be such a hothead!; try to control yourself.

If I was really a hothead, I would have punched that guy.

Usage note: Also as an adjective:

More and more businesses have enlisted anger management services not only to treat hotheaded employees but also to stave off problems before they emerge.

A roof over your head (expression): A place to live

People sometimes think that as long as they are providing a roof over their children's head, clothes on their back, and food on the table, they are being good parents; but it takes more than that.

One way to deal with your debts is to prioritize all your outgoings. Make sure you have a roof over your head, food to eat, and then work out what else you can afford.

Usage notes:

1. This expression is always used with "a"; "*a roof*" here means "*a house*".
2. Another useful expression having to do with "*roof*":
   "As long as you live under my roof, you have to go by my rules".

   American parents often use this line with their children (usually teenagers) who still live at home.

An old head on young shoulders, you can't put (expression): You can't expect a child or young person to think or talk like an older person who has more experience in life.

A street smart tip for your kids: Give them some simple directions on where to go if they are in trouble. But keep it simple. You can't put an old head on young shoulders.

I'd think today's young people are more sophisticated and more prepared than I was, but they obviously still make bad decisions, with worse results. I suppose nobody can put an old head on young shoulders.

Usage note: I accidentally came across this expression on www.famousproverbs.com. Never having heard about or seen it used before, I started to do more research because I wanted to include it in the book. Surprisingly, I found out that it wasn't listed in any idiom websites I went through. It could be that it's no longer in common use.

Beat your head against the wall (v. phr.): To be frustrated with a situation; try an impossible task; struggle uselessly against something

I'm beginning to feel that I'm beating my head against the wall trying to get you to go to the party with me tonight.

You're going to end up beating your head against the wall trying to please your boss. He's never going to appreciate you no matter what.

Usage note: Variations:

Beat your head against a stonewall

Hit/bang your head against a brick wall

Bite someone's head off (v. phr.): To answer in an angry or sharp manner, yelling and putting them down

All I ask is a little money. You don't have to bite my head off.

"No! You can't borrow my car any more. Go buy your own car and stop bothering me!"

"Okay! okay! I'm just asking. No need to bite my head off.

Usage Notes:

1. This is a very common expression.
2. I've always felt that there's a real fine distinction between *"bite someone's head off"* (snap at someone in one's answer, usually brief) and *"jump down someone's throat"* (often done suddenly without any warning or good reason; see under **THROAT**). However, I've noticed from what I've read and heard that people tend to use them interchangeably. I did some checking on this with a lot of American friends. They all seemed to think the two idioms mean more or less the same.

Bury your head in the sand (v. phr.): To refuse to see or face something unpleasant, to ignore a difficult situation

You need to find out more about protecting your finances from the unexpected (accidents, long illness, etc.), especially when you have a mortgage. Don't bury your head in the sand and think that these things won't happen to you.

Burying one's head in the sand and hoping the problem will go away is easier for most than confronting the issue.

Origin: This expression alludes to the ostrich who, when pursued, buries its head in the sand in the belief that because it cannot see its enemy, it cannot itself be seen. There is no evidence to prove that this is true, however.

Usage notes:

1. Variations:
   Hide/have/stick/ your head in the sand

   Your head is in the sand.

2. The opposite is "*get your head out of the sand*".
3. There's also another expression *"to play ostrich"*.

Get inside someone's head (v. phr.): To try to figure out someone's way of thinking (possibly either by observing him/her closely or by pretending to be that person)

Your job as an intelligence analyst is to get inside your opponent's head and figure out what he's going to do next. What motivates him? What will make him side with you or turn against you?

I was trying to talk to him during the match, to get inside his head, and get him off track. But it didn't work. He really stayed focused.

Get it through your head (v. phr.): To start to believe or understand (with the idea that you really have to make a great deal of effort)

Can't you get it through your head that I want out of the marriage?

Usage note: This phrase has a strong put-down tone. Another phrase that is even stronger is "*get it through your thick skull/ thick head.*"

Get/have/keep/ your head on straight (v. phr.): To understand the realities of the situation, have clear goals and an optimistic, can-do attitude

According to this job- hunting guide, the first thing you need to do is to get your head on straight. In other words, understand the realities of the job-hunting process, get into the right frame of mind and have positive thinking.

It was my choice to go back to school – it helps me keep my head on straight if I'm at school learning things.

Usage note: Another similar term is *"to have your head screwed on right/tight/the right way/properly"* (You are thinking clearly, not fantasizing.)

Get your head out of the clouds (v. phr.): To stop daydreaming; be more realistic

Get your head out of the clouds, will you? Come down to earth. Welcome to the real world.

You can dream on your days off, but please get your head out of the clouds when you are at work.

Usage note: "*Head in the clouds*" means "absent-minded, daydreaming":

Anne is a daydreamer. Her head is always in the clouds.

Get your head together (v. phr.): To become organized; to arrange your life properly

I need a few days off from work to get my head together- to think clearly again.

"Thirty-five is when you finally get your head together and your body starts to fall apart."

Author Unknown

Usage notes:

1. Variants: "get your act together" or "get it together", "get with it":

   You'd better start to seriously focus on what you want to achieve and get your act together.

2. Don't get it mixed up with "put our heads together" (to discuss, consult):

   None of us have all the answers but I'd bet we could figure something out if we put our heads together.

Go/get/ to your head (v. phr.): To cause you to be conceited

Her success has gone to her head and she thinks she is much better than anybody else.

I wasn't expecting to get all this attention this early. It makes me feel good, but I'm trying not to let it get to my head.

Usage notes:

1. In Czech, the expression would be *"it has risen to your head"*.
2. Another related expression is *"on a head trip"* meaning, "to be on an egotistical high":

   After he was made partner in the law firm, he went on a head trip that never quit.

   See more about *"head trip"* under **"Head" Bonus**.

3. *"Go to your head"* can also mean "to make you dizzy":

   The alcohol quickly went to his head and he had to lie down for a few minutes.

Go over someone's head (v. phr.): To attempt to accomplish something by bypassing your immediate superior and going directly to a higher-placed person

I'm afraid I have to go over my manager's head to get that cashier fired.

In order to get a pay raise, Paul went over his supervisor's head and straight to the owner.

Usage note: *"Going over someone's head"* is considered a little insulting or not a correct way of doing things (unless you have no other choice) because you're not giving the person involved a chance to take care of whatever the problem is.

Have a big head/give someone a big head (v. phr.): To be conceited; have too high an opinion of your own ability or importance

He's one of the most popular late night talk-show hosts, but he hasn't acted like he has a big head.

Thank you very much for your kind remarks. I hope they don't give me a big head.

Usage notes:

1. Some people might use "*a swelled head*" (or "*a swollen head*") instead; or with the verb "*to swell*":

   Don't give her any more compliments; her head is going to swell.

2. "*A big head*" can also mean "the discomfort feeling from drinking too much liquor":

   That Japanese sake really gave him a big head the next day.

Have a hole in your head (v. phr.): To be stupid; to be crazy

The way he talks-you can tell right away he has a hole in his head.

I must have a hole in my head to invite all these teenagers to my daughter's birthday party.

"Tact is the ability to tell a man he has an open mind when he has a hole in his head."

Author Unknown

Usage note: Also, *"to have a screw loose"*

Have rocks in your head (v. phr.): To have poor judgment, make bad decisions (It's hard to think clearly since your head is so dense like having rocks inside.)

John must have rocks in his head to buy that 20 year-old used car and think it would last a long time.

Usage note: There's an old saying *"They are a good match; the rocks in his head fit the holes in her head."*

Head and shoulders above/ahead of (adj. phr.): To be clearly better, far exceeding

He was an athlete head and shoulders ahead of his peers in terms of sheer athletic ability. His combination of speed, strength and desire earned him all-state recognition in football, wrestling and baseball at his high school.

I voted for Reagan when I was 18. He was head and shoulders above anybody who has come since.

Origin: The phrase comes from the notion that a tall person may tower over a short one. (Rogers, James 1985)

Head over heels (expression): Has several meanings:

1. Completely, deeply, entirely:

   She was head over heels in love with him.

   I'm head over heels for my new video game.

   He was head over heels in debt.

2. In a somersault; upside down, head first

   It was so dark I fell down the stairs head over heels.

3. Hastily, in great confusion

   The kids all hurried in the door at the same time, head over heels.

Usage note: It's true that we often use this phrase to describe people who are madly in love; but we can use it in other situations as well.

Head to head (adv. phr., adj. phr.): In direct competition (between two people or two teams)

The centerpiece of the All-Star Weekend is the All-Star Game, where the NBA's best go head to head.

The Democratic candidate played down a new Newsweek poll that showed him tied with the incumbent President in a head-to-head match up.

Head to toe, (from) (expression): The whole body

The car racer was dressed head to toe in the purple and yellow logos of his sponsor.

That girl is beautiful from head to toe.

Usage notes:

1. I've also seen "from head to foot", or "from top to toe", although I've never heard it used myself.
2. The *"toe"* in this expression is used in a singular form.
3. I've seen it used both with and without *"from".'*

Heads up (interj, n. phr.): Watch out! ; Also an advice or reminder about some problem or mistake that may embarrass you.

Heads up! I just saw one of the kids throwing the ball towards us.

Thanks for the heads up. If you hadn't told me, I would have made the same mistake again.

Heads will roll.(expression): There will be changes in the organization (people will be punished, lose their jobs, or forced to resign, etc.) because something bad has happened or because there is a new boss.

If this project is not finished by the end of the month, heads will roll.

Heads will roll at the Daily News when the new editor arrives tomorrow; she expects a lot and upsets a lot of people.

Origin: The saying dates back to the 1930's.

Usage notes:

1. This expression is used a lot in the news.
2. It can also be used in the past tense, or with "should/must", or with infinitive form:

   There was outrage and heads did roll after Pearl Harbor--there was an immediate investigation and the commanders, Kimmel and Short, were held responsible and forced to resign.

Heads should roll at the Pentagon for their failure to properly plan for postwar developments in Iraq.

Lawmakers called for heads to roll after the name of a CIA agent was leaked and appeared in some newspapers.

Hit the nail on the head (v. phr.): To say precisely the most accurate thing, to express perfectly

The teacher hit the nail on the head when she said that John would become a better speller if he tried to read more.

Wow, you hit the nail on the head! Great article! You got it right!

Origin: This is an old expression. One theory is that it came from the Bible:

Judges 5:26 She put her hand to *the nail*, and her right hand to the workmen's hammer, and with the hammer she smote Sisera, she *smote off his head*, when she had pierced and stricken through his temples.

(my.homewithgod.com/mkcathy/inspirational2/expressions.html)

However, most people think the expression refers more to hitting a nail properly, that is, squarely on the head and alludes to communicating effectively, or being to the point. A bad hit (which bends the nail), on the other hand, is like rambling on and fails to get to the point.

Usage note: A very common expression.

Hold your head high (v. phr.): To feel proud of yourself; to be unashamed

We came to play, refused to give up and could hold our heads high even in losing.

How did she manage to hold her head high after her husband devastatingly betrayed her?

It's all in your head. (expression): Used to describe a problem that doesn't exist and is only imagined

I didn't think I could go on stage without a drink, so I took some whiskey to

help me out. But it's all in your head. You get to where you can learn to do without it and do a lot better.

For years, women have been told PMS (pre-menstrual syndrome) is in their heads. Now it has been proved that it's not an emotional problem, but a physical one.

Usage note: Some people might say, "*It's in your mind*".

In over your head (expression): The situation is too difficult for you.

My sister has a gambling problem. It happened so fast and secretly that I knew nothing of it until she was way in over her head and unable to control it.

He was a very good salesman. But when he was promoted to be the manager of the store, he found himself in over his head. He simply couldn't handle all the extra responsibilities.

Origin: It alludes to an unskilled swimmer who has fallen into the water that is too deep.

Keep a cool head (v. phr.): To stay calm in a difficult situation; keep being unemotional or in total control of yourself

Jim is the kind of guy who can keep a cool head in a hot situation.

How do you manage to keep a cool head in such a hectic, stressful place like this?

Usage note: Notice how *"a cool head"* and *"a hothead"* are used in the following sentence:

The candidate is usually known to have a cool head in a political crisis, but lately he has been such a hothead.

Keep your head (v. phr.): Not to panic, try to think clearly; remain calm when there is trouble or danger.

I'm looking forward to the match. The big thing is to keep my head and stay relaxed.

Our advice is clear: keep your head even though the rest of the world might seem to be losing theirs.

Usage notes:

1. The opposite is "*lose your head*" (discussed later in this section)
2. Compare *"keep your head"* and *"keep a cool head"*.

Keep your head above water (v. phr.): To continue to overcome life's financial difficulties

We're just trying to keep our heads above water now. We have a small savings account; but we haven't added anything to that money for quite sometime.

It is not easy to keep your head above water while you're going through a divorce.

Keep your head down (v. phr.): To avoid trouble

Keep your head down. Get back to your seat. The teacher is coming.

The boss is in a bad mood today. Try to keep your head down. Act busy!

Keep your head up (v. phr.): To remain positive, don't get discouraged

I've got to keep my head up. It's disappointing if I can't play, but I've got to keep a positive attitude and help the team any way I can.

Try to keep your head up, never walk around with your chin dragging.

Usage notes:

1. Don't get it mixed up with "*keep your head.*"
2. Same idea as "*keep your chin up"*

Levelheaded (adj.): Exercising or showing good judgment; sensible

He's smart and he's levelheaded. He knows what he's doing.

More than luck, a major reason for her fortune is that she is extremely

levelheaded in her investment decisions.

Your article was the most sincere, levelheaded, and intelligent analysis of the attacks on the Twin Towers that I've read.

Usage notes:

1. You can use "*levelheaded*" to describe a person as well as an idea.
2. When used with a person, the meaning is pretty close to "*have a good head on your shoulders*". The only difference I can think of (aside from the fact that they are different parts of speech) is that "*have a good head on your shoulders*" is more informal.

Lose your head (v. phr.): To become confused or crazy about, to lose emotional control over something

Everyone calm down! Let's not lose our heads over such a stupid argument.

It's no use losing your head over her. She's not worth it.

Need someone/something/ like a hole in the head (v. phr.): To have no need whatsoever for someone or something

I needed more house guests like a hole in the head.

She needed more problems like a hole in the head.

No, I don't want another piece of pie; I need that like a hole in the head.

Usage note: There is sarcasm in the above sentences since, obviously, nobody needs a hole in the head.

Off the top of your head (expression): Without thinking hard

She probably made the story up off the top of her head.

Off the top of my head, I can remember only a few names of my high school classmates.

Usage notes:

1. The phrase implies that the inside of the head isn't being used to

come up with the answer; you're just giving an immediate reaction and not carefully considered opinion and so it might not be correct.

2. There is an expression *"to talk off the top of your head"* meaning "to speak speculatively, without thorough consideration"

Over your head (expression): Too complicated or difficult to understand

I think the joke was <u>over his head</u>. He didn't laugh, so he must not have understood.

To be honest, I had no idea what these famous professors were talking about. I felt like a guy who suddenly found himself in the middle of a foreign land. It was way <u>over my head.</u>

Usage notes:

1. Compare the difference between *"over your head"* and *"in over your head"*
2. In Portuguese, it would be *"This is too much sand for my truck"*. And in Thai, *" My head can't reach."*

Put/stick/raise/ your head above the parapet (expression): British. To be brave enough to state an opinion that might upset someone

Nobody wanted to criticize the owner's decision because they were all afraid to <u>put their head above the parapet.</u>

<u>To put one's head above the parapet</u> is to invite envy, ostracism or worse.

Usage note: Or, "to be outspoken"

Scratch your head (v. phr.): To feel confused

Some of us <u>are scratching our heads,</u> wondering where the help is going to come from.

Soft in the head (expression): Stupid, dimwitted, not very intelligent in making decisions, having poor judgment

If you quit your job as the vice-president of that big company, you are soft in the head.

Usage note: Roughly the same idea as *"have rocks in your head"* but doesn't sound as harsh

Turn heads/turn someone's head (v. phr.): To catch people's attention

Her looks are so extraordinary that she turns heads everywhere she goes.

George Burns turned Hollywood's head with his memorable performance in the 1975 film "The Sunshine Boys".

My 85 year-old grandmother would walk down the street and actually turn men's heads.

Usage note: The expression *"that will turn your head"* can mean two things: 1. It will get your attention. 2. It will make you feel conceited. (Same as *"go to your head"*)

Two heads are better than one. (saying): Teams or groups typically produce better solutions than individuals do.

I've got a problem with this homework. Maybe you can help me out. Two heads have got to be better than one.

You and your friend need to put your heads together to come up with the solution. Remember what they say? Two heads are better than one.

Usage note: This kind of saying is common in most cultures. Thai has the same exact expression; in Czech, *"More heads know more."* and in Japanese, *"Three people together have the wisdom of Buddha."*

Use your head (v. phr.): To think, use your brain, have common sense

Nobody can tell you what to do. Use your head and figure something out.

"Don't rule out working with your hands. It does not preclude using your head."

Andy Rooney (1919-) American journalist, TV commentator

Usage note: Another term expressed the same idea is *"use your noodle"* (*"Noodle"* is an old word for "head".):

Way to go! That was really using your noodle!

Wrap your head around something (v. phr.): You have difficulty understanding something, but you try really hard to do so

Being a fan of this singer isn't easy. As soon as you wrap your head around what he's doing, he reinvents himself and you have to look at him and his music in a whole new light.

Your head off (adv. phr.): Mightily, a lot, too much

John had to scream his head off before he could get their attention.

She laughed her head off when she heard that joke.

The guy would talk his head off if you let him.

You need/should have/ your head examined. (expression): There's something wrong with the way you think.

If you still want to do business with this guy after all of this, you need your head examined.

"Head" Bonus

An airhead (n.): A stupid person.

My teenage daughter is developing into a classic stereotype of the blonde airhead.

Usage note: Also, *"a moron", "a dimwit", "a fat head", "a lard head"*

An egghead (n.): An intellectual and/or highbrow person or activity

A head (n.): Has two meanings:

1. Common slang for "toilet"

A funny story told by my editor, James Oliver:

The first time James went to England he was walking in London and needed to use the bathroom, he went into a pub and asked the barman:

"Where is your head?"

The barman: *"On top of my neck."*

It was a while before James figured out they were 'two countries separated by a common language' – in England you ask for the *loo.*

Usage note: "Head" in this sense is not technically a body part.

2. A habitual drug user

Usage notes:

1. Sometimes called "a pot head", "a dope head"
2. *"A head shop"* is where dope paraphernalia is sold.
3. *"A head trip"* is what happens to the mind as a result of taking some drugs.

A headbanger (n.): Slang. A fan of heavy metal music

A head shrinker (n. phr.): Slang. A psychoanalyst, often called a *"shrink"*

A sleepy head (n. phr.): A child or person who is tired or sleepy

A talking head (n. phr.): Slang for a television newsreader or analyst whose head and neck (but not the whole body) usually appear on the screen

Have a head for (expression): To be gifted (more an innate ability)

She has a good head for science.

Light-headed (adj.): Dizzy

Not right in the head (expression): Mentally deficient, stupid

HEART

In Their Words:

"A man who works with his hands is a laborer. A man who works with his hands and his brain is a craftsman; but a man who works with his hands and his brain and his heart is an artist."

Louis Nizer (1902-1994)
English-born American lawyer

"If your head tells you one thing, and your heart tells you another, before you do anything, you should first decide whether you have a better head or a better heart."

Marilyn vos Savant (1946-)
American journalist

The heart is often used metaphorically as the seat of our emotions (the heart vs. the head) and as a metaphor for our will (*"he doesn't have the heart to"; "his heart isn't in it"*). It is also used in the sense of 'being in the midst of something' (*"to get to the heart of the matter")*.

A bleeding heart (expression): An extremely softhearted person who feels compassion towards everyone, including those who may not deserve sympathy

My friends call me a bleeding heart because I believe in peace and social welfare.

To my husband, a die-hard Republican, this candidate is just a bleeding-heart, liberal Democrat.

Origin: It started off as a religious term. In the Middle Ages, the *Knights of the Bleeding Heart* (a semi-religious order) honored the Virgin Mary "whose heart was pierced by many sorrows". Its meaning took a negative sense in the 20th century America. At the time, some people felt that government and private charities should have done more to help relieve the suffering of the sick, the homeless and unemployed. In 1930's, Westbrook Pegler, a noted conservative columnist who disagreed with this idea, used the term "*bleeding heart liberals*" to describe these people (www.wordwithyou.com).

Usage notes:

1. I've also often heard *"a do- gooder"*; I think people use it in the same sense as *"a bleeding heart"*.
2. See also *"My heart bleeds for you,"* later in this section.

A change of heart (n. phr.): A reversal of your opinion, attitude or feeling about a certain situation

I had told people I'd never marry, but I had a change of heart when I met my boyfriend.

He abruptly announced a change of heart about the marriage.

Usage note: Similar in meaning to *"change your mind"* (see under **MIND**.), but with an emphasis on 'feeling' rather than 'logic'

A heart-to-heart (talk) (n. phr.): A serious, intimate and straightforward conversation

After my husband's death, I decided to have a heart-to-heart talk with my children about how to manage without him.

You need to have a heart-to-heart with him about substance abuse.

Absence makes the heart grow fonder. (saying): The time spent apart makes you care for a person even more.

I get along better with my parents now since I moved out of the house. I miss them more and always look forward to seeing them whenever I can. Like the old adage says, absence makes the heart grow fonder.

Origin: It dates from Roman times, but only became popular after Thomas Haynes Bayly (1797-1839), a British songwriter and dramatist, used it as the last line of a song in the *Isle of Beauty*.

Usage notes:

1. It can also be used ironically:

The boss has been leaving work real early these days; oh well, absence makes the heart grow fonder.

2. This saying clearly contradicts another old saying: *Out of sight, out of mind.* (See under **MIND**.)

3. The opposite sentiment is expressed by another saying: *Familiarity breeds contempt.*

After your own heart (adj. phr.): Someone who sees things the way you do

You're a man after my own heart. I've had the same feeling when traveling – oftentimes I can't wait to get back to Southern California.

When I saw her interacting with the cats, I knew right away she was a woman after my own heart.

Origin: From the Bible. Samuel 13:14. But now thy Kingdom shall not continue: the Lord hath sought him a man *after his own heart*, and the Lord had commanded him to be captain over his people, because thou hast not kept that which the Lord commanded thee.

Usage note: This expression is listed in most idiom books and websites. I have, however, heard someone use it only once.

Almost/nearly/ have a heart attack (expression): Informal. To be extremely shocked or surprised

I almost had a heart attack when my friend told me she was getting married; I didn't even know she had a boyfriend or was dating anyone.

I bet you almost had a heart attack when you found out you won that big jackpot, didn't you?

Usage note: Other related expressions: *"give someone a heart attack"* and *"get/have/ a heart attack":*

My grandmother would have had a heart attack to see me working with these great movie stars.

At heart (adv. phr.): Basically; in reality, in spite of the appearances

He might have rough manners but he is a kind person at heart.

Even though we live in a big city, I'm still a country girl at heart.

Usage note: There's an expression *"young at heart"*:

She may be sixty, but she's still young at heart.

Bless your heart! (expression): Phrase used to express a sincere desire for increased blessings to come someone's way.

"He's such a well-behaved baby, bless his heart!"

"That woman just turned 100 years old a few months ago."
"Bless her heart! She does look good, doesn't she?"

Our long-haired Chihuahua, bless his heart, now has a new home.

Customer #1: "Here comes the lady with hot coffee!"
Customer #2: "Bless her heart!"

Usage note: This expression is a staple of southern conversation. It can be a term of endearment, a way to nod to an eccentricity or excuse a blind spot, or an expression of sympathy in the face of misfortune:

No one noticed that Aunt Greta - bless her heart -forgot to put the sugar in her famous strawberry lemonade.

Bless his heart! You have to at least give him credit for hanging in there after what happened.

This same expression can also be added to any insulting statement. It has been noted that a southerner can get away with the most outrageous kind of insult just as long as it is prefaced or followed with the word *"bless his/her heart"*:

She's dumber than a door knob, bless her heart!
www.dobhran.com/humor/Grhumor72

"That newspaper columnist is as dumb as a box of rocks", he said. "Bless his heart!" she replied. ("I agree with the unkind thing you have just said but do not wish to say so myself.")
www.edcone.com

Break someone's heart (v. phr.): To give someone very bad news, or make someone feel very bad, sad or disappointed

The breakup with her boyfriend really broke her heart.

He broke his mother's heart when he dropped out of school.

The San Francisco game broke his heart.

Usage note: This idiom is used not only in the romantic sense; it can be used in other situations as well.

By heart (adv. phr.): Memorized completely or word by word

My cousin knows most of Elvis' songs by heart.

I haven't been there in 10 years, but I still know the route by heart.

Usage note: In the second sentence, you can also say *"know it like the back of my hand"*; see under **HANDS**.

Close/dear/near/to your heart (adj. phr.): Loved by or very important to you and you have strong feelings about it

This particular painting was near to the artist's heart.

Her youngest son is dear to her heart.

Cold-hearted (adj.): Unsympathetic, lack of empathy

She is a cold-hearted, vain woman who always looks out for her own interests.

He reminded me of that tight-fisted, cold-hearted Scrooge in "Christmas Carol".

Usage note: The opposite is *"warm-hearted"*.

Cross my heart (and hope to die) (v. phr.): To promise that you are telling the truth or promise to perform an act in the future.

To make his point stronger, the boy said, "cross my heart and hope to die, I didn't touch your money."

I'll pay you back next week. Cross my heart.

Usage notes:

1. Most often used by children – they sometimes say the longer form while making a sign of a cross over the heart at the same time. It's a form of oath swearing, not commonly used by adults.
2. Other alternatives: *"Honestly", "Seriously", "Trust me", "(You've got to) take my word for it"*, *"I swear!"*

Do your heart good (expression): Old-fashioned term. To lift your spirit; make you feel good emotionally

Her get-well card really did my heart good.

It did my heart good to see a wholesome show like that.

Usage notes:

1. Or, *"It makes me feel good."*
2. There's also an expression *"do your body good":*

"Milk does your body good." (Milk is good for your body.)
An ad

Don't have the heart to (expression): To feel unable to do something because you think it would be unkind

I didn't have the heart to tell her to stop talking, even though it was hard for me to try to listen to her and concentrate on work at the same time.

She didn't have the heart to disappoint such a cherished friend by missing his wedding.

Eat your heart out (expression): Has two meanings:

1. Be jealous of someone for something they have

She hated to see him with his new girlfriend; she was <u>eating her heart out.</u>

It is often used by a person who wants to gloat:

<u>Eat your heart out</u>, I'm going on a cruise for three weeks.

2. To worry excessively

It's no use <u>eating your heart out</u> about things that can't be helped.

My son is suffering so much it's <u>eating my heart out.</u>

Usage note: The #1 meaning is a more common usage.

***Faint heart never won fair maiden*.** (old saying): Literally, if you don't speak up because you're afraid of rejection, you'll never get a lady's attention. Figuratively, you must make a lot of effort if you want to achieve something difficult.

Usage note: *"The faint of heart"* or *"the faint-hearted"* are "people who are timid, not courageous."

Skydiving is not for <u>the faint of heart.</u>

"The future doesn't belong to <u>the faint-hearted;</u> it belongs to the brave."

Ronald Reagan (1911-2004)
The 40th U.S. President (1981-1989)

Find it in your heart (v. phr.): To be disposed or willing to do something unpleasant or difficult

Can you <u>find it in your heart</u> to forget about the problems you two had in the past?

He didn't think <u>he could find it in his heart</u> to forgive his wife for her adultery.

Usage note: This expression is often said with the implication that you are doing a great favor (Rogers, James 1985).

Follow your heart (v. phr.): To do what you wish to do rather than to follow the voice of reason

Instead of accepting a lucrative deal with a professional football team, he followed his heart and joined the army instead.

From the bottom of your heart (expression): To sincerely mean what you say or do, to deeply feel about something

Thank you from the bottom of my heart for helping me out today.

Trust me, she's sorry from the bottom of her heart for having hurt your feelings.

Get/go/ to the heart of the matter (of something) (v. phr.): To understand the most important thing about something

If I were the owner of this company, I'd try to get to the heart of the matter of the employees' low morale.

The artist's images got to the heart of the matter: war is a great tragedy.

Usage note: Because of the heart's position and importance in the body, it becomes the center or 'core' of things.

Have a heart (expression): A pleading exclamation meaning, don't be so cruel, have some feelings, have some sympathy, be merciful

Have a heart, boys. This was only my first mistake.

"Have a heart, save a heart."

An ad

Have a soft spot (in your heart) for someone/ something (expression): To have a particular fondness for someone or something

I have a soft spot in my heart for my oldest nephew, probably because I was so close to him when he was growing up.

My brother has a soft spot for puppies, but not for big dogs.

Have the heart (v. phr.): To have the passion, courage or emotional strength

One must have the heart and the motivation for wanting to change.

The Cowboys had the talent. The Steelers had the coaching, and the heart.

Usage note: Notice the difference in meanings between "*have a heart*" and "*have the heart*".

Have your heart in your mouth/ Your heart is in your mouth. (expression): To get a choking feeling from fear or nervousness.

I had my heart in my mouth when I heard that loud bang.

He nervously proposed to her with his heart in his mouth.

Usage notes:

1. When your heart starts pounding so much that you can feel a thumping in your throat, it may feel like you "*have your heart in your mouth*". This is quite an old expression. A modern equivalent would be *"to be scared to death."*
2. Also, *"your heart sinks into your boots"*
3. In German, it would be *"your heart falls into your pants"*.

Have your heart set on something/set your heart on something (v. phr.): To wish for intensely, to desire greatly

She has her heart set on buying a new car as soon as she can afford it.

Usage note: Or, "*to set your sights on something*":

He/she has a big heart. (expression): He/she is very caring and thoughtful.

He has such a big heart. He always tries to be there for his friends who need help.

Usage notes:

1. Notice that it's a good thing to "*have a big heart*", but bad to "*have a big head*"
2. Similar in meaning to "*heart of gold*", but more informal

Heart and soul (n. phr.): All of your effort, your entire energy or passion

I put my heart and soul into that project.

Usage note: It can also mean the key or critical component:

She's our heart and soul. She allows the team to get more out of its skilled players.

Our defense has always been the heart and soul of this team.

Heart and soul, with (all your) (adv. phr.): Fervently, enthusiastically, wholly; engaging all of your interest or emotions

I love you with all my heart and soul.

I've learned what I can do. Then I do what I can with all my heart and soul.

Usage note: We often hear "*with all my heart*" but not often "*with all my soul*". Putting them together helps intensify the statement.

Heart of gold (n. phr.): Gentle, generous nature; very caring about others

She was known to have a heart of gold and a real concern for people in unfortunate circumstances.

People shouldn't try to take advantage of the man's heart of gold.

Heart of stone (n. phr.): Cold, unforgiving nature, unsympathetic. It can also mean unresponsive to love or romance.

Nothing fazes him; he has a heart of stone.

Commanding officers sometimes have to act like they have a heart of stone. It's the only way to keep things in order in their units.

He brought her flowers, took her to expensive restaurants, but was unable to melt her heart of stone.

Heart races. (expression): It works extremely fast because of excitement, drugs, etc.

A glimpse of his bare chest set her heart racing.

There's nothing like a good shock to get the heart racing.

I was hot and had a racing heart after taking that new medication.

Usage note: Also, *"mind/pulse/ races."*

Heart-wrenching (adj. phr.): Emotionally draining

The TV coverage from Russia was heart- wrenching. I could feel the pain of those parents and grandparents. And not since 9/11 have I been so angry.

My cat had cancer that spread to all parts of his body. After hearing him cry out in pain at 3 a.m., my family and I made the heart-wrenching decision to have him put to sleep.

Usage note: Stronger than "*heart-breaking*".

In a heartbeat (expression): Immediately, without hesitation

If I had to do it again, I'd do it in a heartbeat.

Growing up happens in a heartbeat. One day you have them in diapers; the next day they're gone.

Usage note: I was told that another common expression is *"in a New York minute"*; I've never heard it used myself.

In your heart of hearts (expression): Truly, at the deepest level in your heart; in your most secret and true thoughts

I didn't want to believe the news, but in my heart of hearts, I knew it was true.

It may look like they're not going to make it, but I think in my heart of hearts, they are going to be fine as long as they are together.

Usage note: Used to emphasize the true essence of your being

Light-hearted (adj.): Happy and not serious; being in or showing good spirits

It was a fairly light-hearted discussion.

In this play, the writer made a light-hearted jab at love, marriage and infidelity.

I like light-hearted people, not people who take themselves so seriously.

Lose heart (v. phr.): To stop believing that you can succeed; to become demoralized

Don't lose heart just yet. There are more chances you might get a promotion.

The old samurai wrote that one enthusiastic swordsman could defeat ten demoralized fighters. "Attack them boldly, so they lose heart and scatter".

Usage notes:

1. Variant: "*to get discouraged*"
2. The opposite is *"to take heart"*.
3. Another idiom "*lose your heart to someone*" – similar in wording but different in meaning. It's an elaborate way of saying "*you fall in love with someone*".

My heart bleeds for you. (expression): Phrase often used humorously or sarcastically to mean the opposite of what it says

My friend complained she might not be able to go on a cruise again this year. My heart bleeds for her!

"I'll think about you while I'm breaking my back working during Christmas holidays".
"And making dough hand over fist! My heart bleeds for you!"

Usage note: It is rarely used to express sympathy; some other terms used instead are *"I feel your pain.", "I feel great pain for you.", "I feel for your loss."*

Open your heart to someone (v. phr.): To tell someone about your problems or secrets

He seemed to be very understanding. I felt like I could open my heart to him.

Put your heart into something (v. phr.): To try hard, do your best

My sister is such a hard worker. She puts her heart into everything she does.

Put your heart into helping others, which you're good at, and forget the mindless gossip.

Usage note: Or, *"to give it your best shot"*.

Straight from your/the/ heart (adv. phr.): Sincerely, honestly

I could see by the expression on her face that her offer to help came straight from her heart.

Every musical note that he plays is full of warmth and straight from the heart.

Usage note: Compare: *"straight from the shoulder"*; see under **SHOULDERS**.

Strike at the heart of something (v. phr.): To damage something severely by attacking the most important part of it

The 9/11 attacks struck at the heart of our sense of security.

Take heart (v. phr.): To regain courage and strength

Take heart, guys, the work is almost done.

Take heart, USC fans, the coach may have choked in a few big games lately, but he's a proven coach with a winning record and an ability to recruit top athletes. Now is not the time to change coaches.

Take to heart (v. phr.): To take seriously and be affected or troubled by

If I were you, I wouldn't take your mother's criticism to heart and get defensive.

"We Take Matters of the Heart, to Heart."
An ad

The way to a man's heart is through his stomach. (saying): Feeding a man good food will cause him to love you.

They say the way to a man's heart is through his stomach. This really applied to a cold hungry hiker like me on that fateful day!

I don't believe that the way to a man's heart is through his stomach. If I had believed that, I would never have married my wife. She's not a good cook at all.

Usage note: Other cultures probably have similar kind of advice. The one I'm most familiar with is a Thai saying, *"(With) the charm at the tip of a ladle, (your) husband will love you to death!"* (a word-by-word translation)
Or, as one would say in German: *"Kissing doesn't last but cooking does"*
One has to admit that food does play an important role in the art of wooing!

To your heart's content (expression): Until you are completely satisfied; as long as desired

Stop by, have a cookie and a cup of warm cider and browse to your heart's content.

I like living in the country. My dog can run around in the open space to his heart's content.

Warm the cockles of your heart (expression): To please you, make you feel good; to arouse your innermost feelings in a pleasant way

I enjoyed being with my grandmother. Just thinking of her warmed the cockles of my heart.

"Lassie" is the kind of movie that will warm the cockles of just about anybody's heart.

Origin: The expression turned up first in the mid 17th century and that the earliest form was "rejoice the cockles of your heart". The word "cockles" is used either as a comparison of the shape of the heart with that of a cockleshell, or because the zoological name for "cockles" is "cardium" (heart), or because the Latin name for the ventricles (the chambers) of the heart is "cochleae cordis" ("cochleae" means "snail-shells). This last explanation sounds the most likely. (http://users.tinyonline.co.uk/gswithenbank/sayingsw.htm)

Wear your heart on your sleeve (expression): To show your feelings clearly and openly; to be frank or impulsive

Everybody can tell she is in love with the guy—she simply wears her heart on her sleeve.

I'm the type that wears my heart on my sleeve. I cannot hide exactly how I'm feeling from anybody who knows me.

Origin: It was once a custom for a young man to attach to his sleeve a gift from a young lady he loved, thus displaying his feelings.

Usage note: Whether it's good or bad to *"wear your heart on your sleeve"* depend on what the context is and/or how you look at it. In certain situations, it might be better to *"play your cards close to your chest"* (see under **CHEST**).

Win the heart and mind (of someone) (v. phr.): To make them like you and have a good opinion of you

Vietnam taught us that to defeat a guerrilla army, you must win the hearts and minds of the people. How many hearts and minds did we win there?

Usage note: Also, *"lose/change the heart (of someone)*

Your heart goes out to someone. (expression): You feel very sorry for someone.

Please accept my sympathy on the loss of your son. My heart goes out to you.

We would like to offer condolences for the victims of the latest attacks in your country. Our hearts go out to the families that lost their loved ones.

Your heart is heavy. (expression): You are stricken with grief and sorrow.

Even now, my heart is still heavy when I think of my only son who died in a car accident a few years ago.

Usage note: Also used as a noun, *"a heavy heart":*

He went to his mother's funeral with a heavy heart.

"A light purse makes a heavy heart."
Author Unknown

Your heart is in the right place. (expression): You have good intentions.

I know that her heart is in the right place even though she didn't give me the kind of birthday gift I had hoped for.

I believe in the President politically. I may not agree with him on all the issues, but I think his heart is in the right place. He really cares about the people.

Usage note: Often applied to situations where someone means well and intends to do good deeds, but things don't turn out as well as they were supposed to.

Your heart isn't in it. (expression): You don't feel interested or enthusiastic about something.

If your heart isn't in this kind of work, you should go look for something you might like better.

I wanted to drive across the country. But when the big day came, my heart wasn't in it.

Your heart/spirit/ sinks. (expression): You feel disappointed or lose hope.

Her heart sank when she realized she couldn't afford that house.

Your heart stops/stands still. (expression): You are paralyzed with fright or are astonished by something

My heart stopped when I saw the face on the TV special news report. That was my own brother and the police were after him!

"Heart" Bonus

A black heart (n. phr.): A wicked person, evil by nature

A heart as big as all outdoors (expression): Extremely generous or compassionate

A heartthrob (n.): An object (usually a person) of romantic love or infatuation

A Purple Heart (n. phr.): An American medal given to soldiers who have been injured in war

'Be still my heart!' (expression): A whispered prayer to help gain composure

Harden your heart (v. phr.): To make yourself stop feeling kind or friendly to someone

You've got to harden your heart and say 'no' to him.

Heartless (adj.): Without feelings, compassion

Make a half-hearted effort (expression): Not to give your full effort

Make (your) heart flutter (expression): You find someone very physically attractive and you feel excited when you see or talk to them.

He has been making hearts flutter since the first day he started working here.

Play on your heart strings (expression): To cause you to feel emotional or sentimental

HEELS

In Their Words:

"Time wounds all heels."

Jane Sherwood Ace (1905-1974)
American actress

(A play on *Time heals all wounds.*)

"Grief walks upon the heels of pleasure; married in haste, we repent at leisure."

William Congreve (1670-1729)
English playwright

--- ---------------------------

There are the heels of your feet and there are also the heels of your shoes. The idioms discussed below involve both kinds of "heels."

Achilles' heel (expression): A seemingly small but actually crucial weakness in a person or system that can result in its failure

A misbehaving cabinet member is undoubtedly regarded as the government's Achilles' heel and is often pressured to resign.

The question of religious freedom is the Achilles' heel in this Asian country's human rights record.

Origin: The term alludes to Greek legend about heroic warrior Achilles. His mother tried to make her infant son immortal by holding him by the heel and dipping him into the River Styx, whose water was believed to confer invulnerability, but his heel remained dry because her hand was cupped over it. Eventually he died as a result of a wound from an arrow that struck him in that heel.

Usage notes:

1. The "*ch*" in the name is pronounced with a "k" sound.
2. I've seen it used both ways: *"Achilles' heel"* and *"Achilles heel"*
3. We also refer to the strong tendon that connects the muscles of the calf of the leg with the heel bone as the "Achilles tendon" or "Achilles heel". An athlete who hurts this tendon may need

surgery and expect a long recovery.

Bring to heel (v. phr.): To force to obey

The prisoners were immediately brought to heel.

Origin: The term transfers the idea of commanding a dog to come close behind its owner to similar control over human beings. (Ammer, Christine 1997)

Cool/kick/ your heels (v. phr.): To be kept waiting, especially when it's annoying and boring

The star center sometimes charges too hard, getting himself into foul trouble and forcing his coach to cool his heels on the bench.

The doctor kept Linda cooling her heels for over two hours.

Origin: The term originally meant to cool one's feet when they became hot from walking, and began to be used ironically for being forced to rest (or wait) in the early 1600's. (Ammer, Christine 1997)

Dig in your heels/dig your heels in (v. phr.): To refuse to change your mind, plans or ideas, especially when someone is trying persuade you to do so

She dug in her heels, refusing to give in, and soon held her tongue.

To dig your heels in and fight may win you an immediate battle but may also rupture a long-term working relationship with your colleagues.

Down at the heels (adj. phr.): Untidy, in poor conditions or circumstances; poor, destitute

Those kids were all down at the heels.

Usage notes:

1. The term refers to the sad state of a person's worn-out shoes.
2. Also, *"out at the heels"* ("having holes in one's socks or shoes")
3. The opposite is "*to be well-heeled*", meaning "rich, well-off"
4. See also "*out at the elbows*" under "**Elbow" Bonus**.

Drag your heels (v. phr.): See "*drag your feet*" under **FEET**.

Head over heels (expression): See under **HEAD**.

On/at/ your heels (prep. phr.): Directly behind, immediately following

The dog is always at his master's heels.

How do you feel about the fact that the other two golfers are right there on your heels and will be closing in on you tomorrow? Will it affect your game? Make you nervous?

Usage note: "*Hot*", "*hard*", "*close*" may be added to intensify the idea.

On/at/ the heels of (prep. phr.): Immediately following

On the heels of the hurricane, there was a snowstorm.

The movie stars' quiet wedding came on the heels of their previous high-profile relationships with their former partners.

Usage notes:

1. It has the same meaning as "*on your heels*", but is used to describe events or things.
2. You can add either "*hot", "hard"* or *"close"* to intensify the idea.

Kick up your heels (v. phr.): To celebrate, have a good time

The guest of honor was kicking up his heels and singing songs after the state banquet.

We finally finished the project. Let's go out and kick up our heels.

Origin: The irony of this expression is that it used to mean "to die". The modern sense probably alludes to the action of high spirited horses and /or exuberant dancers. (Ammer, Christine 1997)

Set back/knock back/ on your heels (v. phr.): To give an unpleasant surprise; to shock; stop or turn back your progress

John had been bragging about how good a player he was, so it set him back on his heels when his coach told him he wasn't that good.

Sally was doing so well in school until the flu knocked her back on her heels.

Origin: It comes from a graphic image of someone being pushed back.

Show your heels/ show a clean pair of heels (v. phr.): To move rapidly; make a fast getaway

I wanted to ask her out but she showed her heels before I had a chance.

Origin: The backs of the heels are exactly what is seen when a person (or an animal) is running away. The "*clean*" probably is meant that "they are unencumbered by a pursuer" (Rogers, James 1985).

Usage note: Another term used is "*take to your heels*":

The robbers took to their heels before the police showed up.

Turn on your heel (v. phr.): To turn around suddenly and sharply

I tried to ask him how his mother was doing, but he simply turned on his heel and walked away.

Origin: It alludes to making a sharp about-face similar to military step but usually implies a sudden departure. (Ammer, Christine 1997)

"Heels" Bonus

A heel (n.): Slang. A dishonorable person

I'm glad she stopped dating Ted; he was really a heel.

Usage note: Also, "*a cad*", "*a lout*" and "*a rat*"

She has round heels. (expression): American slang. She's easy. (promiscuous; a loose woman sexually)
www.rootsweb.com/~genepool/amerispeak/traits.htm

HIPS

In Their Words:

"One moment on the lips... forever on the hips."
Author Unknown

"A husband is a guy who tells you when you've got on too much lipstick and helps you with your girdle when your hips stick."
Ogden Nash (1902-1971)
American poet

There's a body part "hip" and there's slang "hip"; the latter has many meanings, sometimes with subtle differences of meaning:

1. Aware of what's going on concerning tastes and attitudes
   She looked quite hip in her new retro style dress.

2. Comprehending, on top of it
   He was hip to what was happening within the State Democratic Party.

There's also another usage of "hip" (approval) as in *"hip, hip hooray!" (hurray)* - an expression called out often by a group of people at the same time to express approval of someone:

Hip, hip, hooray! Let's hear it for Nancy, who hasn't had a smoke for three whole months!

The expressions discussed below are the body part "hip".

Joined at the hip (expression): Always together, or doing the same thing, thinking alike

Whenever I see Lucy, I also see Rosie. They're always together, like they were joined at the hip.

Shoot from the hip (v. phr.): To act or speak quickly and without thinking, to be startlingly direct or behave impulsively

He'd never make it as a diplomat. He always shoots from the hip.

We should tell Lisa that her dress is inappropriate to wear to the funeral. But don't let John tell her. He shoots from the hip and will surely offend her.

To be honest, I wasn't that thrilled about what I said either. I did shoot from the hip too much at the meeting.

Origin: The term probably alludes to the notion that when a person draws the gun from the holster (attached to the hip) and shoots, he usually doesn't spend as much time aiming at the target like he would do if he were to use a rifle over his shoulder.

Usage note: The term implies someone who doesn't know how to be tactful in his/her approach to others; often used in the negative sense.

"Hips" Bonus

Hip huggers (n. phr.): Tight fitting pants; the waistline sits at the hip level

Smite them hip and thigh (old expression): To attack your foes unmercifully, defeat utterly

Avoid conflict and trouble; but when you are attacked, smite them hip and thigh.

Origin: The phrase is from the Bible, relating what Samson does to the Philistines: And he *smote them hip and thigh* with a great slaughter. (Rogers, James 1985)

Usage note: Very rarely used

JAW

In Their Words:

"Wrigley was the first man to discover that American jaws must wag, so why not give them something to wag against?"

Will Rogers (1879-1935)
American actor, author, humorist,

(Note: Wrigley is the most well-known name in the chewing industry.)

"Relieving tension is closing the eyes and relaxing the jaw. Do not form a picture."

Author Unknown

"Jaw" is the lower part of your face that moves when you open your mouth *(a broken jaw; he has a square jaw.)*. It can also mean either of the two bones in your mouth that holds your teeth, the upper jaw and the lower jaw.

"Jaws" is the mouth of a person or a large, fierce animal.

Flap/bat/beat/ wag/ your jaw (v. phr.): To talk non-stop, talk a lot

Quit flapping your jaw! (Be quiet!)

Usage notes:

1. Used in the negative sense, same as *"flap your gums"*; see under **MISCELLANEOUS.**
2. Also, *"a jaw flapper"*:

   What did those jaw flappers on TV say about the new tax law?

Make your jaw drop (expression): To surprise or impress you

The last scene in this film will make your jaw drop.

Usage note: Also used in its adjective form "*jaw-dropping*":

She has worked so hard to go from being just a "looker" to being

recognized as a real actress, with jaw-dropping performances in such films as "The Burning Bed" and "Extremities".

Your jaw drops (open) (expression): Informal. Your mouth falls wide open with surprise or shock, or when you are greatly impressed

I'm shocked! My jaw dropped!

My jaw dropped the second I saw him. He's absolutely gorgeous!

Usage note: Variant: *"Your jaw drops a mile."*

"Jaw" Bonus

Glass jaw (n. phr.): A boxer's tendency to succumb to a hit to the chin

Jawbone/jaw (v. phr.): Slang. To apply pressure

Don't jawbone me! There's no way I'll do that.

Jawbreaker (n.): Informal. A word or name that is difficult to pronounce

Usage note: It's also the name of the very hard, long lasting candy.

Jaws of death (n. phr.): Something dangerous

"My idea of walking into jaws of death is marrying some woman who has lost three husbands."

Kin Hubbard (1868-1930)
American humorist, writer

Jaws of Life (n. phr.): A trademark for a large pneumatic tool used to save people that are trapped in a wrecked car

The firefighters, using the Jaws of Life, snatched the little girl from the jaws of death.

KNEES

In Their Words:

"The real glory is being knocked to your knees and then coming back. That's real glory. That's the essence of it."
Vince Lombardi (1913-1970)
American football coach

"I saw this on a sign outside of a church, "God answers knee mail."
www.pioneerthinking.com

Bring someone/something/ to his/her/its/ knees (v. phr.): To defeat, humiliate, or ruin them utterly; to reduce to a position of submission

The pain can <u>bring even the heartiest person to their knees.</u>

The tsunami <u>has brought Thailand's economy to its knees.</u>

Origin: The term probably comes from the notion that when an opponent is losing in a fight, he would fall to his knees to beg for mercy that the fight should end and he be spared. Or if he has been hit hard enough, he would fall to his knees from the blow itself.

Get/go/ weak at the knees (v. phr.): To be overcome by emotion

A lot of women probably would <u>get weak at the knees</u> if they saw a good-looking guy like Tom Cruise.

Usage note: I've seen it used both ways: *"weak <u>at</u> the knees"* and *"weak <u>in</u> the knees"*; the latter is probably the American version.

Knee-jerk reaction (n. phr.): A reaction to something in a habitual way without reflection

Getting angry when someone cuts you off in traffic is a normal <u>knee-jerk reaction;</u> but you shouldn't try to retaliate.

Knee-slapping (humor, jokes, etc) (adj.): Really enjoyable or very funny

Go see this movie for some good old-fashioned knee-slapping laughter.

Usage note: Variants: *"gut-busting", "rib-splitting" "bone- tickling"*

On bended knees (expression): Humbly, pleading

Our nonprofit group is very desperate for money; we're asking for contributions on bended knees.

Origin: It alludes to a traditional attitude of supplication

Usage notes:

1. "*Bended*", the past tense of "*bend*", survives only in this idiom. Elsewhere it has been replaced by "*bent*". (Ammer, Christine 1997)
2. Another expression with similar idea is *"hat in hand"*. See under **HANDS**.

On your knees (expression): Has a few meanings:

1. Kneeling
   My mother usually gets on her knees and prays every night before she goes to bed.

2. Exhausted
   After spending the whole morning cleaning the house, she was literally crawling on her knees.

3. Begging
   There were people down on their knees begging not to be sent back to their country, as they knew they would be killed, jailed or tortured.

Take down at the knees (v. phr.): To be severely punished

My dad took me down at the knees for lying to them about my grades.

Origin: From the criminal method of punishing someone by shooting or crushing their kneecaps

"Knees" Bonus

At your mother's knees (old expression): Said of truths, lessons that were first learned or heard when you were very young

Be the bee's knees (old expression): Something/someone/ that is outstanding or the best in the class; terrific, excellent

Everybody agreed that my sister's diamond earrings were just the bee's knees.

He was voted the best citizen of the year. Now he thinks he's the bee's knees.

Origin: In the 1920's, it was fashionable to use nonsense terms for excellence; some other examples are *"the snake's hips", "the monkey's eyebrows"* and *"the gnat's elbows."*

Usage notes:

1. Often used sarcastically about a person, suggesting that he/she has an inflated opinion of him/herself
   Also, *"He/she thinks he/she's God's gift to mankind."*
2. I was told that this term is rarely used nowadays.

Knee baby (n. phr.): Southern U.S. Next to the youngest child in the family

Knock knees (n. phr.): A medical condition when a person walks or runs with his/her knees very close together, or even touching when walking. The opposite is *"bow legs"*.

Housemaid's knee (n. phr.): Swelling of the fluid-filled sac (that acts as cushion between tendons, bone and skin) in the knee due to trauma or excessive kneeling on a hard or raised surface for long periods. Also known as *"roofer's knee"* or *"carpet layer's knee"*.

Knee high to a grasshopper (old expression): Very young

He's grown so much! He was just knee high to a grasshopper not long ago.

Walk on their knees (expression): Implying habitual and continuous prayer

KNUCKLES

In Their Words:

"In our workaday world, I would compare humor with the runner's second wind or the socket wrench that allow you to tighten up without breaking your knuckles."

Author Unknown

"Even a gentleman may use bare (or brass) knuckles when he is being hit below the belt."

Author Unknown

Get your knuckles rapped/rap someone's knuckles (v. phr.): To be punished/to reprimand, scold

Son, don't talk back to me, or you'll get your knuckles rapped!

The teacher rapped Paul's knuckles for copying someone else's homework.

"Remember this: They that will not be counseled cannot be helped. If you do not hear Reason, she will rap your knuckles."

Benjamin Franklin (1706-1790)
American author, public servant

Origin: From the old school punishment of rapping the knuckles of a child with a ruler

Knuckle down (v. phr.): To address seriously the business at hand

Summer is over. You have to knuckle down now that school has started.

Time to knuckle down to work! You've been talking too much.

Origin: From the *Morris Dictionary of Word and Phrase Origins* by William and Mary Morris (Harper Collins), quoted in www.phrases.org.uk/blletin_board/1/messages/2098.

There are two theories:

The first is that the knuckles once meant any bone joint, including those of the spine. Thus, *"to knuckle down"* meant "to put one's back into the job, to work as hard as one could".

The other theory is taken from the game of marbles. A boy can play marbles fairly casually, but when he is keenly contesting a match, he *"knuckles down"* with his fist to the earth to direct his shot better.

Knuckle under (to someone/something) (v. phr.): To acknowledge defeat or another's mastery

The New York Yankees knuckled under to the Boston Red Sox in the baseball World Series opener.

They don't want the President to knuckle under to the demands and the pressure from the big financial contributors.

No one could reasonably expect him to knuckle under.

Origin: The saying might have gone back to the late 17th tavern habits of knocking the underside of the table when beaten in an argument; they put their knuckles under (www.briggs13.fsnet.co.uk/idiomslist.htm).

Another theory is that at one time the end of a bone at any joint, such as the knee, was called a knuckle. When one went to one's knees, one was knuckling; hence bending the knees in respect or submission. This theory seems to be cited more than the first one.

Near the knuckle (adj. phr.): Borderline on the indecent or obscene

The star-studded ceremony is renowned for its unpredictable nature, unbleeped expletives and near the knuckle comments.

On stage, the comedian's material is spellbinding. It's usually about sex and sometimes can be a little near the knuckle.

Origin: When carving a joint of meat one may get 'near the knuckle' (i.e. the bone) and be unable to cut any further, thus a remark that is near the knuckle is one close to the borderline of propriety.

Usage note: Possibly British; used in the same sense as *"near the bone"*

"Knuckles" Bonus

A knuckle dragger (n. phr.): A caveman mentality, a stupid brute; someone who resembles a caveman in attitude

A knucklehead (n.): Someone who does not think

What a knucklehead! She keeps making the same mistake over and over again.

Brass knuckles (n. phr.): Small, heavy, hard weapons into which the fingers fit so that a thrown punch causes much damage

Give someone a knuckle sandwich (expression): To give someone a punch in the mouth

Usage note: An aging term that is still used, often in a light-hearted way

White knuckle (n. phr., adj. phr.): Something that's tense, fast, exciting, frightening

This TV show is a real white knuckle; you may want to reinforce the arms of easy chairs and couches so they can withstand vigorous gripping.

What a white-knuckle ride! I wouldn't want to do it again.

LEGS

In Their Words:

" Coward: One who, in a perilous emergency, thinks with his legs."
Ambrose Pierce (1842-1914)
American Journalist

"Darling, the legs aren't so beautiful; I just know what to do with them."
Marlene Dietrich (1901-1992)
German-born American actress

A leg man (n. phr.): Someone who performs messenger services

He worked as a leg man for a law firm while going to college.

Origin: In the old days this kind of work (collecting information) involved the legs, i.e. lots of walking and traveling.

Usage notes:
1. I've seen it used both ways: *"a leg-man", "a leg man".*
2. When used as a slang term, *"a leg man"* means a man who judges women by their legs or who is sexually aroused by women's legs. There are also *"an ass man"* and *"a boob man".*

A leg up (on someone/something) (n. phr.): An advantage, a good start

Several employers said that older workers' high literacy rates gave them a leg up on their younger counterparts in acquiring computer skills.

He had a leg up on the field due to his years of training.

"Sometimes you have to put your foot down to get a leg up."
Pierre Jean de Beranger (1874-1936)
French lyrical poet

Origin: The phrase comes from the act of an equestrian receiving help mounting a horse. The helper would create a foothold by cupping the hands to heft the rider upward, throwing a leg up and over the horse.

Usage note: A very common expression

Break a leg! (expression): A wish for good luck; to do well

I hope you do well on the speech. Break a leg!

We wish all nominees a lot of luck. Break a leg!

Origin: This expression originated in the theater and is steeped in superstition. It was once believed that spirits or ghosts enjoyed wrecking havoc and causing trouble. Wishing an actor good luck would 'tempt the gods' and cause bad luck, so negative expressions were substituted - sort of medieval reverse psychology.

In French, one says *Merde! ("Shit!")* when an actor is about to go on stage. In German, it's *Hals und Beinbruch! ("Neck and leg fracture!")*. The leading theory is that the English expression came from German, via Yiddish.

(Mark Israel, alt-usage-english.org/excerpts/fxbreaka)

Get your sea legs (v. phr.): To adjust to a new situation

I know people are still somewhat concerned about the candidate's slippage in Aug., but I think he's now getting his sea legs back.

Origin: The phrase dates back to the days when sailing ships ruled the high seas. A new sailor was said to have 'gotten his sea legs' when he could walk steadily across the deck of a ship in stormy weather.

Give/find/ the (new) legs (v. phr.): To give new life

Smart marketing can give a product new legs.

After having been rejected in the lower courts, the case found new legs in the U.S. Supreme Court.

Have a hollow leg (v. phr.): To be able to drink or eat excessively without visible repercussions

I can't believe he can drink that much coffee. He must have a hollow leg.

Her friend told her that when it comes to food, she has a hollow leg.

Usage note: I was told that this is an old expression; I still hear people use it from time to time.

Have a leg to stand on (v. phr.): To have support for your assertion, have facts to support your claims

How could you accuse me of stealing your money? You don't have a leg to stand on.

He doesn't have a leg to stand on as far as his excuses for not finishing his job goes.

"A rumor without a leg to stand on will get around some other way."
John Tudor

Legwork (n.): Difficult aspects of a project that are time and labor-consuming

My secretary usually does all the legwork for the proposal and I just fine tune the language.

On its/his/her/ last legs (expression): In a very bad condition, very tired or old, at the end of your career

My car is on its last legs. I need to replace it or get it repaired soon.

After bad performances the last few seasons, any sports fan can tell the quarterback is on his last legs of his pro career.

Pull someone's leg (v. phr.): To try to make someone believe something which is not true, especially as a joke; to play a trick on someone

John is a perennial trickster, always trying to pull someone's leg.

I want to ask you something and I want a straight, honest answer, no pulling my leg.

"You're pulling my leg!" (You're not serious, are you?)

Origin: It alludes to the practices of street thieves tripping their victims as a prelude to robbing them, either with their foot or with a cane or the like. To "pull someone's leg" thus meant to trick, disorient and confuse a person, a meaning which lives on today in the "just kidding" sense.

The original belief was the phrase referred to pulling the legs of someone being hanged to speed up the process. This theory has now been discounted (www.word-detective.com).

Usage notes:

1. If you suspect that someone is trying to play a joke on you, you can say, "*Pull the other one (leg)! It's got (brass) bells on.*" It's a way of telling them that you don't believe them; that you know what they're up to.
2. The 'leg-pulling' expression in other languages:
   Spanish – "*You're taking my hair!*"
   French – *"You're treating yourself to my head!"*
   German – *"You want to take me in your arm!*
   (http://everything2.com/?node-id=1297932)

   Also, in Russian, *"You put noodles over my ears!"*

Put your tail between your legs (v. phr.): To run away in defeat or fear; retreat quickly

I think they should break up the team. They started falling apart as early as the second quarter. They put their heads down and their tails between their legs.

Origin: This is an allusion to the way a dog behaves when it is cowed – it puts its tail between its legs showing submission.

Puts on his pants one leg at a time, he (expression): He's human, like everybody else.

Come on! If he can do it, you can do it too. He's not a superhuman; he just puts on his pants one leg at a time, like the rest of us.

Origin: This is a 20th century expression. The "pants" is an abbreviation of "pantaloons."

People wore "trousers" before they came to be known as "pants."

Shake a leg (v. phr.): To hurry up

<u>Shake a leg</u>! You're going to be late for work.

They're waiting for us in the car. Let's <u>shake a leg.</u>

Origin: The phrase is derived from an old navy saying to *"show a leg"*. When ships were put in port, the crew would be restricted to the ship to avoid desertion. Their wives, however, were allowed to join them aboard ship. When the petty officer came through the compartments rousing the men in the morning, a woman could avoid being dumped out of the hammock by "showing a leg" making it known that the occupant was female and not required to turn in for work. The phrase has somehow been twisted from *"show a leg"* to *"shake a leg"*.

Usage note: Usually used as an order.

"Legs" Bonus

Bow legs (n. phr.): A condition in which the legs curve out to leave a gap between the knees after the period of infancy has passed

Crooked as a dog's hind leg (expression): Dishonest (when referencing a character trait) (www.rootsweb.com/~genepool/amerispeak/traits.htm)

Dog leg (n. phr.): A sharp angle or bend as in a road or a golf fairway

Fresh legs (expression): Sports term. New players or players who have been rested

He's busier than a one-legged man at/in/ an ass-kickin' (butt-kickin') contest. (expression): He's extremely busy; he's a workaholic (www.rootsweb.com/~genepool/amerispeak).

Usage note: Perhaps there are several meanings to this expression. My editor, James Oliver, pointed out that he has always heard this expression used as a description of futility, for example:

He had about as much chance of going out with that movie star as a one-legged man in an ass-kicking contest.

Leg (n.): A stage of a journey or course, air flight pattern, etc.

In the second leg of the relay she dropped the baton and her team was eliminated.

Leggy (adj.): Long legs

The colt looked like he was built for speed. He was tall, well muscled, and leggy.

My leg just went to sleep. (expression): My leg went numb.

Usage note: Also, *"to have pins and needles in your legs"*- used to describe uncomfortable sensation in your leg often when it is waking up.

Stretch your legs (v. phr.): To go for a walk, especially after a lengthy period of sitting

After sitting in front of the computer the whole morning, I felt the need to get up and go stretch my legs for a while.

(To be) a blackleg (expression): British. A derogatory term for someone who declines to join a strike; someone who is considered to be out of step with opinions held by his/her peer group

LIPS

In Their Words:

"Oh how sweet it is to hear one's own convictions from another's lips."
Frank Gifford (1930-)
American football player, sports commentator

"Smile – It's the second best thing you can do with your lips."
Author Unknown

Like the tongue and the mouth, the lips get mentioned quite often in the Bible - *"to shoot out the lips"* (Psalms 22:7), *"perverse lips"* (Proverbs 4:12), *"uncircumcised lips"* (Exodus 6:12,3), *"feigned lips"* (Psalms 17:1), *"lying lips"* (Psalms 3:18), *"righteous lips"* (Proverbs 16:13), to name just a few. (www.searchgodsword.org. The International Standard Bible Encyclopedia)

Here, we'll deal with the more 'worldly' kind of *"lips"* expressions.

Bite your lips (v. phr.): To force yourself to remain silent, not to reveal your feelings

It's not easy to bite one's lips and remain silent in the face of a slanderous attack.

I had to bite my lips when I heard my boss give the wrong orders.

Usage note: Similar idea to *"to bite your tongue"*; see under **TONGUE**.

Button your lip (v. phr.): To keep your mouth shut, be quiet so that you don't give away a secret or say mean things about others or talk when it's not appropriate

Why don't you button your lip? You're always squawking about something. You've got more static than a radio.

The spokesperson for the company was ordered by his director to button his lip when it came to dealing with the media.

Usage notes:

1. Often used as an order
2. I've seen it used in the singular form.
3. Other slang expressions with the same meaning are *"zip your lip"*, *"zip it"*, *"put a zipper on it"* (a picture of a closed zipper on one's mouth), *"put a lid on it"* (a picture of a jar with its lid closed).

Famous use: There were two U.S. slogans during World War II using this expression. One was *"Button your lip! Loose talk can cost lives."* (with a cartoon character of a U.S. soldier with buttons on his lips; the image promotes vigilance.) The other slogan said *"Somebody blabbered.....don't talk about ship movements!...don't talk about war production. Button your lip!"*

Curl your lip (v. phr.): To show scorn or despise

That rich kid is so arrogant. He never wants to join in and play with other kids, always standing alone curling his lip.

The editor curled up one corner of his lip when he saw an article written by someone who didn't bother to learn how to spell.

From your lips to God's ears (expression): I hope what you've just said comes true.

"I'm pretty sure your new business plan will succeed."
"From your lips to God's ears!"

My cousin made a comment that he hoped it snowed while we were in Colorado. From his lips to God's ears, within 10 hours, the whole city was blanketed in 12 plus inches of snow!

Keep a stiff upper lip (v. phr.): To bear trouble without emotions, to keep brave and maintain one's composure

British men, especially the upper class, are taught to keep a stiff upper lip and show no emotion.

Even though the candidate and his advisors attempted to keep a stiff upper lip, the slew of losses weighed down a campaign that had once seemed unstoppable.

Origin: According to James Rogers (1985), this saying arises from the fact that a prelude to crying is a trembling of the upper lip; the advice is to keep it firm and not to weep.

Keep a tight lip (v. phr.): To stay silent

As a Special Operations Force soldier, he has to keep a tight lip; not being able to talk about the specifics of his two missions in Afghanistan.

I'll keep a tight lip on those other issues until I've done some private digging of my own.

Usage notes:

1. Also used as an adj. *"tight-lipped"*:

   The police refused to comment on the report that the actor may have been killed over the locket. The district attorney's office was tight-lipped too.

2. Another expression used is *"mum's the word"* meaning "let's keep quiet about this". (*"mum"* comes from the sound when one's lips are closed):

   I don't want him to know about the present until Christmas. Mum's the word!

   I've also seen it used the following way:

   The Presidential candidate has been mum about whom he wants to be in his cabinet.

Lick/smack/ your lips (v. phr.): To show eagerness or zeal for something, to look forward to it

She couldn't help licking her lips when she saw that piece of chocolate cake, even though she was pretty full

Lip service (n. phr.): All talk, no action

Our veterans' sacrifice deserves more than lip service. They require and deserve the medical care and benefits they have earned through their noble

service to our country.

Origin: The original meaning has more of an emphasis on the difference between the lips (superficial) and the heart (deep felt).
From Matthew 15: 7-8: You hypocrites! Isaiah was right when he prophesied about you: "These people honor me with their lips, but their hearts are far from me."

Usage note: Often used in the expression *"pay lip service"* or *"give lip service"* meaning "to agree or obey only in speech and not by action".

Every presidential season, Republicans pay lip service to the idea of reaching out to black voters. Then, after the election, these voters are forgotten.

He's just giving you lip service; nothing will be done about it.

Loose lips (n. phr.): Careless talk; tendency to gossip and not able to keep secrets

Loose lips can easily ruin another's reputation or introduce mistrust into a relationship.

If you have loose lips, your words will eventually return to haunt you.

Usage note: This term is often associated with another expression *"loose lips sink ships"*; which is discussed next.

Loose lips sink ships. (expression): Safety and well being of others (or yourself) depends on you keeping quiet.

Some view "loose lips sink ships" campaign as part of an overall White House policy to stop all leaks about everything, not just the war in Iraq.

If you've been arrested, do not talk to the police without an attorney present. If you talked to them, you were likely to blurt something out that could potentially harm your cause. As they say, "loose lips sink ships". Keep quiet.

Origin: The saying was an US slogan during World War II to warn the soldiers to be cautious about discussions that might jeopardize the security of the country and fighting forces overseas. Because so many civilians volunteered and were drafted during the war, the U.S. government was afraid they wouldn't know how to conduct themselves and would inadvertently disclose information. As a result, rules of conduct that included ten prohibited subjects were given to each soldier. They were warned that *"loose talk is direct delivery to the enemy"* and *"your lips must remain sealed."*. One poster actually read *"Loose lips sink ships"*. (www.WiseOldSayings.com)

My lips are sealed. (expression): I can't or won't tell you (with the implication that the person has pledged himself/herself to secrecy)

I'm sorry, but I can't tell you who she is. My lips are sealed.

Don't worry, my lips are sealed. I won't tell the boss you were late again.

Famous use: When it was rumored that King Edward VIII of England would abdicate so that he could marry Mrs. Wallis Simpson and the Prime Minister Stanley Baldwin was asked about the situation, he responded, *"My lips are sealed."*

Usage note: A creatively modified (or exploited, depending on how you want to look at it) expression, but probably not yet become institutionalized, is *"my lips are zipped"*.

On everyone's lips (expression): Being talked about by a lot of people

The question on everyone's lips is when interest rates will start to rise.

This is the year the name of this band will be on everyone's lips.

Read my lips! (expression): A command, ordering someone to listen carefully

Read my lips! No more commitments.

Why would I lie to you? I'm telling the truth. Read my lips!

Origin: It comes from *"to lip read"* by deaf people.

Famous use: George H.W. Bush (1924 -), the 41st U.S. President (1989-1993) said in his acceptance speech (as the Republican Presidential nominee) at the Republican National Convention:

"The Congress will push me to raise taxes, and I'll say no, and

they'll push, and I'll say no, and they'll push again. And all I can say to them is <u>*read my lips:*</u> *No New Taxes"*

After he became President, he raised taxes anyway.

Usage notes:

1. This expression is often said very slow (i.e. you really enunciate the words.) to emphasize your point (and probably also to give time for the listener to follow what you're trying to tell him/her).
2. In some contexts, this can be a rather impolite, or rude way of telling somebody to listen to you. It may not be appropriate in many situations. In other circumstances, it's a colorful way to emphasize the speaker's point.

There's many a slip between the cup and the lip. (expression):
Between the time we decide to do something and the time we do it, things often go wrong; don't be so sure that the plan is going to work because anything can go wrong at anytime.

Many of us want to lose weight and get fit, but <u>*there's many a slip between the cup and the lip.*</u>

There are a lot of things that get said, but don't always come to fruition in this game. <u>*There's many a slip between the cup and the lip.*</u>

Origin: The story is that Ancaeus, a son of Neptune, had a beautiful vineyard and was harsh with the slaves who worked it. Once an overworked slave predicted that Ancaeus would never get to taste the wine produced that year. When the first juice was pressed from the grapes, Ancaeus poured out a cup of wine for himself and called for the slave in order to demonstrate the prophecy was wrong. As Ancaeus raised the cup to his lips, the slave said, "There's many a slip between cup and lip." Just then another slave came running in with the news that a wild boar was destroying the vineyard. Ancaeus dropped the cup, raced to the scene and lost his life when attacked by the boar (Rogers, James 1985).

Usage note: Also, *"There's many a slip 'twixt (the) cup and (the) lip."*

"Lips" Bonus

A fat lip (n. phr.): A hit on the lip, an injured lip

The comic's wisecracks pay him millions now; but in high school they often gave him a fat lip.

Cleft lip (n. phr.): A birth defect that occurs when the upper lip doesn't join in the middle, leaving one or more vertical openings that may extend up to the nose

Usage note: It is sometimes called *"hare-lip"* (because a hare's lip is similarly cleft) or *"hair lip"* (misspelling of *"hare-lip"*) (en.wikipedia.org/wiki/Hare-lip)

Does a chicken have lips? (expression): Sarcasm. Stating the obvious, a kind of "duh!" statement

Lip (n.): Back talk, impudent talk, rude talk

I don't want any more of your lip. Knock it off!

Lip lock (n. phr.): Slang. A term for kissing

Lip sync (v. phr.): To pretend to be singing a song

The Louisville Lip (expression): A name given to the young Cassius Marcellus Clay, born in Louisville, Kentucky, who later changed his name to Muhammad Ali; it refers to his early style of braggadocio, swagger, cockiness—often creating clever, humorous poems about his opponents.

Thunder lips (n. phr.): One who will try to prove a point by talking or shouting the loudest

MIND

In Their Words:

"Little minds still are little, even when they are made professors."
Author Unknown

"Great minds discuss ideas. Average minds discuss events. Small minds discuss people."
Author Unknown

Mind is the part of a person that enables one to think, feel emotions and be aware of things:

I'm not clear in my mind about what I want to do yet.
Of course I'm telling the truth -why do you always have a suspicious mind?

It can also mean a person of great mental ability, a very clever person:

I've always heard Yale has some of the best minds in the country.
I think this writer is the greatest mind of all time.

Be at/in/the back of your mind (v. phr.): To not consciously or immediately think of (something); to be in the remote part of your mind

That idea was at the back of my mind all the time.

Being close to her aging parents has always been in the back of her mind.

Be of two minds (v. phr.): To be undecided between two alternatives

I'm of two minds about this new job. I like it because it's closer to home. Yet, I don't like it because the pay is not good enough.

It's so hard to come to a final decision. I'm still of two minds.

Usage note: The British would say *"be in two minds"*.
(http://dictionary.cambridge.org)

Bear/keep/ in mind (v. phr.): To remember

Bear in mind that I can't work as fast as you do.

Keep your constituents in mind when you give a speech tomorrow.

Blow your mind (v. phr.): To surprise or impress you in a very strong way

The concert was amazing; it blew my mind.

That one observation just blew my mind. It changed my entire perspective on the subject!

I was thinking about buying my dad a Cadillac. That really would blow his mind away.

Usage notes:

1. The adjective is *"mind-blowing"* meaning, "extremely impressive or surprising."
2. Also, *"a mind-blower"*:

   Nowadays, guys no longer always pick up the tab when they go out on dates. This has been a mind-blower for me. When I was growing up, guys always paid. Girls never did.

3. *"Blow your mind"* is also a common expression for drug use. In the days of the *Grateful Dead* (a rock band), the *Dead Heads* (the followers of the band) were known to 'blow their minds' (i.e. they took a lot of drugs).

Boggle your mind (v. phr.): To bewilder, astonish or confuse you with complexity, novelty, or the like

The fact that scientists now believe that there are clusters of galaxies evenly spaced throughout the universe, 500 million light years apart, boggles my mind.

"Strangely enough," said the comedian, " I've actually been making a living at telling jokes. This still boggles my mind."

Usage note: The adj. "*mind-boggling*" means "extremely surprising and difficult to understand or imagine":

That's quite a mind-boggling victory.

Understanding the nuts and bolts of the caucuses in the American political system can be a little mind-boggling.

Change your mind (v. phr.): To form a new opinion about something that is different from your old one

It's not easy for him to change his mind; it takes guts to admit it also.

Usage notes:
1. Compare: "*(have) a change of heart*" under **HEART**.
2. Also, *"to change someone's mind"*

Come to (your) mind (v. phr.): To cause to be remembered; to be remembered

When I hear Dr Martin Luther King's name, the first thing that comes to my mind is the sound of his voice in his "I Have a Dream" speech.

The poll asked an "open-ended question," meaning respondents were allowed to offer any names that came to mind.

Usage note: Also, *"pop into your mind/head"*, *"bring to mind"*, *"enter your mind"*, *"spring to mind"* ; the first two are the more common ones.

Cross your mind (v. phr.): To suddenly think of (something), to suddenly realize something

Has it ever crossed your mind that maybe you shouldn't have said it?

It never crossed my mind that Larry would be playing in college and of course, not the Super Bowl, not with his size and ability back in school.

Usage note: Also, *"pass through your mind"*, although I think *"cross your mind"* is more common.

Do you mind? (expression): Said to someone when you feel annoyed with them for what they have just done or said

<u>Do you mind?</u> We're having a serious conversation right now.

<u>Do you mind?</u> The newspaper you're reading is mine.

Usage note: The expression *"Do you mind if………?"* is used to ask permission:

<u>Do you mind if</u> I smoke?

Ease your mind (v. phr.): To make you feel better

If you think it will help <u>ease your mind,</u> go ahead and do it.

Usage note: See also *"set your mind at ease/at rest"*.

Frame of mind (n. phr.): Mental or emotional attitude or mood

Many writers say they are at their best when they are in turmoil or pain; but I feel I write better when I am in a good <u>frame of mind.</u>

Usage note: A similar way of saying is *"state of mind"*.

Give someone a piece of your mind (v. phr.): To criticize someone strongly and angrily

If my mother-in-law tries to humiliate me in public again, I'm going to <u>give her a piece of my mind.</u>

I'm going to <u>give him a piece of my mind.</u> How dare he trash me to everyone like that?

Go out of your mind (v. phr.): To lose your sanity, lose your mental stability, become insane, often used as a humorous exaggeration

I think I'm <u>going out of my mind</u> trying to get this book finished on time.

Usage note: Similar to "*lose your mind*"

Have a good mind to do something (v. phr.): To be strongly inclined to do something, often because something has annoyed you

I've got a good mind to go by myself if he's going to take his time like that.

I have a good mind to call the parents and complain about their son's bad behavior at school.

She's got a good mind to drop that guy!

Usage note: Also, *"to have a mind to"* if less certain
And *"to have half a mind"*

Have a mind/memory/ like a sieve (expression): To be very forgetful

I have a mind like a sieve. I forget everything.

Usage notes:

1. A sieve is a utensil of wire mesh or closely perforated metal, used for straining, sifting or pureeing. If your mind is like a sieve, it wouldn't be able to hold on to anything, i.e. you wouldn't remember anything.
2. This is an older expression but is still in use.
3. The idiom *"to be absent-minded"* is more common.

Have a mind like a steel trap (expression): To have a very quick and understanding mind; to have a mind that is quick to catch an idea.

She may be old, but she still has a mind like a steel trap.

He was very well read and had a mind like a steel trap, but he never made people around him feel inferior.

Origin: The term likens the snapping action that shuts an animal trap to a quick mental grasp (Ammer, Christine 1997).

Have a mind of its/his/her/ own (expression): Has two meanings:

1. Used humorously-- said of a machine or other object that seems to be controlling the way it behaves or moves independently of the person using it.

The phone has a mind of its own. *It hangs up by itself when it wants to.*

I can't guarantee the cake is going to come out good. I have an oven with a mind of its own *when it comes to holding a consistent temperature.*

2. Said of a person-- it means the same as *"know his/her/ own mind"*:

   I have a mind of my own *when it comes to writing this book. I know who my audience is, what I want to put in the book and how I want it to come out.*

   He knows his own mind. *He knows exactly what he's going to be doing in the next five years.*

Have/keep/ an open mind (v. phr.): To wait until you know all the facts before forming an opinion or making a judgment

Don't rush to a conclusion yet. Keep an open mind!

Usage notes:

1. Also, *"with an open mind"*:

   If I were you, I would go into that relationship with an open mind.

2. The adj. *"open-minded"* can be used to describe something as well as someone:

   You need to learn to be more open-minded.

   I think Dear Abby's responses are usually fairly open-minded.

3. The opposite is *"narrow-minded", "with a narrow-mind"*; and the extreme: *"closed-minded", "with a closed mind"*

Have (a) one-track mind (v. phr.): To have a tendency to think about only one subject or one thing

Sex, sex, sex! Is that all you can think about? You have such a one-track mind!

He has had a one-track mind *ever since he decided to win that chili cook-off*

competition.

Origin: The term came from the times when railroads had only a single track for trains.

Usage note: It is often associated with (talking about) sex, but you can use it for other things as well.

(Have) something in mind (v. phr.): To have a plan or intention

I didn't start exercising with weight loss in mind. As I become active and am exercising on a daily basis, it's going to come off any way.

Do you have anything in mind for your sister's birthday present?

Have something on your mind (v. phr.): To be worried about something

This is not a good time to talk to him; he's got a lot on his mind right now.

I can't seem to concentrate on work today. I just have too many things on my mind.

Usage note: Don't get it mixed up with *"to be on someone's mind"* meaning, to be on someone's thoughts:

I think of him all the time; he was especially on my mind that day.

If you don't mind me saying (so) (expression): Used as a polite way to begin a criticism

If you don't mind me saying, I think your chicken stir-fried dish was a little too bland this time. Usually it's real tasty.

In your mind's eye (expression): See under **EYES**.

It keeps my mind busy. (expression): It helps me mentally.

I enjoy writing. It keeps my mind busy.

Usage note: Variants: *"It keeps my mind going.", "It keeps my mind occupied."* and "*It keeps me going.*"

Lose your mind/ lose your reason (v. phr.): To become mentally ill, or to start behaving in a foolish or strange way; to become overwhelmed

Don't be so hard on your mother. She's 85 years old; she's starting to lose her mind.

I thought my sister had lost her mind when she said she was going on a safari by herself.

I would be losing my mind if I had to do your job all day.

Usage note: As I understand it, this expression is often used to describe a process; one step further and you'll be *"out of your mind"*. In many cases, however, people tend to use *"lose your mind"* and *"out of your mind"* interchangeably.

Make up your mind (v. phr.): To decide

We finally made up our minds to buy that house.

Usage note: Also often used, "*Your mind is made up.*"

Mind-set (n.): A fixed mental attitude that predominates a person's responses to and interpretations of situations

There is a mind-set out there that in the future only the computer literate will have jobs. I don't buy it, though. We are going to need plumbers and teachers and doctors and dentists.

When it comes to classical music, he has a negative mind-set; he thinks it's boring.

Usage note: See also "*to set your mind (on something)*"

Mind your p's and q's (old expression): To be on your best behavior, mind your manners

The article offers a few tips on how to mind your p's and q's in the workplace.

Origin: No one has been able to pinpoint the exact origin of this expression. The following are some of the explanations advanced in various places:

1. Advice to a child learning penmanship and spelling to be careful not to mix up the handwritten lowercase letters p and q.
2. Similar advice to a printer's apprentice—in the early days of printing, typesetters had to be careful not to mix up the blocks they used to print letters, particularly the p's and q's, which look quite similar.
3. A bar term—in the pub, bartenders would keep a "tab" on the amount of pints ("p") and quarts ("q") consumed by their patrons. "Minding your p's and q's" was a way to keep track of how much money was owed and also a way to keep some drinkers from over-indulging.
4. An abbreviation of "mind your please's and thank you's". (http://expert.about.com/q/1474/3207509.htm) (www.worldwidewords.org/articles/psandqs.htm)

No doubt in my mind (adj. phr.): Without doubt, no question about it

We will win. There's no doubt in my mind that we will win.

As soon as I saw him, my heart skipped a beat. There's no doubt in my mind that what I felt that day was truly love at first sight.

Not in his/her/ right mind (expression): Signifying extreme stupidity or bad judgment

No one in their right mind would go skiing in the snowstorm like that.

Anyone in their right mind would not have said such a hurtful thing!

Usage note: Similar to *"out of your/his/her/ mind"*

Out of your mind/out of your head (expression): Has two meanings:

1. Unable to deal with things normally because something has made you very worried, unhappy or angry:

She was out of her mind with grief from the death of her son.

2. Extremely stupid; same as *"not in his/her/ right mind", "lose your mind":*

   He must be out of his mind spending all his paycheck on a pair of shoes!

Out of sight, out of mind (saying): (Said to emphasize that) when someone or something cannot be seen, it's easy to forget them

I moved away and soon I forgot all about him. Out of sight, out of mind, I guess.

The American servicemen and women stationed overseas may be out of sight, but they should not be out of mind.

Peace of mind (n. phr.): To have no concerns regarding a particular activity

The decision I made gave me the peace of mind I had not known for years.

Your peace of mind is guaranteed at our bank.

Put your mind to something (v. phr): To be focused

People could do whatever they put their minds to.

"How did you lose all that weight?"
"Just put my mind to it, mostly"

Put something out of your mind (v. phr.): To force yourself not to think about something

It's over; put it out of your mind!

Read someone's mind/read someone's thought (v. phr.): To know what someone is thinking without them telling you

If you didn't tell me what you wanted, how could I read your mind?

I've known her so long I can read her mind.

Usage notes:

1. I've also heard "*Do you read minds?*" -used humorously
2. And, "*a mind reader*"- often used humorously:

Waitress: "Would you like more coffee?"
Customer: "Yes, you're a mind reader!"

Set/put/ your mind at ease/at rest (v. phr.): To reassure, relieve your anxieties

"I want to set your mind at ease," said the doctor. "You'll be able to go back to work in two weeks after surgery."

Usage note: Compare: "*ease your mind*". Usually, something "*eases your mind*"; someone/ something "*sets your mind at ease*".

Set your mind on (v. phr.): To be determined to, decide to

My sister has set her mind on going back to Thailand to live once she and her husband are retired.

Usage note: Similar to "*set your eyes on*", "*set your sights on*", "*set your heart on*"

Slip your mind (v. phr.): To be overlooked or forgotten

I meant to call you yesterday, but it slipped my mind.

Speak your mind (v. phr.): To be outspoken about what you are thinking

John has a reputation for speaking his mind, so he wasn't bashful about offering his opinion on the new management.

I can't get into the details because it's in litigation, but in due time I'll speak my mind.

Stick out in your mind/your memory (v. phr.): To remember something

His name always sticks out in my mind, no matter how long it has been.

(Take) a load off your mind (expression): To be relieved to hear

It's a load off my mind to hear that my mother is doing fine after the surgery.

It was a load off my mind I didn't have to make that speech after all.

Usage note: Used when a problem that has been worrisome is resolved or dealt with

Take your mind off something (v. phr.): To stop you from thinking about a problem or pain, often by forcing you to think about other things

The good thing about going to the gym is that it takes my mind off any problems at work and any worries at home.

To be mindful of (v. phr.): To be very aware of

You've got to be mindful of the consequences of the words you use, especially when you're in public office.

The FBI has warned people to be mindful of identity theft on line.

Your mind goes blank./Your mind is a blank. (expression): Has two meanings:

1. You can't remember a particular thing or you can't remember anything.

   I tried to think of the name of that restaurant, but my mind went completely blank.

   My mind was a blank and I couldn't explain what happened before the accident.

2. You can't think of what to say.

   As soon as I got up to make a speech, my mind went blank.

   Usage note: See also *"lose your* tongue*"* under **TONGUE**.

Your mind is in the gutter. (expression): You have a dirty mind, that is, thinking only about sex.

A lot of things have sexual undertones, but not everything. And not everybody's mind is in the gutter, believe it or not.

I prefer to just think of it as any male whose mind is in the gutter would think about it.

Usage note: Also, *"get your mind out of the gutter":*

Get your mind out of the gutter! There's nothing to it; he and I are just good friends.

"Mind" Bonus

All great minds think alike. (expression): Humorous. Smart people make the same decisions.

Usage notes:

1. Often used to prove your intelligence by referring to someone else's same opinions or decisions
2. I've also heard *"Geniuses think alike":*

Geniuses think alike. It doesn't take long to come to the same conclusion.

Be of like mind (expression): Formal. To agree with one another

Don't mind him/her! (expression): Don't listen/ pay attention/ to him/her!

Meeting of the minds (expression): A group of people sharing their thoughts and opinions

Mental block (n. phr.): An inability to have a clear thought process about something, sometimes considered a consequence of repression or caused by emotional tension

I have a mental block about names. I never can seem to remember them.

She has a mental block about getting intimate with her boyfriend.

Mind over matter (n. phr.): The mind is stronger than the body –believing you can do it, using the mind's power.

When your brain controls your heart rate, it's mind over matter.

Usage note: A play on this phrase might be *"mind over mattress"* (years ago, as college students, when the final exams caused us to study all night we often invoked this mantra).

'-Minded suffix': Used to express a particular character, interest or way of thinking about things, for example, *"reformed-minded", "politically-minded"* and *"strong-minded"*

A lot of reformed-minded journalists in this country have been jailed.

Never mind that (expression): Informal. Despite the fact that

He went out and bought another car, never mind that he still owes me money!

Usage note: Compare: *"never mind"* – used to tell someone not to worry about something because it's not important

Of sound mind/of unsound mind (expression): Legal term. To be completely sane/insane

My dad is 90 years old, but he's still of sound mind and body.
(He still has a good mind.)

Play mind games (v. phr.): To manipulate a desired effect

He tried to kill her. She survived, however, and decided to take her revenge by playing mind games with him. His life has spiraled downwards since then.

To be bored, drunk, etc. out of your mind (expression): Informal. To be extremely bored, drunk, etc.

MOUTH

In Their Words:

"Lord, please put your arm around my shoulders and your hand over my mouth."

Author Unknown

" It is better to keep your mouth shut and appear stupid than to open it and remove all doubt."

Mark Twain (1835-1910)
American author and humorist

"A shut mouth catches no flies."

Miguel de Cervantes (1547-1616)
Spanish dramatist and novelist

Like most languages, English is full of proverbs and sayings warning us to watch our mouth. But where else can you find such unique and vivid expressions as "*put words in someone's mouth*", or "*take the words right out of someone's mouth*"?

A mouthful (n. phr.): Has several meanings:

1. A profound, meaningful, true statement

   When you said it is important to have honest employees, you said a mouthful.

   That is a mouthful. I know it took a lot of courage to say it.

2. A tirade, a tongue lashing

   My dad really gave me a mouthful. I didn't realize I upset him that much.

3. Humorous. A long word that's difficult to pronounce

   Your name is a real mouthful!

A smart mouth /a mouth (n. phr., n.): American. Informal. Someone who talks to other people in a way that shows a lack of respect; someone who makes sarcastic remarks

I hate to say it, but my daughter really has a smart mouth on her. She's not even a teenager yet and already she's convinced she knows everything.

Teenagers are such smart mouths; they always have a comment about something.

Usage notes:

1. Used with verb "to be" or verb "to have"
2. Also as an adj., for example: *"smart-mouthed little rascal"*

Another mouth to feed (expression): Another person in the house, especially a new baby

That's all we need, another mouth to feed!

Usage note: The use of "a mouth" to mean "a person" in this case is called "*synecdoche*"(a part of speech wherein a part of something is used as a reference for a whole). Other examples: "wheels" for "cars"; "threads" for "clothes" and "heads" for "cattle".

Bad-mouth (v. phr): To say unkind, unflattering, embarrassing (and probably untrue) things about someone

I never said anything bad about my ex-husband. My philosophy was he was my sons' father and I didn't want to bad-mouth their father.

Be all mouth and trousers/be all mouth and no trousers (expression): To be boastful and without just reason

Don't listen to him! He's all mouth and trousers. He promises a lot of things but never delivers.

Usage notes:

1. This is probably a British expression.
2. Judging from the 'trousers' part, this expression is probably used more by women as a put down to men who are pushy and over-confident (or at least it might have started that way).

3. Other expressions with the same idea: *"to be full of hot air", "to be all show and no go"*

Big mouth (n. phr.): An obnoxiously outspoken person; also a term of address

Be careful with John. Don't tell him anything. He's such a big mouth. As soon as you tell him something, the whole office is going to know about it.

You, big mouth you!

Born with a silver spoon in his/her/ mouth (expression): Born rich, born to wealth and comfort and/or high social standing

"Every man was not born with a silver spoon in his mouth."
Cervantes in *Don Quixote* (1615)

I wasn't born with a silver spoon in my mouth, and I don't believe in fancy cars, overpriced clothes or wasting hard earned money on material things.

Origin: It was a tradition for godparents to give spoons as a christening gift. Among the wealthy, it was usually a silver spoon (silver symbolizes riches, just as gold does). Presumably a child receiving silver spoons was from a wealthy family and would never be without money.

Usage notes:

1. Sometimes the term is used as a putdown against someone born into a wealthy family who never has to work for a living.

2. The Japanese have a similar saying:

   "He hasn't ever picked up anything heavier than chopsticks."

3. The reverse situation is described with the expression: *"born with a wooden spoon in his mouth."*
   I'm not really sure where I got this. It may not have become institutionized yet; somebody might have come up with it as a parody to *"born with a silver spoon in his/her mouth."*

Butter wouldn't melt in his/her/ mouth (expression): This phrase has two opposite meanings, depending on the context:

1. To stay calm, composed, be in control

   Most of my friends think I'm such a sunny, happy person that butter wouldn't melt in my mouth, but occasionally I do get ticked about certain things.

2. Used to refer to a cold, aloof person, or somebody who appears gentle or innocent while typically being the opposite (i.e. they are capable of doing unpleasant things)

   "When a visitor comes in, she smiles and languishes, you'd think that butter wouldn't melt in her mouth; and the minute he is gone, she flares up like a little demon and says things fit to send you wild."
   William Thackeray's *Pendennis*, quoted in The Mavens' Word of the Day
   www.randomhouse.com/wotd/index.pperl?date+20000901

   I have a problem with someone who tries to keep a 'butter wouldn't melt in his mouth' image when clearly he's as immoral as the next person.

Usage note: This expression is not altogether easy to understand, even to the native English speakers themselves sometimes (based on what has been asked/or answered about its meaning on different web sites). According to the Mavens' Word of the Day, its intended meaning, positive or not, often depends on the context. The general metaphorical sense of butter refusing to melt in the mouth suggests an aura or attitude of coolness. On the other hand, it could suggest that such a person is so cold or aloof, and has no warmth to him/herself..

Cry/talk/ poor mouth (v. phr.): To be constantly complaining about how poor you are

If you can't pay the bills for your indulgences, you shouldn't cry poor mouth and expect any handouts.

The baseball owners often cry poor mouth yet one baseball team recently was sold for a record $660 million.

Down in/at/ the mouth (adj. phr.): Sad, depressed

My teenage son has been down in the mouth since he found out that his

favorite rock band decided to go their separate ways.

Origin: It alludes to the way one looks when the corners of one's mouth are turned down in disheartenment or disappointment.

Usage note: Or, you can say "*down in the dumps*".

Foam at the mouth (v. phr.): To be furiously angry

Coming in late to class and making a loud entrance all the time is sure to make any instructor foam at the mouth.

He snarled and foamed at the mouth the minute he saw her walk through the door. I wonder what she did to make him that angry.

Origin: More than likely this term comes from animals (e.g. dogs) that are affected by rabies. Such animals may behave in an erratic or menacing way.

Keep your mouth shut (v. phr.): To stop talking, especially not to reveal a secret

My advice to you is to keep your mouth shut, mind your own business and pretend you don't know what is going on if you are in a bind.

We need to learn to keep our mouths shut sometime. Rarely will keeping quiet get us into trouble.

Usage notes:

1. The opposite would be "*open your (big) mouth*"
2. There is also an expression *"shut your mouth";* often used imperatively.

Laugh out of the other side of your mouth (expression): See *"be laughing on the other side of your face"* under **FACE.**

Leave a bad taste in your mouth (expression): To cause a bad impression, make or feel disgusted

The way he treats people leaves a bad taste in my mouth.

Last night's loss really left a bad taste in our mouth. We didn't distribute the basketball correctly. We didn't think before we shot.

Origin: The term alludes to how a person feels when he/she eats something bad, rotten, gross, etc.

Make your mouth water (v. phr.): To smell or look very good to eat

As full as I am, that piece of chocolate cake really makes my mouth water.

Just looking at the dessert list is making my mouth water.

Usage notes:

1. Also as an adj.: *"mouth-watering"*:

   What a mouth-watering piece of cake!

2. The opposite would be *"make your mouth dry"*:

   That medication will make your mouth dry.

Melt in your mouth (v. phr.): To be so tender as to seem to need no chewing; to taste very good

The turkey was so tender it melted in your mouth.

The carrot cake at this restaurant will really melt in your mouth.

Mouth off (about something) (v. phr.): To complain or express your opinions too loudly and indiscreetly

There he goes again! Mouthing off about politics while others are trying to eat in peace!

Mouth off (to/at/ someone) (v. phr.): To give someone back talk or to speak out of turn

If you mouth off one more time, I'll ground you for two weeks.

Hold it! Don't just mouth off! Wait for your turn.

Put your money where your mouth is (v. phr.): To be willing to back up what you have said with money

The National Rifle Association has, in fact, put its money where its mouth is, having trained thousands of law enforcement officials in the safe and lawful use of firearms over the years.

Americans have been clamoring for more healthful choices in restaurants. But they don't put their money where their mouth is. The McLean Deluxe was pulled because it didn't sell. Taco Bell not only scaled back its Border Lights menu, it introduced huger, richer selections, including double tacos topped with bacon and rich sauce.

Put words in someone's mouth (v. phr.): To make an unfounded claim about what someone else thinks or feels, speak for another without right

I've never said I'm against abortion. You're just putting words in my mouth.

I'm not here to put words in your mouth. You'll know what to say yourself.

Run off at your/the/ mouth (v. phr.): To talk too much, particularly in a situation where it would be better if one said little or nothing; to have "diarrhea of the mouth"

There's nothing in sports worse than a guy who runs off at his mouth and doesn't deliver when it counts.

Nobody's perfect. We sometimes carelessly run off at the mouth, but it's not a good habit to have.

"Don't let your mouth run off till your brain is in gear".
Author Unknown

Origin: The picture here is of someone who talks so much that the words flow out of his mouth like a liquid.

Shoot off your mouth (v. phr.): To express opinions that are uncalled for; to speak hastily without consideration, be too bold verbally

If you hadn't shot off your big mouth, we wouldn't be in trouble now.

No one else could get a word in with John continuously <u>*shooting off his mouth.*</u>

If she's going to keep <u>*shooting off her mouth,*</u> *I can't stop her. It doesn't make me mad. I just kind of laugh about it and move on.*

Usage note: *"Shoot off your mouth"* and *"mouth off about something"* convey similar idea, with the first one implying more of 'bragging'.

Speak /talk/ out of/from/ both sides of your mouth (v. phr.): To say things which are contradictory

We may sometimes <u>*talk out of both sides of our mouth*</u> *and end up giving mixed messages.*

What do I think of him? He's a fake, <u>*talking out of both sides of his mouth.*</u> *He even upholds opinions against his own values.*

Usage note: Compare: *"speak with (a) forked tongue"*; see under **TONGUE**.
From my observation, a lot of people use the two terms interchangeably even though they don't mean exactly the same.

Take the bread out of someone's mouth (v. phr.): To deprive someone of their very means of living

You just can't lower your employees' wages. It would be like <u>*taking the bread out of their mouth.*</u>

"That new fancy restaurant across the street is definitely going to <u>*take the bread out of our mouth,*</u>*" complained my restaurant manager.*

Take the words right out of someone's mouth (v. phr.): To say what another person was just going to say, put another's thoughts into words

I totally agree with you. You <u>*took the words right out of my mouth.*</u>

"That guy is so good looking!"
"<u>*You took the words right out of my mouth!*</u> *I was about to say the same thing.*

Out of the mouths of babes (expression): The phrase used when a child has just said something sensible; kids say the damndest things

Out of the mouths of babes comes wisdom and universal truth.

Parents can learn a tremendous amount from their children- from those 'out-of-the-mouths-of-babes' moments.

" Jesus is my friend. I can talk to him anytime and I don't even need the phone," little Michael said. Out of the mouths of babes!

Origin: The term comes from the Bible, although the meaning has changed somewhat. The original meaning is "childlike simplicity".

Psalm 8:2 *Out of the mouth of babes* and sucklings hast thou ordained strength because of thine enemies, that thou mightest still the enemy and the avenger.

Mathew 21:16 And said unto Him, Hearest thou what these say? And Jesus said unto them. Yea, have ye never read *Out of the mouth of babes* and sucklings thou hast perfect praise?

Word of mouth (n. phr.; adj. phr.): The spread of information informally, without organized advertising or publicity

Our radio station has been presenting its "adult alternative" format since 1994. The audience is loyal and word of mouth is growing.

Since premiering last weekend, the movie has had to depend almost entirely on word of mouth to pull in audiences.

I've heard through word of mouth that the food at this restaurant is good.

Asked about his popularity, the writer credited good reviews, winning the PEN/Falkner award, and a lot of word-of-mouth recommendations.

Usage notes:

1. I was told that it is used in both the positive and the negative sense. I personally have heard it used more in the positive sense.
2. Another expression often used is *"(heard it) through the grapevine"*.

"Mouth" Bonus

A blabbermouth (n): Someone who doesn't know how to keep a secret

A garbage mouth (n. phr.): One whose speech is rude, crude, and lewd—often with a lot of obscenities

Usage note: Also, *"a trash mouth"*

Hush your mouth! (expression): A more polite way of saying "shut up!"

Usage note: Also, *"hush"* and *"shhhhhhh"*

Mealy mouth (n. phr., adj. phr., v. phr.): A contemptuous term we apply to those unwilling to state facts or opinions directly

Your goal is unattainable and your mealy mouth is becoming tiresome.

These proposals are just mealy-mouth ideas that say very little, but take the maximum number of words to wind around what little they do say.

If you mealy mouth around, you're not effective.

Origin: It may have come from the German saying *"mehl im maule behaltem"* (to carry meal in the mouth, that is, not to be direct in speech)
(www.hauntedpalace.net/library/archieves/2004/11/28/408/)

Mouthpiece (n.): Has several meanings:

1. An actual part of musical instrument, telephone, etc. that is directly used by the mouth
2. A protective piece of gear used by boxers, hockey players and other athletes
3. Slang for a spokesman
4. Slang for a defense lawyer

Mouth the words (v. phr.): To utter words in a mechanical fashion without conviction and/or understanding

MUSCLES

In Their Words:

"It takes seventy-two muscles to frown, but only thirteen to smile."
Author Unknown

"We should take care not to make the intellect our god; it has, of course, powerful muscles, but no personality."
Albert Einstein (1879-1955)
German-American physicist, regarded as the greatest scientist of the 20th century

----

Flex your muscles (v. phr.): Informal. To show off your strength; to psyche yourself up

Don't worry, he's not going to sue us; he was just flexing his muscles.

Tripling the aid money to the earthquake victims would prove how generous our country could be when we flex our muscles.

Muscle (n.): The power to do difficult things or to make people behave in a certain way

The evangelical leader threatened to use his political muscle against some politicians.

This cable network has considerable financial muscle and can afford to pay top journalists.

We lack marketing muscle to compete with other big companies in the same business.

Muscle in (v. phr.): Informal. To force yourself in between two people; to force your way into a situation and make sure you are included, although you are not wanted

She muscled in to the ticket counter because she didn't want to stand in line

like other people.

The restaurant owner knew I write a food column for a local newspaper; so he tried to muscle in on my review when I was there the other night.

Is it true that she muscled in on your meeting yesterday?

Muscle in on (the act) (v. phr.): To take advantage of something that someone else started

We did all the hard work getting this business started and now they all wanted to muscle in on the act.

Not move a muscle (v. phr.): To stay completely still, not move even a little

He didn't move a muscle to help us get things ready for the party.

We were so shocked to see what happened we didn't move a muscle.

Usage notes:

1. It can imply criticism, as in the first sentence.
2. It is usually used in the negative sentences.

Pull (a) muscle(s) (v. phr.): To injure or strain (a) muscle(s) by stretching it/them too far so that it's very painful

The player pulled a muscle in his back early in the game.

I laughed so hard I pulled muscles in my face.

"Muscles" Bonus

Abs (n.): Abdominal muscles

A charley/charlie/ horse (n. phr.): A bruise in the leg or arm that is typically followed by a painful hardening or tightening of the afflicted muscles

Origin: It was originally American baseball slang, dating from about

1880's. Most sources list the origin as obscure; there are lots of theories, however.

One persistent story was that the original Charley was a lame horse of that name that pulled the roller at the White Sox ballpark in Chicago near the end of last century. Others say that it is named after Charlie "Duke" Esper, a left-handed pitcher who walked like a lame horse. Another theory is that the term comes from a lame horse owned by Charley, the groundskeeper in a Sioux City ballpark. Some other experts, however, suggest that the term revolves around Hall of Fame pitcher Charley Radbourn (1853-1897), nicknamed "Old Hoss", who suffered this problem during a game in the 1880's. (www.randomhouse.com/wotd/index.pperl?date=20001012)

A muscle man (n. phr.): Literally, a man who has a firm, toned body

Usage note: This term has several different meanings and depending on the tone of voice can imply different things. Generally it is used in a slightly derogatory sense (when referring to someone as a muscle man, you are implying that perhaps he isn't too bright, perhaps vain and superficial).

A six-pack (n.): Toned stomach muscles.

Origin: Named after a six-pack of beer because the abdominal muscles when toned and knotted to the extreme begin to resemble a six-pack when seen from above

Muscle-bound (adj.): To have your muscles hard and tight from too much exercise that you can hardly move

A good athlete must learn to train properly so as not to become muscle-bound.

Muscle memory (n. phr.): A physical skill that we have mastered so thoroughly that we no longer have to "think" to perform it, like tying our shoes or walking down the stairs (www.phrases.or.uk/bulletin/2/messages/159.htm)

NAILS

In Their Words:

"Like the fingernail and the flesh beneath."
Indonesian Proverb
(Each is dependent on the other for their mutual survival.)

"See what will happen if you don't stop biting your fingernails!"
Will Rogers, to his niece on seeing the Venus de Milo

A nail-biter (n.): A tense situation or close contest

The Hawks eliminated the Pacers in a nail-biter, 89-88.

Bite your nails/fingernails (v. phr.): To be nervous or frustrated

Everyday we see people die on the nightly news, in plane crashes, in drive-by shootings. As a result, we bite our nails on airline flights and spend millions on alarms and guns for protection against murderous strangers.

Fight tooth and nail (v. phr.): See under **TEETH**.

Hold/hang/on by your fingernails (v. phr.): To make a desperate last chance effort to keep your position/ to hang on

Our country has not been pushed out of the business of building microcomputer chips just yet. It's still holding on by its fingernails.

"Luck consists largely of hanging on by your fingernails until things start to go your way."
Aaron Allston (1960-)
Science fiction author

"Nails" Bonus

Onychophagia (n.): The habit of biting your nails

NECK

In Their Words:

"If the Creator had a purpose in equipping us with a neck, he surely meant for us to stick it out."

Arthur Koestler (1905-1983)
Hungarian-Jewish novelist, philosopher

"When you feel steamed up, remember the teakettle –it is always up to its neck in hot water and it still sings!"

Author Unknown

A millstone around your neck (expression): An intolerable burden, a heavy obligation

Like a lot of people, the high mortgage on our house is now a millstone around our neck.

I feel like I had a millstone around my neck with all these assignments from my boss.

Origin: This idiom has its root in the miller's trade. A millstone is a large, heavy, flat circular stone with a central hole, turned by the action of a water wheel at a mill. It was used to grind or crush grains. The typical millstone was four feet in diameter, ten inches thick and weighed several hundred pounds (Rogers, James1985).

A pain in the neck (n. phr.): A bother, a troublesome thing or person

Christmas shopping can be a fun thing for some people, but a pain in the neck for others.

I've learned to get along better with my mother-in-law, but I still feel she can be a pain in the neck sometimes.

Usage notes:

1. As I've mentioned elsewhere, use *"a pain in the neck"* instead of *"a pain in the butt"* or *"a pain in the ass"*, in polite company.

2. Sometimes shortened to *"a pain"*

An albatross around your neck (expression): Something you have done or are connected with that keeps causing problems and stops you from being successful

The failed real estate deal has become <u>an albatross around the realtor's neck</u>. Now he can't seem to be able to attract any investors to his newer projects.

Rare is a politician without at least <u>one albatross around his/her neck.</u> Unlike Coleridge's sailor, however, politicians carry the bird more to display their sins rather than to cleanse them.

Origin: An albatross comes from a Spanish word for 'pelican' and it is regarded as bad luck to kill one of these birds. The expression itself comes from Samuel Coleridge's1798 narrative poem *The Rime of the Ancient Mariner*. (Note: *"Rime"* is the spelling used by Coleridge; more common is "*rhyme*".) In the poem, a mariner shoots the bird, for no clear reason, thus bringing a curse upon his ship. When the ship is becalmed near the equator and runs out of water, his shipmates blame him and force him to wear the dead bird around his neck. The other sailors die from the curse; the mariner is left alone, sees a vision and offers a prayer, after which the albatross falls off his neck into the sea. The outcome is that the mariner has to walk the Earth telling people his story and what he has learned.

The figurative use of this expression was first found in the 1930's. Even though many people are now unfamiliar with the allusion, the expression is still quite common.

Be up to your neck in something (v. phr.): To be exceptionally busy or deeply involved in something, especially a troublesome situation

The senator has appeared to <u>be up to his neck in</u> assorted cover-ups.

I don't think I can afford to go on vacation this year. I'<u>m up to my neck in</u> debt.

Usage note: I've also heard "*to be neck-deep in something*".

Break your neck (expression): To try your hardest, do all you possibly can

He nearly broke his neck trying not to be late for class.

You can go to the market for me if you have time, but don't break your neck over it.

Usage note: A secondary connotation of this expression is "to proceed with reckless abandon or rushing speed", a sense that is conveyed by such terms as *"breakneck pace/speed"*, *"breakneck schedule"*:

The breakneck pace of construction is causing alarm in financial circles of this country.

Speaking during a brief pause in his breakneck schedule, the singer seemed pleased with his successful career but unruffled by all the fuss.

Breathe down someone's neck (v. phr.): To threaten by pursuing closely; to watch or monitor closely, often annoyingly

Stop breathing down my neck, will you?

Since I was laid off from work, I've got creditors breathing down my neck. I've got to file bankruptcy this year and start all over again.

Dead from the neck up (adj. phr.): Very stupid or of little intelligence

I hate to say this, but I think the guy is dead from the neck up. He has no clue what we're talking about.

Usage note: A derogatory term

Get it in the neck (v. phr.): To be severely rebuked or punished

You'd better pay what you owe him, otherwise you'd get it in the neck.

Usage note: I've also seen "*take it in the neck*".

Have someone/something/ hanging around your neck (expression): To be limited in what you can do by someone or something

I don't need to have babies hanging around my neck right now. I want to

finish college first, get a good job and do some traveling before I settle down and have a family.

Neck (v.): Old-fashioned term. To kiss and hold a person in a sexual way

I saw your boyfriend necking with some girl at the party last night.

Neck and neck (adj. phr.): Competitors who are level, each with an equal chance of winning

The race between the two candidates was neck and neck up until the Election Day.

That was quite a neck-and-neck battle between USC and UCLA.

Usage note: Variants: *"too close to call", "a horse race down to the wire"*

Save your neck (v. phr.): To save yourself from trouble or danger

When John heard that the police were coming to arrest the demonstrators, his first instinct was to save his neck and flee the scene as soon as possible.

Usage notes:
1. Same idea as "*save your skin*"
2. Also, *"save someone's neck"* (to help someone avoid being getting in trouble)

Stick your neck out (v. phr.): To risk your safety to help

I always stick my neck out for you, helping you in any way I can, but you never appreciate anything I do for you.

Origin: The term likely alludes to the chopping off the head of a chicken with an ax.

Usage note: Other alternatives:
Put your neck on the line
Go out on a limb
Put your ass on the line (bad language)

"Neck" Bonus

A leatherneck (n.): Slang. A United States Marine

Origin: The early uniform had a leather neckband.

A redneck (n.): The term comes from the South (of U.S.). It refers to anyone who works outdoors, especially in the farm field, where after a while all that sun exposure gives one a very red neck (from bending over a lot in the fields). Over the years, the term has started to imply that someone is backward, a racist or with fixed uncompromising views.

A turkey neck (n. phr.): A neck that gets wrinkles (like those of a turkey) usually as one gets older

A turtleneck (n.): A sweater with a high turned-down collar fitting tight about the neck

I'll wring your neck! (expression): Something you say when you are very angry with someone

I bet he was so aggravated he wanted to wring her neck!

NERVES

In Their Words:

"He that wrestles with us strengthens our nerves and sharpens our skill. Our antagonist is our helper."

Edmund Burke (1729-1797)
Irish statesman

"I don't like money actually, but it quiets the nerves."

Joe E. Lewis (1902-1971)
American comedian and singer

A bundle/a bag/ of nerves (n. phr.): Informal. An extremely jittery, tense, or fearful person

I hate job interviews. Every time I have one, I'm a bundle of nerves.

My mother was a bundle of nerves for months after that car accident.

Usage note: Another term that I've often heard a lot of people use is *"a nervous wreck"* (a person suffering from extreme agitation or worry):

I was a nervous wreck until the police arrived at the scene of the accident.

Get on your nerves (v. phr.): To annoy or irritate you

He got on my nerves because of his constant talking.

I know you like baseball; but you keep talking about it and it starts to get on my nerves. Can we please talk about something else?

Usage notes:

1. Another similar expression is "*drive you up a/the/ wall*"
2. In French, it would be "*to break your feet*".
3. I've also heard *"get on your last nerve"*; I was told that this is quite a new expression.

Nerve (n.): Has several meanings:

1. The rudeness to do something that you know will upset other people

   He has such a nerve! He always blames other people for things that are his fault.

   You have the nerve to lecture me about being on time when you yourself are late for work everyday?

   "The government deficit is the difference between the amount of money the government spends and the amount it has the nerve to collect."
   Sam Ewing (1920-2001)
   American writer, humorist

2. The courage or audacity to do something difficult or unpleasant

   It takes a lot of nerve to be a building demolition expert.

   It took me a long time to build up my nerve to ask her out.

   The anchorman told his friends he'd always wanted to get an ear pierced, but never had the nerve to do it because of his high-profile job.

Nerves (n.): Worry or anxiety about something that's going to happen

My brother smokes like crazy. He said it helps calm his nerves.

A lot of people suffer from nerves when they are speaking in public.

The spokesman denied that the new First Lady was facing nerves as some media reports have suggested.

Nerves of steel/nerves of iron (n. phr.): Ability to speak or act calmly when facing risk or danger

He's got nerves of steel. The bigger the magnitude of the game, the calmer he is. Nothing rattles him. He probably thrives for the big games.

These police maneuvers take nerves of steel and tons of practice.

Set/have/ your nerves on edge (v. phr.): To make you feel uptight with irritation

If the sound of the guns was not enough to set the whole neighborhood's nerves on edge, the bullet that went through my living room glass door was.

The staff at the hospital already is stressed and the prospect of war has people's nerves on edge.

Usage note: See also "*set your teeth on edge*".

Strike/touch/ a (raw) nerve (v. phr.): To raise a sensitive subject unintentionally

The team owner didn't realize how condescending he came off when talking about his players; he struck a raw nerve with a whole lot of them.

Marketing Professor Lee's resignation touched a nerve among university recruiters hoping to hire out-of-state educators to balmy and pricey Southern California.

Strong nerves (n. phr.): An ability to not be upset by unpleasant things

Everyone should see this movie, but they'll need strong nerves.

To be a leader requires strong nerves.

Some say that the poker- playing process is for people of strong nerves.

Unnerving (adj.): Something that catches you off guard, uncomfortable, disarming

The atmosphere is very, very negative. Very few people are going to make the team. I don't want to look into those faces and see people cry. It's unnerving.

War of nerves (n. phr.): A conflict marked by psychological tactics, such as intimidation and threats, that are intended to confuse, exhaust and demoralize an enemy

The lawyer claimed that his client's employer tried to use the war of nerves to

make her resign from her job.

Political campaigns can get so ugly once people from both sides start to use the war of nerves.

To many people, Anthrax terror has been more than a war of nerves.

Origin: It alludes to tactics used in World War II. (Ammer, Christine 1997)

"Nerves" Bonus

A nervous nellie (n. phr.): Informal. A timid person who lacks determination or courage

We'll win this thing if we stop being nervous nellies.

The U.S. stock market lost 46 billion dollars last month as nervous nellies withdrew their mutual funds and quit.

Usage notes:

1. It's either *"nellie"* or *"nelly"*
2. A similar expression is *"a worry wart."*

NOSE

In Their Words:

"Hard work spotlights the character of people; some turn up their sleeves, some turn up their nose, and some don't turn up at all!"
Sam Ewing (1920-2001)
American writer, humorist

"To see what is in front of one's nose needs a constant struggle."
George Orwell (1903-1950)
English novelist, essayist and critic

Our nose is one of the first things a person notices about us, due to its prominent central location.
Linguistically speaking, the nose idioms are easy to visualize; some of which, however, are not really pleasant! Consider, for example, *"it's no skin off my nose"*, *"cut off your nose to spite your face"*, *" pay through the nose"*, *"get your nose out of joint"* and *"brownnose"*

As plain as the nose on your face (expression): Very easy to see or understand, very clear

You're telling me you don't know why your girl friend is mad at you? It's as plain as the nose on your face. You forgot her birthday!

He's not happy being here – that's just as plain as the nose on your face.

Brownnose (v.): Slang term. To be excessively attentive and overly nice in an attempt to curry favor with someone

He got a promotion by buying his boss gifts, running errands, and general brownnosing.

No wonder Jane got an A in chemistry. She had been brownnosing the professor the whole semester.

Origin: This phrase is a humorous way of saying *"kissing (someone's)*

ass" or *"butt kissing"*. It alludes to ass kissing when the backside being kissed is less than clean (and that's why one could potentially get a 'brown' nose).

Usage notes:

1. Despite its rather graphic origin, I don't think it sounds as vulgar as *"kiss someone's ass"*. However, it's the kind of word that you would generally use talking about a person, and not directly to the person.
2. The person doing it is "*a brownnoser*" or *"a brownnose"*.
3. Other less offensive terms are *"to curry favor"*, *"kiss someone's feet"*, *"lick someone's boots"*, *"apple polish"*
   Also, *"to suck up"* (slang)

Can't see beyond the end of your nose (v. phr.): To be narrow-minded, mentally near-sighted; lack foresight, envisioning only immediate events or people

Sally is so selfish and self-centered she can't see beyond the end of her nose.

He never learned to save money or make plans for the future; he just couldn't see beyond the end of his nose.

Origin: From an old French proverb, "*Il ne regard plus loin que le bout de son nez.*" ("He can't see any further than the end of his nose.")

Usage note: Variable versions:
Can't see past the end of your nose
Can't see (any) further than the end of your nose
See no further than the end of your nose

Cut off your nose to spite your face (expression): To take rash or single-minded action (out of anger) that hurts your own cause in the end

By walking off the job when the job market was so bad, he cut off his nose to spite his face.

You only cut off your nose to spite your face if you stay away from the family reunion just because someone who has done you wrong will be there.

Origin: In the late 16th century, King Henry IV of France was ready to destroy Paris to punish the people who objected to him being the monarch. One of his men remarked that to do so would be like 'cutting his nose to spite his face' (i.e. a self-defeating action). The expression didn't reach the English language until the 19th century.

Usage note: Similar sayings have been popular in other languages and cultures, including the Chinese: "*Do not burn down your own house even when you're angry with your wife's mother.*" (Note: In Asian cultures, adult children sometimes stay with their parents even after they get married.)

Follow your nose (v. phr.): Has two meanings:

1. To go straight ahead, continue in the same direction; to go any way you happen to think of

   Just follow you nose, you'll see it.

   I'm not sure yet where I want to go. I think I just follow my nose and see what happens.

2. To be guided by instinct; to trust your own feelings rather than obeying rules or being influenced by others' opinions

   John had no formal business training but became a success and owned a big corporation by following his nose.

   Just take a chance, follow your nose –things may turn out right for you.

Get/put/ someone's nose out of joint/Someone's nose is out of joint. (expression): To offend or upset someone especially by taking their place as the center of attention or by getting something that they were wanting themselves; to humiliate someone's pride

His nose was really put out of joint when the new employee got a pay raise and he didn't.

My nose would not be out of joint just because my husband is a better cook than me.

Usage notes:

1. The nose doesn't really have any joint. But if your nose really were 'out of joint', it would be very painful and impossible to

ignore. Similarly, a severe case of jealousy would make your entire existence miserable (www.word-detective.com).

2. Also used as a noun:

There are more than a few noses out of joint since the advent of Benson's increased presence.

Get up someone's nose (v. phr.): Mainly British. To irritate someone, provoke hostility

If you put these two kids together in a room, they'd get up each other's nose in a hurry.

She got right up my nose with her constant whining.

Usage note: The term provides the idea along the line of *"get on someone's nerves"*.

Hard-nosed (adj.): Unyielding, unbending, very determined in achieving something

The Union representatives took a hard-nosed position during the talks for a new contract.

He's an acknowledged hard-nosed player, but has to prove he also can accept blame when necessary.

The Lakers finally got a hard-nosed victory on the home-court.

Usage note: The term usually carries a positive tone.

Have a (good) nose for something (v. phr.): To have an aptitude for doing or finding something; to be good at figuring things

A good reporter usually has a nose for a good story.

My sister has a good nose for a bargain.

I think he's got the best instincts of any junior college basketball player I've seen this year in the state. He has excellent hands and a nose for rebounding.

Origin: This expression probably alludes to the fact that certain animals, especially dogs, are very good (and even better than humans) in using their sense of scent to find things.

Have your nose in the air (v. phr.): To be snobbish

Kelly has her nose in the air now that she's married to a millionaire.

Have/keep/ your nose in a book (v. phr.): To like to read; to read intently

He was always more interested in boxing than keeping his nose in a book.

Stop reading for a few minutes, will you? You always have your nose in that book!

Usage note: Variant: *"have your head buried/stuck/ in a book"*

Hold your nose (v. phr.): To accept with reluctance or disdain

I know you don't like any of these candidates, but at least you should hold your nose and choose the least crooked one.

It's no skin off my nose. (expression): It doesn't matter to me; it makes no difference to me one way or the other.

Go ahead if you want to date my ex-husband. It's no skin off my nose.

It's no skin off my nose if he didn't take my advice.

Origin: The term may allude to a fight or boxing, in which one has scratched one's opponent while remaining unscathed oneself. Or it may derive from the admonition to keep one's nose out of another's business. If one refrains from interfering, one is unlikely to lose skin from one's nose.

Usage note: Variants: *"It's no skin off my butt/tail/behind/back/ass/teeth/ear/brow".*

Keep your nose clean (v. phr.): To avoid breaking the law, or getting into trouble

Now that you're out of jail, try to keep your nose clean.

Origin: An Americanism dating back to the late 19th century, it's a metaphorical reference to a child maintaining proper hygiene in polite company, in particular children with runny nose. (www.wordorigins.org/wordork.)

Keep/put/ your nose to the grindstone (expression): To stay diligent, work steadily, keep working on the task at hand

They definitely keep their nose to the grindstone; they look more haggard than the other campaign teams.

Talking about keeping your nose to the grindstone, my girlfriend said she would work till she dropped this summer in order to save enough money to buy a brand new car.

Origin: A grindstone is a rotating stone wheel used for sharpening, shaping or polishing. It's also another name for a "millstone" (see also *"a millstone around your neck"* under **NECK**.)

In the old mills, the fineness of the flour is determined by the separation between the two grinding stones. The most diligent millers learned to close the gap down until they could just smell the flour browning, then ease the stones apart enough to prevent burning. This required constant attention and much effort to keep the stones aligned at the optimum distance; hence the origin of the term. (www.waynesthisand that.com)

Usage note: There is a difference between "*keep your nose to the grindstone" and "put* your *shoulder to the wheel"* (see under **SHOULDERS**). The former gives the notion of steady, seemingly endless boring task while the latter implies a finite task; you set to work with vigor to get something done, especially something difficult. In practice, the two are often used interchangeably. (The Mavens' Word of the Day – www.randomhouse.com)

Lead by the nose (v. phr.): To cause another person to follow submissively

He took his girlfriend for granted and would lead her by the nose.

Origin: It probably alludes to the way we do with animals, leading by a nose ring.

Look down your nose at someone/something (v. phr.): To regard someone or something with disdain and scorn

She thinks they look down their nose at her because of her job as a waitress.

My sister only goes for real nice expensive china; that's why she looks down her nose at the plastic cups I use.

Usage note: Variant: *"look down on someone/something"*.

Nose around/about (v. phr.): To look for something kept private or secret; to pry, snoop around

The secretary was nosing around her boss' office wanting to know what was going on.

Usage notes:

1. The adj. is "*to be nosy*":

   I think she's a very nosy person with a lot of gall, always wanting to know what's going on in other people's lives.

2. Also, "*a nosy body*"

On the nose (adj. phr., adv. phr.): Very precise, exact, exactly, precisely right

His stock prediction was on the nose.

Your guess about the price of my new car was on the nose.

Origin: The term comes from radio broadcasting in the U.S. where the producer would signal to the performers that they were "on air" by touching his nose. (www.briggs13.fsnet.co.uk/book/no)

Usage note: Variants: *"on the dot"," on the money"* and *"right on"*

Pay through the nose (v. phr.): To pay too high a price for something, pay excessively, be overcharged

You have to *<u>pay through the nose</u>* *to get a house in Beverly Hills.*

Origin: As early as the 17th century, "*rhino*" was slang for "*money*". "*Rhinos*" is Greek for "*nose*". Noses bleed and someone who pays over the odds can also be said to bleed.

The other theory goes back to the days of the Danish invasion of Britain in the 9th century. The Danes imposed a tax on the Irish called the "Nose Tax". Failure to pay this tax was met with harsh punishment - the debtor has his nose slit open. (www.briggs13.fsnet.co.uk/book/no)

Usage note: Whereas "*cost an arm and a leg*" means the original price is expensive, "*pay through the nose*" implies someone is taking advantage of a specific situation and charging you more.

Powder your nose (v. phr.): A polite or humorous way of saying "to go to the toilet"

Excuse me for a minute, I need to go *<u>powder my nose.</u>*

Usage notes:

1. It's a term used by women only.
2. This is an old expression that I still hear some people use from time to time. Most people nowadays probably just say "*I need to use the restroom/bathroom.*"

Right under your nose (prep. phr.): In an obvious place, in plain view

How many times have you looked for something on your desk and couldn't find it, only to have it appear *<u>right under your nose</u>* *later? Happens all the time.*

She dated the guy for three years before she discovered he had two affairs going on *<u>right under her nose.</u>*

Usage notes:

1. Other expressions used in this sense:

"*You can't see your nose in front of your face.*"
"*If it was a snake, it would have bitten you already.*"

2. There is also an expression *"from under one's nose"* or *"out from under one's nose"*; used about something bad which happens in an obvious way but in a way that you don't notice or can't prevent:

   She stole the purses from under the saleslady's nose.

Rub someone's nose in it (v. phr.): To say or do things that make someone remember that they failed or got something wrong

My roommate failed his last course and didn't get to graduate, so just to rub his nose in it, I put my diploma up on the wall!

I know I was all wrong, but you don't have to rub my nose in it.

Origin: It alludes to the practice of housebreaking a dog by rubbing its nose in its feces when it does something wrong (Ammer, Christine 1997).

Stick/poke/your nose into something (v. phr.): To interfere in something which does not concern you

I shouldn't stick my nose into your personal life. I'm sorry.

Don't you dare stick your nose into her financial matters!

Usage note: The opposite is *"keep your nose out of something"*.

Take a nose dive (v. phr.): To go down fast, or fail miserably at something

The airplane took a nose dive into the mountain and everyone was killed.

His business took a nose dive because of the recession.

The nose knows. (expression): Phrase used to emphasize the power of the sense of smell.

Go ahead, smell the food. The nose knows what it's doing.

The dog's nose knows it all.

Thumb your nose at someone (v. phr.): To indicate extreme contempt, express scorn or ridicule by placing the thumb on the nose and wiggling the fingers

Somehow God loves the people of Israel who thumbed their noses at him again and again.

He had been thumbing his nose at the international community before we decided to invade his country.

Usage note: This gesture is also known as "giving the five-finger salute" and "cooking a snook". (www.word-detective.com)
Or, *"to give five fingers to"*

Turn up your nose at something (v. phr.): To reject something because you think it's not good enough for you

Vegetarian eating is "in" nowadays, even among teenagers. The same kids who turned up their noses at vegetables when they were younger are turning back to them in greater numbers.

Win by a nose (v. phr.): To just barely succeed or win

He came in first at the cooking contest, but I heard that he just won by a nose.

Origin: The term comes from horseracing, referring to a finish so close that only a portion of the horse's nose reached the finish ahead of the second horse.

Usage notes:

1. Notice that this expression is used with the article "a"
2. Also, "*win by a whisker*" or "*win by a hair*", which is an even narrower margin

"Nose" Bonus

A Roman nose (n. phr.): A nose with a high prominent bridge (that is higher than usual at the top)

A snub nose (n. phr.): A nose that is short and turns upwards at the end

Usage note: *"A snub nose 38"*, on the other hand, is a pistol with an extremely short barrel.

Count noses (v. phr.)/***Nose count*** (n. phr.): (To make) a count of members, attendees, or participants by noting bodily presence.

It helps to do a nose count several times during the students' field trips.

Usage note: Also, *"count heads"*

Nose candy (n. phr.): Something that smells really delicious. Also a slang term for an illegal drug that is inhaled; cocaine

Nose job (n. phr.): A slang term for plastic surgery on the nose

Nose of wax (n. phr.): A person easily influenced. The term is rarely heard nowadays. (www.word-detective.com/back-j2.html)

Nose to tail (expression): One closely behind the other

I couldn't find a place to park; there were cars nose to tail the whole street.

You're Pinocchio! (expression): You're lying!

Origin: Pinocchio is a wooden puppet – a character created by Carlo Collodi in 1881 and made into a movie by Disney in 1940. Every time Pinocchio lies, his nose gets longer.

Usage note: Because of Disney movie, the term has become very American.

PALM

In His Words:

"At 30 a man should know himself like the palm of his hand, know the exact number of his defects and qualities, know how far he can go, foretell his failures – be what he is. And, above all, accept these things."
Albert Camus (1913-1960)
French writer and philosopher

Cross someone's palm/hand/ with silver (v. phr.): To give money to someone especially for some information

I'll tell you everything I know, but first cross my palm with silver.

Origin: The phrase is often attributed to the gypsies. It alludes to the old practice of placing silver coins across a gypsy fortuneteller's hand so that he/she will tell you what will happen to you in the future.

Usage notes:

1. Today it's sometimes used in a playful way to ask for a bribe or a tip (Ammer, Christine 1997), as in the examples.
2. This could be an older expression. I've asked many American friends about it; only a few older ones knew what it means.

Grease someone's palm/hand (v. phr.): To secretly give someone money in order to persuade them to do something for you, to bribe

If you want extra service from him, you should grease his palm a little.

We might have to grease the city officials' palms to get our building permits approved.

Origin: This expression may have come from the U.S. music industry. The record producers would pay radio stations extra money to have their songs played more often, so as to help boost the sales.

Usage notes:

1. The 'money' is the 'grease' (used in the sense of "to enrich") that

helps for a smooth transaction
2. Also used, *"oil someone's palm/hand"*, but not as common
3. It's different from *"cross someone's palm with silver"* in that it can be used with any kind of service.
4. Another term used to express the same idea is *"to pay someone under the table"*.

(Have) an itchy/itching/ palm (v. phr.): To have strong desire for money, especially from bribes

The mayor is known for his itchy palm.

The man was born with an itchy palm.

Origin: The term alludes to placing the money in the palm of the hand.

Usage note: There's an old wives' tale that if the right hand itches, you will have money coming your way. If the left palm itches, you will be paying out money. This is the only version I know. There might be some other versions, however.

Have someone eating out of the palm of your hand/have someone in the palm of your hand (v. phr.): To have them trust you and do what you want them to do

When he first came to work for the company, we were suspicious of him. Now he has us eating out of the palm of his hand.

It quickly became clear that the guest lecturer did not lose his powers. Within minutes he had the listeners in the palm of his hand.

"Palm" Bonus

Sweaty palms (n. phr.): Signifying being anxious and worried

Before he went in to see his boss, he definitely had a case of sweaty palms.

SHOULDERS

In Their Words:

"You will find men who want to be carried on the shoulders of others, who think that the world owes them a living. They don't seem to see that we must all lift together and pull together."

Henry Ford (1863-1947)
American businessman

"The burden is light on the shoulder of another."

Russian Proverb

A good head on your shoulders (expression): See under **HEAD.**

A shoulder to cry on/to lean on (expression): A person to tell your troubles to

A shoulder to cry on or an ear to listen might be what we need from time to time.

I still care for her, and I'll be there if she ever needs a shoulder to lean on.

Usage notes:

1. Variants: "*someone to talk to*", "*someone to confide in*"
2. Also, "*to cry on/lean on someone's shoulder*":

   Try to avoid being insensitive to your friends' needs because you might have to turn around and lean on someone's shoulder when things get stressful for you.

Carry (the weight of) the world on your shoulders (expression): To appear to be burdened by all the problems

She seemed to be carrying the weight of world on her shoulders, being a single mother and having to raise three young kids on her own.

"Drop the idea that you are Atlas carrying the world on your shoulders. The

world would go on even without you. Don't take yourself so seriously."
Norman Vincent Peale (1898-1993)
Author of the self-help classic *The Power of Positive Thinking*

Origin: From the Greek mythology about the war between the Titans and the Olympians: After Zeus and the Olympians defeated the Titans, Atlas (a Titan) was condemned to hold up the heavens at the edge of the world, ensuring the continued separation of Sky and Earth.

Usage note: Variants: *"have all the cares of the world on your shoulders", "(have) a huge burden on your shoulders"*

Have a chip on your shoulder (v. phr.): To behave anti-socially, rudely or aggressively, to be sensitive, to feel resentful about something, especially unreasonably; to harbor a grudge

He seems to have a chip on his shoulder. He's always angry and short-tempered with people around him.

A wise friend of mine remarked, "It's difficult to walk through doorways with a chip on one's shoulder."
Bobbie Lieberman

Origin: It comes from the common practice of picking a fight in the 19th century America. A boy who thought he was pretty tough would put a wood chip (something that was common during the pioneer days) on his shoulder and dare anyone to knock it off.

Usage notes:

1. This is quite a common expression. It refers to anyone who is "touchy" or takes offense easily. (Usually one feels inferior or thinks one has been treated unfairly.)
2. In Italian, somebody like that would be described as "*he/she has flies on his/her nose"*
3. Also, *"to knock the chip off someone's shoulder"*

Head and shoulders above/ahead of (adj. phr.): See under **HEAD**.

Give someone the cold shoulder/turn a cold shoulder to someone (or something) (v. phr.): To ignore, to behave in an intentionally unfriendly way

After those notorious murder charges, the former movie star has been given the cold shoulder by a lot of people who used to be his friends.

The critics loved this movie, but the moviegoers, especially in the heartland, turned a cold shoulder to it.

Origin: In the old days, guests were usually welcome with a nice meal of beautifully hot joint of roast mutton. If the visitors stayed too long, the host would switch to a cold shoulder of mutton (which was considered a less desirable cut) as a way of passing a subtle message that they should move along.

Some dismiss this as one of those colorful word-origin tales that is not true. They argue that 'the shoulder' in question was not a cut of meat, but of the 'host' who had turned one's back and shown one's shoulder in 'cold' dismissal, i.e. it refers to rude body language as the cure for a pest. (www.worddetectives.com)

Usage notes:

1. Notice the use of the article in *"give (someone) the cold shoulder"* and *"turn a cold shoulder"*. Also, one *"gets a cold shoulder"*.
2. Other expressions with the same idea are " *brush someone off*", *"shrug someone off"* or *"be as cold as the other side of the pillow"* (This last one is new to me; I'm not sure how common it is.)

Look over your shoulder (v. phr.): To look behind yourself to check things out as a precaution

Every coach is looking over his shoulder. They know they can be gone anytime.

Americans don't like to finish second in anything. When you're no.1, you're always looking over your shoulder to see who is coming up from behind. On the other hand, when you're no. 2, you spend all your time explaining to your family why you failed.

"It's a terrible thing to look over your shoulder when you are trying to lead – and find no one there."

Franklin D. Roosevelt (1882-1945)
The 32nd U.S. President of (1933-1945)

Look over someone's shoulder (v. phr.): Has two meanings:

1. To observe someone's activity

    I hate it when you look over my shoulder like that.

    "Somebody just back of you while you are fishing is as bad as someone looking over your shoulder while you write a letter to your girl."
    Ernest Hemingway (1899-1961)
    American novelist and short-story writer

    Usage note: Some people consider it to be rude to do something like that, but it depends more on the context.

2. To watch someone to scrutinize or find something wrong with them

    I can feel the pressure at my new job right away. The boss is always there looking over my shoulder.

Put your shoulder to the wheel (v. phr.): To work vigorously to get something done, especially something difficult

If only you had just put your shoulder to the wheel, you could have been half done already.

Work hard! Put your shoulder to the wheel and – with a little bit of luck - you can make it just as I did.

Origin: The image is the way you would thrust your shoulder against a wagon wheel when the going got heavy for the horse because of mud, a hill or the weight of the load.

Usage note: Compare: "*put your nose to the grindstone*". See under **NOSE**.

Round shouldered (adj. phr.): Has two meanings:

1. Literally, having shoulders that curve down and forward

    She has become noticeably round shouldered from sitting in front of a computer all the time.

    The more round- shouldered you are, the more your torso (and your chest) slumps.

2. Figuratively, having a defeated or dejected spirit or attitude

   Don't walk with a resigned, round-shouldered look on life. Your posture does tell the rest of the world how you feel –about yourself, and about others.

Shoulder the blame (v. phr.): To admit it is your fault

The quarterback is the one who should shoulder the blame for his team's big loss yesterday.

The Governor must shoulder some of the blame for the state budget stalemate.

As a child, she could charm her way out of any situation, leaving her sister to shoulder the blame for their various transgressions.

Usage notes:

1. The phrase is not limited to talking about people, for example:

   I don't think our food industry should shoulder all the blame for America's growing obesity problem.

2. Variant: *"to take the blame"*

Shoulder the load (v. phr.): To take your share of responsibility in work

I do my part in shouldering the load by cleaning the house every other week.

If they want to win the championship this year, their bigger players need to shoulder a bigger load than they do now.

Usage note: Variant: *" to pull one's weight"*

Shoulder to shoulder (adv. phr.): Side by side

In the photo, the Mayor is seen shoulder to shoulder with the President and other dignitaries.

Usage notes:

1. Sometimes it is used to mean physically side by side; other times it's a metaphor for "working with" or "sticking out for" someone:

"The friends who grew up with you deserve a special respect—the ones who stuck by you shoulder by shoulder, in a time when nothing was certain, all life lay ahead, and every road led home."
Author Unknown

2. See also *"elbow to elbow."*

Square your shoulders (v. phr.): To stand strong and ready to face adversity; to mentally prepare yourself for a task

He squared his shoulders and entered the game without showing any signs of being sick.

She knew it wasn't going to be easy, but she squared her shoulders, stepped up to the microphone and started her speech to the hostile audience.

Origin: The expression equates standing erect and raising the shoulders so as to give them a square appearance, to the situations calling for this stance.

Straight from the shoulder (expression): Frank and forthright, truthful (answer or opinion)

Carol always gives it to me straight from the shoulder.

Will you give us a straight from the shoulder opinion on the situation in the Middle East as of today?

Origin: The term comes from boxing (Rogers, James 1985).

Usage notes:
1. Another similar expression is *"to be plain spoken and to the point"*
2. Compare: *"straight from the heart"* - this one has to do more with 'your feeling' (of being sincere).

"Shoulders" Bonus

Angel on your shoulder (old expression): Someone is looking out for you.

Broad shoulders (n. phr.): This is the term we English language learners sometimes fail to use correctly. In English, one usually uses the adjective 'broad' to describe the shoulders; whereas in some other languages, such as Thai, Chinese and Portuguese, one would use "wide".

Usage notes:

1. The term *"broad shoulders"* can also be used metaphorically. When used this way it means "courage, strength, pride":

   Larry (a man with very narrow shoulders) exhibited very broad shoulders when he took on the entire I.R.S.

2. You can also use *"broad"* to describe chubby people.
3. *"Broad"* (slang) means a woman or a girl. Could it be that its origin/derivation has something to do with females being wider in the hips?

On the shoulders of the giants (expression): (One's success) was built on the work of one's predecessors.

Usage notes:

1. It's an expression of humility in genius.
2. The phrase was quite commonly used by authors and thinkers of the Middle Ages and the Renaissance. Sir Isaac Newton's reference is probably the best known today:

   "If I have seen further than others, it is by standing upon the shoulders of giants."
   His quote in a letter to a fellow English scientist and rival Robert Hooke

3. Some other related quotes:

   "A dwarf standing on the shoulders of a giant may see further than a giant himself."
   Robert Burton (1577-1640)
   English writer

   "If I have not seen as far as others, it is because giants were standing on my shoulders."
   Harold Abelson
   Professor of Computer Science at MIT, writer

SKIN

In Their Words:

"Beauty is only skin deep, and the world is full of thin-skinned people."
Richard Armour (1906-1989)
American poet

"None of us is responsible for the complexion of his skin. This fact of nature offers no clue to the character or quality of the person underneath."
Marian Anderson (1902-1993)
American musician

Beauty is only skin deep. (saying): One's real beauty comes from within; so we shouldn't judge a person by physical features.

If the adage 'beauty is only skin deep' is true, how come our culture places such priority on appearance?

I know what they say – beauty is only skin deep, but I still do care about looking good anyway.

Usage notes:

1. Another saying with similar meaning is "*You can't judge a book by its cover*".
2. The adj. *"skin-deep"* means "only on the surface, superficial, shallow; not carefully considered or strongly felt":

   Anybody can tell that her friendliness with me is only skin-deep.

Comfortable in your own skin (expression): To be comfortable with yourself

According to body language experts, in an informal setting, the President comes across well; he's really quite comfortable in his own skin.

"Why do you think that he's not comfortable in his own skin?"
"Because he changes personalities, drifting from one to another along with the crowd that he's trying to impress. He likes to change his

skin, just like a snake".

Origin: As the second example suggests, this expression probably comes from the notion that reptiles often change the color of their skin to fit their environment in order to fool predators.

Usage note: *"Being comfortable in your own skin"* is an idea that doesn't translate easily. It suggests having self-confidence, knowing yourself, your capabilities and your strength. People who are comfortable in their own skin are not self-conscious or easily hurt. Nor are they competitive or attention-grabbing.

Get under your skin (v. phr.): To irritate, to annoy

Our goal is to try to shut down the other team's line, frustrate, get under their skin, make them lose their concentration.

It irritated me so much. It really got under my skin.

Jump out of your skin (v. phr.): To jump with fright, become very scared

I almost jumped out of my skin when the gun went off. It was such a loud bang.

Save your skin (v. phr.): To save yourself from something unpleasant or dangerous

We live in a world today where everybody is looking to save his own skin.

If he wants to save his political skin, he has to address his constituents again and admit he lied under oath.

Usage note: Also, *"to save your neck"*; see under **NECK**

Skin alive (v. phr.): To punish harshly

My date's dad would skin me alive if I didn't take her home before midnight.

Don't do that or I'll skin you alive!

Usage note: This is an overstatement to make a point. ("hyperbole")

Skin and bones (n. phr.): See under **BONES**.

Thick-skinned, thick skin (adj., n. phr.): Tough, toughness

He had so many problems but he was so thick-skinned he made it through.

It takes a thick skin and a lot of patience to make it in show business.

"A thick skin is a gift from God."
Konrad Adenauer (1876-1967)
West Germany's first chancellor

Usage note: In English, this term is usually used in a positive sense – 'to be thick-skinned' is considered a good quality in a person. In some other cultures, especially Asian, the term has a completely opposite connotation: you're an insensitive person; you simply don't care how other people think and feel about what you've done.

Thin-skinned, thin skin (adj., n. phr.): Oversensitive to criticism, easily hurt

My sister is so thin-skinned it's hard to joke around with her.

He has learned to roll with the punches. If he had thinner skin, he would have never survived. The system would have gotten him.

Usage note: Certain cultures (particularly Asian) consider 'thin-skinned' a good character trait. It means you are considerate of other people's feelings.

English learners from such backgrounds, therefore, have to take this into account when they use the English *"thick-skinned"/ "thin-skinned".*

"Skin" Bonus

A skin flick (n. phr.): U.S. slang. A movie that revolves around sex and nudity

A skin flint (n. phr.): A very cheap person, a miser

A skin game (n. phr.): A crooked gambling game set up with the intent to swindle

Alligator skin (n. phr.): Skin that is very rough, coarse, bumpy and damaged

Usage note: A skin lotion company had an advertisement with the final line: 'see ya later alligator'

Red skin (n. phr.): Slang (offensive). An Indian from North America

Skin diving (n. phr.): Underwater swimming, spear-fishing, exploring often with scuba gear (self contained underwater breathing apparatus)

Skinny dip (v. phr.): To go into the ocean, lake, river, etc. in the nude

SOUL

In Their Words:

"Begin to see yourself as a soul with a body rather than a body with a soul."
Wayne Dyer (1940-)
American self-help book author

"Years may wrinkle the skin, but to give up enthusiasm wrinkles the soul."
Samuel Ullman (1840-1924)
American businessman, poet, humanitarian

Soul (spirit): Some people believe that the soul is the part of a person that continues to exist in some form after the body has died:
He suffered so much when he was alive, so let us pray that his soul is now at peace.

Soul (your essential nature): It reveals your journey through life—the pain and changes that have formed you. It also means authenticity and /or inspiration:
Many musicians, though technically proficient, lack soul.
When he played the blues we believed he had lived it; his music was pure soul.

We can also talk about the soul of a non-human:
This political party has lost its soul.

A soul (n.): A person of a stated type

She's a happy, little soul.

I'm looking for a creative soul, a passionate woman who loves to express herself.

Usage note: *"Not a soul"* means "no one":

I can walk down my street and not know a soul. Before, I spent half my time saying hello to everybody.

Bare/pour out/ your soul (v. phr.): To reveal your secret thoughts or feelings to someone

I am more or less content to make music for fun because for me it's just like recreation more than anything. I have to do it to bare my soul.

Although these female writers live in a society that worships thin, they are not afraid to bare their souls about being fat.

Usage note: Also, "*bare your heart*"

Can't call your soul your own (expression): To be so much under someone else's influence as to have lost your independence

Followers of this (religious) cult couldn't call their soul their own. They blindly followed their leader and finally committed mass suicide.

Captain of one's soul (expression): In charge of one's own destiny

Martin Luther King responded to the call of his conscience, in the face of fierce opposition and institutionalized beliefs. He was truly the captain of his own soul.

Origin: The thought (and the phrase) was made memorable in a poem by William Ernest Henley in the late 19th century. See details under *"bloody but unbowed"*.

Usage note: Other expressions with similar idea: *" be his own man", "be his own master"* or *" be at the helm of his own life"*

Feel like a lost soul (v. phr.): To feel sad and lost, feel like there's no other way out

I feel like a lost soul. Why do I attract the same type of man into my life over and over again? Why do I keep getting what I've always gotten?

Heart and soul (n. phr.): See under **HEART**.

Keep body and soul together (v. phr.): To survive, to stay alive

He barely makes enough money to keep body and soul together.

Origin: This expression alludes to the religious belief that the soul gives life to the body, which therefore cannot survive without it.

Usage note: Today it is used mainly to refer to earning a living.

Life and soul of the party (n. phr.): Someone who is energetic and witty and at the center of activity at social occasions

John is a fun-loving and outgoing person who enjoys being the life and soul of any party.

A quiet and shy girl will generally not be looking for a 'life and soul of the party' type whereas a real party girl will be most interested in a man who looks like he can really enjoy himself.

Usage note: You can also simply say "*the life of the party*", but making it "*life and soul*" does help intensify the statement.

Rest his/her/ soul / May God rest his/her/ soul. (expression): May his/her/soul rest in peace.

I remember when Joe, rest his soul, saved my sister's life when she was drowning.

"I don't want to talk ill of the dead." As an afterthought he added, "May God rest her soul."

Sell your soul (to the devil) (expression): To get what you want, you are willing to do things that are improper or immoral

The idea of selling your soul to the devil to get what you want in life goes against everything that our parents have taught us.

Origin: The expression may have been in usage earlier, but came into prominence because of Christopher Marlowe's play "*Dr Faustus*". According to the storyline, the devil offers Fautus 24 years of unlimited pleasure and power in exchange for his soul.

Soul searching (n. phr.): Searching your conscience, completely and thoroughly

She has done some serious soul-searching and come to the conclusion she couldn't live without him.

Usage notes:

1. Often used in the expression "*do (some/a lot of) soul*-searching".
2. You can also use the verb form "*to search your soul*" (or "*search your heart*"):

   I spent a lot of time searching my soul, trying to decide whether I was guilty of anything.

   The teacher searched her heart, trying to decide if she had been unfair in failing some students.

3. Also as adj. "*soul-searching*":

   That was quite a soul-searching sermon about the thoughtless ways people hurt one another.

"Soul" Bonus

Bless my soul! (expression): Used to express surprise

Usage notes:

1. It's an old-fashioned term.
2. Also, "*bless me!*" or "*well, I'm blessed!*"

Blue-eyed soul (n. phr.): The name given to those non-Blacks whose music reveals a great deal of soul

Origin: The term was coined for the duo *The Righteous Brothers* in the 1960's.

Soul food (n. phr.): The food of the Southern Black Americans

Origin: Back in the time of slavery the slave workers would cook for the plantation owners and then were given the parts and leftovers that the whites wouldn't eat (for example, ham hock and collard greens). These 'less desirable' foods became the staple of and genesis for soul food.

Nowadays it is sometimes considered trendy.

Soul of discretion (n. phr.): Someone who can keep secrets and does not say things to annoy others

"Can you trust him with this?"
"Yes, he's <u>the soul of discretion</u>." (He will not tell other people.)

Soul kiss (n. phr.): Another name for a French kiss

Soul mate (n. phr.): Someone who is a perfect match, at the soul level.

Origin: The concepts of soul mates arose from Greek Mythology: The myth was that our ancestors once had 2 heads 4 arms. They did something to offend a god; so the god punished them by splitting them down the middle, resulting in the creation of humans. As a punishment, we are condemned to spend our lives searching for the other half, our soul mate.

Soul music (n. phr.): Heartfelt music developed by American blacks combining the music of the church (Gospel) with Rhythm and Blue (R&B)

Your body and soul (expression): Your boyfriend or girlfriend. The phrase signifies complete love for that person.

SPINE

In Their Words:

"To understand others, you should get behind their eyes and walk down their spine."

Rod McKuen (1933-   )
American poet, composer, singer

"An observation about the boss: He gives accident victims new hope for recovery. He walks, talks, and performs rudimentary tasks, all without the benefit of a spine."
www.fortunecity.com/roswell/séance/134/jokes/oquotes.html

Send chills/a chill/ (up and) down your spine (v. phr.): To make you feel very frightened

It sends chills up any parents' spine when you use the words 'car' and 'teenager' in the same sentence.

Usage note: Also, *"make chills run up and down your spine"*, *"a chill goes down your spine"*:

"Every time Bush talks about trust, it makes chills run up and down my spine."

Bill Clinton (1946-   )
The 42nd U.S President (1992-2000)

A total chill went down my spine at the eeriness of the scene.

Send shudders/a shudder/down your spine (v. phr.): To cause you to feel extremely anxious or frightened

When I thought what might have happened at the accident, it sent shudders down my spine.

Usage note: To me, it has a similar meaning to *"send chills down your spine"*, maybe with a stronger sense. From what I've heard/seen, people tend to use *"send chills..."* more.

Shiver (up and) down your spine (n. phr.): A frightened /excited feeling

The word 'open wide' at the dentist's office usually sends shivers down my spine.

The guy has an incredible voice. Whenever I hear him sing, I feel a shiver down my spine.

Spine-chilling/spine-tingling (adj.): Alarmingly or eerily frightening

That's quite a spine-tingling horror story.

"In Africa, some of the native tribes have a custom of beating the ground with clubs and uttering spine-chilling cries. Anthropologists call this a form of primitive self-expression. In America, we call it golf."

Dave Barry (1947-)
American humorist

Spineless (adj.): Lacking determination and the willingness to take risks

We all came to the conclusion that this guy is simply a spineless person.

Usage notes:

1. Variant: *"to have no spine"* (similar to *"to have no backbone"*):

   You just let your boss walk all over you. You have no spine!

2. Also, *"to show some spine"*:

   It's time for the President to show some spine on this issue.

"Spine" Bonus

Spine (n.): Used figuratively. A central part, a vital part

These mountains form the spine of Italy.

"Vocation is the spine of life."

Friedrich Nietzsche (1844-1900)
German philosopher

STOMACH

In Their Words:

"By swallowing evil words unsaid, no one has ever harmed his stomach."
Winston Churchill (1874-1965)
Prime Minister of Great Britain during WW II

"It is an unfortunate human failing that a full pocketbook often groans more loudly than an empty stomach."
Franklin D. Roosevelt (1882-1945)
The 32nd U.S. President (1933-1945)

Stomach-related terms, like *"guts"*, are often used to describe deeply felt feelings.

Get/have/ butterflies (in your stomach) (expression): To get a nervous feeling before doing something or waiting for something to happen

Jane got butterflies in her stomach while waiting for the result of her job interview.

A lot of people have butterflies in their stomach when they have to make a speech.

Origin: The term likens a nervous feeling to that resulting from swallowing live butterflies that fly about inside your stomach. (Ammer, Christine 1997)

Usage notes:

1. Often shortened to *"get/have/ butterflies"*
2. You can also say "*to feel/experience/ the jitters*".

Get sick to your stomach/make you sick to your stomach (v. phr.): To be or feel nauseated

I always get sick to my stomach when I sit in the back of the car.

It's so ridiculous you get sick to your stomach.

The images of the dead servicemen floating on the water with certain parts of the body missing and a makeshift morgue just made you sick to your stomach.

Usage note: Used both literally and figuratively.

Have/get/a bad feeling in the pit of the stomach/feel it in the pit of your stomach (expression): You just seem to have a "bad feeling" or feel uneasy about things.

She admits that even now, when she thinks about that incident, she gets a bad feeling in the pit of her stomach.

I empathized with her plight and felt it in the pit of my stomach.

Usage notes:

1. The 'pit' is the very core, the deepest part of your stomach. This 'uncomfortable' feeling is like a knot; it could be something you've done in the past, something you wish you had done, or you just feel unsettled about how things turned out for you.
2. I did some google-search and found out this expression is quite widely used.
3. Other substitutions for "*bad*" are "*ill, sick, sinking, empty, heavy, nagging, deadening*".
4. I've also seen it used simply as "*to feel the pit in your stomach*":

   Have you ever felt the pit in your stomach that just never seems to go away?

Have a strong stomach (v. phr.): To be able to smell, taste or see unpleasant things without feeling ill or upset

You really need to have a very strong stomach to watch the surgery scenes in this movie. (similar to *"to have strong nerves"*)

Do you think you have a strong enough stomach to try this hot, spicy food?

Usage note: The opposite is *"to have a weak stomach"*.

Have no stomach for something (v. phr.): To not feel brave or determined enough to do something unpleasant

I'm not an outdoorsman in the classic sense. I like hiking and camping, but I'm not much of a fisherman and I have no stomach for hunting.

She has no stomach for quarrels. Anytime someone tries to start one, she just walks away.

Usage note: Also, *"not have the stomach for something"*

Make your stomach churn (v. phr.): To agonize you

The news was so grim it made my stomach churn.

Usage note: Its adj. form *"stomach-churning"* is very similar to *"gut-wrenching"*; see under **GUT**.

On an empty stomach (expression): Without food in your stomach

It's hard to be cheerful around the holidays on an empty stomach.

You can't start the day on an empty stomach.

On a full stomach (expression): Soon after eating a meal

It's common knowledge that one should not run or do strenuous exercise on a full stomach.

Stomach (v.): To be able to accept an unpleasant idea or watch something unpleasant; to bear or put up with

I can't stomach the idea that this guy might become my boss.

"The truth does not change according to our ability to stomach it."
Flannery O'Connor (1925-1964)
American author

The way to a man's heart is through his stomach. (saying): See under **HEART**.

Turn your stomach (v. phr.): To make you feel sick

Watching you eat that raw fish really <u>turns my stomach!</u>

There was so much blood and violence in this movie that all it did was <u>turn my stomach.</u>

Your eyes are bigger than your stomach. (expression): See under **EYES.**

"Stomach" Bonus

Lie down/sleep/ on your stomach (expression): To lie down with your face down

The doctor asked him to <u>lie down on his stomach.</u>

Usage notes:

1. The opposite is *"lie down/sleep/ on your back"*.
2. Also, *"sleep on your side"*
3. These are useful phrases for us foreign learners of English. It took me a long time, after so many years of living in the U.S. to learn how to use them right.

Your stomach is /starts/ growling (rumbling). (expression): Your stomach starts making noises when you get hungry.

SWEAT

In Their Words:

"It takes sweat to work on things, but it only takes saliva to criticize things."
Taiwanese Proverb

"No one has ever drowned in sweat."
Lou Holtz (1937-)
College football coach

Literally and figuratively, talking about 'sweat' often conjures up an image of 'hard work'. This is probably true in any culture.

Break a sweat (v. phr.): To begin to sweat or perspire

I hardly break a sweat when lifting but sweat like a sloth when performing cardio.

Break out in a cold sweat/break into a cold sweat (v. phr.): To feel terrified or nervous

She broke out in a cold sweat the minute she looked over the cliff.

Bring up the subject of downsizing and some homeowners break into a cold sweat.

Origin: It refers to perspiring accompanied by a feeling of cold, which can be induced by acute fear (Ammer, Christine 1997)

By the sweat of your brow (expression): Through your own hard work

Lee built up his business by the sweat of his brow.

I know I'll succeed, but only by the sweat of my brow.

Origin: From the Bible: it's one of the punishments God lays on Adam for eating the forbidden fruit, "*In the sweat of thy face* shall thou eat bread, till thou return unto the ground."

Usage note: Variant: "*through your own sweat*".

Don't sweat (it)! (expression): Don't worry about it!

Don't sweat! I'll take care of it.

"I wonder why the boss wants to talk to me tomorrow in his office."
"Don't sweat it!. He probably just wants to show you the new computer system we'll be using."

Don't sweat the small stuff. (expression): To try to pick a few really important things to worry about and let the rest slide; getting worked up over every little thing will only increase your stress.

Don't sweat the small stuff. Learn to enjoy life every moment one moment at a time.

"Rule Number 1 is, don't sweat the small stuff. Rule Number 2 is, it's all small stuff. And if you can't fight and you can't flee, flow."
Robert S. Elliot
World famous cardiologist

Make someone sweat (v. phr.): To make someone wait anxiously

It seemed that the police had delayed the news about our son's whereabouts just to make us sweat.

No sweat (expression): Slang. Has two meanings:

1. Easily done or handled, not very time-consuming

   This is no sweat. We'll be done in a few minutes.

2. No problem!

   "Thanks, man, for the help."
   "No sweat!"

Sweat blood (over something) (v. phr.): See under **BLOOD**.

Sweat it out (v. phr.): To endure a difficult or unpleasant situation to the end, especially to wait for a long time in nervous anticipation

I knew raising a son would be tough, but I also knew that with a little love and a little patience, we could somehow sweat it out.

She wanted to leave the party because she didn't know anybody there. But not wanting to offend the host, she sweat it out and tried to socialize with other guests the best she could.

Sweat like a pig (expression): To sweat profusely

He doesn't know much about the game itself but he heads the league in foul body odor. He's sweating like a pig on a spit roast.

Origin: This is a curious expression because pigs don't sweat – they don't have sweat glands and they have to cool themselves off by wallowing in puddles and mud.

According to Ken Greenwood at www.wordwizard.com, the idea that pigs sweat profusely could have come from the fact that they smell, with the assumed cause being 'sweat.'

Usage notes:

1. Variants: *"sweat like a horse"* (horses do sweat and they sweat a lot, especially when they're running) and *"sweat buckets"*:

   I sweat buckets and stain all my clothes. It's unappealing and gross. I have yet to find an antiperspirant that works.

2. Another expression *"sweat bullets"* - this slang term also means to sweat so much, but under a certain degree of stress:

   I sweat bullets over that job interview.

   The airlines employee who checked the 9-11 hijacking ringleader said that he was sweating bullets and that he was running late for the flight.

Work up a sweat (v. phr.): To work hard or exercise

My husband was out in the hot sun digging up weeds, really working up a sweat.

I can show you a way to earn a living without working up a sweat.

"I don't feel right unless I have a sport to play or at least a way to work up a sweat."

Hank Aaron (1934-)
Retired American pro baseball player

"Sweat" Bonus

Flop sweat (n. phr.): Theater term. Sudden, nervous perspiration; it contains fatty oils that react with the bacteria on the skin's surface, generating a sour smell (http://www.phrases.org.uk/bulletin-board/18/messages/594.html)

"I still get flop sweat before every interview," said the star.

Sweat (v.): Informal. To interrogate someone under duress to extract information

After the lineup the police put him in the interrogation room to sweat out a confession.

Sweat hog (n. phr.): The term can mean one of the following:

1. A difficult student singled out for special attention (may have come from the TV sitcom, "*Welcome Back Kotter*" in the 70's)
2. An unattractive female
3. A promiscuous female
(www.wordwizard.com)

Sweatshop (n.): A shop or factory where employees work long hours for low pay under very bad conditions

TEETH

In Their Words:

"The man with a toothache thinks everyone happy whose teeth are sound. The poverty-stricken man makes the same mistake about the rich man."
George Bernard Shaw (1856-1950)
Irish dramatist, literary critic

"Parents are the bone on which children cut their teeth."
Peter Ustinov (1921-2004)
English actor

A kick in the teeth (n. phr.): A sudden disappointment, a humiliating snub, especially at a time when you need support

It was a kick in the teeth to get fired from the job like that, after all the work I've done for them.

The home team defeat was a kick in the teeth, due to the unfair decision by the referee; at a time they desperately needed a win to be qualified to go into the playoffs.

Armed to the teeth (adj. phr.): Fully or even excessively well prepared

Most of the companies in America were armed to the teeth against the dreaded glitch of the Y2K.

By the time the trial began, the prosecutor's team was armed to the teeth.

Usage note: The phrase *"to the teeth"* means "completely, fully". It has been used as an equivalent to *"up to here"* (with hand signal indicating the neck region) for quite a long time. You can say "fed to the teeth" if you had a big meal, or if feeling really exasperated, "be fed up to the teeth". (www.word-detective.com/090699.html)

A tooth for a tooth (saying): See "*an eye for an eye*" under **EYES**.

By the skin of your teeth (expression): Just barely escape a dangerous situation; barely qualified for something

He escaped by the skin of his teeth.

I passed the driving test by the skin of my teeth.

Origin: From the Bible: Job 19:20
Jonah first used it after getting out of a big fish's belly (commonly thought of as a whale):
"My bone cleaveth to my skin and my flesh, and I am escaped *with the skin of my teeth."*

Usage note: In a sense it's closer than close because teeth don't have skin; this is a ridiculous overstatement to make a point.

Cut your teeth/eyeteeth (v. phr.): To learn as a beginner or at the start of your career, most often as a young person but not necessarily

They both started their journalism careers in New York radio, and went on to cut their journalism teeth as young TV correspondents in Vietnam.

Like a lot of business leaders of his generation, he cut his management teeth by chewing out subordinates.

Origin: The term possibly derived from how a baby's teeth seem to cut through its gums.

Usage note: See more about the definition of "eyetooth/eyeteeth" under *"give your eyetooth/eyeteeth/for."*

Fight tooth and nail (v. phr.): To fight or argue aggressively, fiercely

They fought tooth and nail over the changes in the movie script.

I will fight tooth and nail to make sure the bill gets passed.

Get out with your eyetooth (v. phr.): To escape relatively unharmed

I was lucky to get out with my eyetooth seeing what they asked for those cars.

Give your eyetooth/eyeteeth/ for (v. phr.): To be willing to give anything to have something

I would give my eyetooth for nice legs like Meg's.

Origin: The eyeteeth are the four pointed teeth next to the front teeth on either side of both jaws. They are called "eyeteeth" because they sit directly under the eyes (or because the nerves for these teeth are close to the eyes). They are also known by such other names as "canines" and "dog teeth" (especially pronounced in dogs) and "cuspids" (from a Latin word for "point"). Since non-human mammals use their eyeteeth mainly for biting and chewing food; it would be a disaster if they lost those teeth. So apply this metaphorically to humans, to give them away is a very great sacrifice indeed. (www.randonhouse.com/wotd/index.pperl?date+20010412)

Usage note: Used in the same sense as *"to give one's right arm"*

Grit your teeth (v. phr.): To prepare to endure a difficult time; to carry on, though upset, try to conceal your anger

As they say, the true test of a mature person is to be able to grit one's teeth during the most trying of moments.

He's hateful, and I've often gritted my teeth over things he has said about me. But I don't deny him the right to say it.

Origin: It alludes to the "gritting" or "grating" one's teeth that one does literally at such a moment (Rogers, James 1985).

Lie through your teeth (v. phr.): To tell very obvious lies and do not seem to be embarrassed about them

Politicians often mask their feelings and lie through their teeth.

"My car will go 150 miles an hour", he said, lying through his teeth.

Like pulling teeth (expression): Very difficult

Trying to get the foreign students to talk during the pronunciation class was like pulling teeth. They really did not want to speak.

Long in the tooth (adj. phr.): Of advanced years, past your prime, old

Your dog is awfully <u>*long in the tooth.*</u> *It's not a good idea to enter him in that dog race.*

Today, TV sitcoms often get <u>*longer in the tooth*</u> *than a walrus. Five years is usually a good run for a sitcom. The joke is usually over after that.*

"I'm too <u>*long in the tooth*</u> *to think we can make demands on life and expect that they will be granted, like waving a magic fairy wand."*

Annie Lennox (1954-)
Scottish singer

Origin: The term was originally used to describe horses. As horses age, their gum recedes, giving the impression that their teeth are longer. The longer the teeth look, the older the horses. Thus a horse ready for retirement was said to be *"long in the tooth"*.

Set your teeth on edge (v. phr.): To make you wince with irritation

My parents' endless bickering and nagging is <u>*setting my teeth on edge.*</u>

His totally self-absorbed persona with rampant overtones of paranoia can <u>*set one's teeth on edge.*</u>

Usage note: Compare: "*set your nerves on edge*"; see under **NERVES**.

Sink/get/ your teeth into something (v. phr.): To have something real or solid to think about or go to work on seriously

Now, that's an idea you can really <u>*sink your teeth into.*</u>

The book was such a good read that it was easy to <u>*sink one's teeth into.*</u>

Origin: It transfers the literal sense of enjoying a plate of food to the figurative sense of completely involving oneself into doing something.

Show/bare/your teeth (v. phr.): To show that you are capable of fighting or defending yourself

I'd <u>*show my teeth*</u> *only if my property is in danger.*

Origin: It probably alludes to the way a dog acts when it gets mad and ready to start a fight.

Take the bit between/in/ your teeth (v. phr.): To take control of a situation, push aside restraints and forge ahead

He's taking the bit between his teeth to carry out the project without delay.

Origin: The term comes from horsemanship. The bit is the metal mouthpiece on a horse's bridle that enables its rider to direct it. The horse is only sensitive to the rider's direction while the bit is in the right place in its mouth. If it takes the bit between its teeth it will no longer feel the pull of the reins and the rider loses control of it. This expression dates back to the ancient Greek, with the original meaning of obstinate self-will. Only recently has it developed the sense of determinedly setting out on a task, without negative overtones. (http://www.users.tinyonline.co.uk/gswithenbank/sayingst)

"Teeth" Bonus

Fat tooth (n. phr.): Tendency to be drawn to food with a high fat content

There's evidence that fat people have a fat tooth, not a sweet tooth. Obese people appear to prefer foods with a higher fat content, but less sweet than foods liked by thin people.

Sweet tooth (n. phr.): Tendency to like sweets, a craving for sugar.

Teeth (n.): Used in the sense of enforcing something. A law with *teeth* in it would have the power to execute said law

Usage note: The opposite is *"toothless"*.

Teething problems (n. phr.): Problems that a project has when it's starting (the same way with babies when their teeth start to come out)

All the teething problems from the first CD have been ironed out, and the music of this second album is first class.

THROAT

In Their Words:

"A good listener is not someone with nothing to say. A good listener is a good talker with a sore throat."

Katherine Whitehorn (1926-)
British writer

"If you want to cut your own throat, don't come to me for a bandage."

Margaret Thatcher (1925-)
Prime Minister of Great Britain (1979-1990)

At each other's throat (expression): In a heated argument, disputing

As friends, rivals, and in-laws, both men were as frequently at each other's throat as well as at each other's side.

They'd been at each other's throat for quite some time and felt this was the last straw.

Cut your own throat (v. phr.): To ruin your own chances for success, usually unintentionally

The candidate cut his own throat by accepting illegal contributions.

I think she cut her own throat through repeated absences.

Usage note: Same idea as "*shoot yourself in the foot*". See under **FEET**.

Cut someone's throat (v. phr.): To be the means of someone's ruin

I know his type. He would cut anybody's throat that got in his way.

"A real diplomat is one who can cut his neighbor's throat without having his neighbor notice it."

Trygve Halvdan Lie (1896-1968)
Norwegian politician, First United Nations Secretary-General

Cut one another's/each other's/ throat (v. phr.): To engage in destructive competition

Car dealerships cut one another's throat through their price war.

Usage note: It gave rise to the term "*cutthroat*":

Some voters said they were turned off by cutthroat attack ads.

After college, she encountered more cutthroat competition in the job market. It took her almost five months before she could find a job.

Get/feel/have/bring/ a lump in your throat (v. phr.): To get/feel/ a sensation of tightness in your throat usually caused by a buildup of emotion

It's hard for me to talk about my mother's death without getting a lump in my throat.

To this day, whenever that song comes on, she still feels a lump in her throat.

Some movies have the ability to bring a lump to one's throat.

Have a frog in your throat (expression): To have difficulty in speaking because your throat feels dry and you want to cough

John had a frog in his throat and had to excuse himself from the table.

Origin: The frog's name in Old English is *'frogga'* meaning 'hoarseness'. Aside from this, there are a few speculative connections between this creature and the condition (of the throat), for example, the shared sliminess of the frog and the phlegm, the sounds made by a sore throat and by frogs, and an ancient folk medicine belief of tiny frogs infecting/infesting one's throat (caused by drinking water from streams that contained their eggs). (http://platearpress.com.au.wfw/froginyo.htm)

Usage note: It is also used when someone can't think of an appropriate response:

"Got a frog in your throat?"
(Thanks to Japhet Ward for this.)

Jump down someone's throat (v. phr.): To criticize or answer someone severely and angrily, usually suddenly without warning or any good reason

The boss jumped down Jane's throat for no apparent reason.

I don't understand why he always jumps down her throat.

Usage note: Compare: "*bite someone's head off*"; see under **HEAD**.

Shove/ram/ something down someone's throat (v. phr.): To force someone to accept or consider something

I think that as soon as he gets elected President, he'll shove a tax increase down our throats.

I hate it when people try to ram their political or religious beliefs down my throat.

Loosen up! Don't try to shove your puritanical morals down other people's throats!

Stick in your throat (v. phr.): To be unable to say something; to be so offensive that you can't tolerate it

He wanted to ask for his wife's forgiveness, but the words stuck in his throat.

The obscene language in that movie really stuck in my throat.

Usage note: Variants: "*stick in your craw*"
"*stick in your gizzard*" (the place in a bird's digestive tract where food is ground up)

"Throat" Bonus

Clear your throat (v. phr.): To give a small cough to clear your voice

She cleared her throat a few times before starting her speech.

Deep throat (expression): A secret informer, especially one who reveals detailed inside information about a scandal to a journalist.

Origin: It was a nickname (suggested by Howard Simmons, managing editor of the Washington Post) given to the secret Government source who aided Washington Post reporters Bob Woodward and Carl Bernstein in exposing the Watergate scandal that led to President Nixon's resignation in their best-selling book *All the President's Men* (1974). The name was based on *Deep Throat,* a very popular pornographic film (1972).

The book was later made into a movie in 1976 starring Robert Redford as Woodward, Dustin Hoffman as Bernstein and Hal Holbrook as Deep Throat.

On May 31, 2005, the legendary source Deep Throat was identified by Vanity Fair magazine and The Washington Post as W. Mark Felt, now 91, associate FBI director in the early 1970's.

Hold/put/have/ a knife to someone's throat (expression): To give someone an ultimatum

Usage note: Also, *"to hold a gun to someone's head"*

Strep throat (n. phr.): A severe infection of the throat

Throaty voice (n. phr.): A guttural sound that can be hoarse and husky, sounding like it comes from deep in the throat

THUMBS

In Their Words:

"In the absence of any other proof, the thumb alone would convince me of God's existence."

Sir Isaac Newton (1642-1727)
English mathematician and physicist

"I always wondered why babies spend so much time sucking their thumbs. Then I tasted baby food."

Robert Orben (1927-)
American humorist, speechwriter, editor

All thumbs adj. phr.): Awkward, clumsy, having difficulty fixing things or working with your hand

My sister is all thumbs when it comes to drawing.

Today, I'm all thumbs. I dropped everything.

Usage notes:

1. The idea behind "*all thumbs*" is that if your all other fingers were to turn into thumbs, you would have quite a difficult time using your hand.
2. Variant: *"(to be) klutzy"*
3. Compare: *"butterfingers"*; see under **FINGERS**.
4. See also: *"(have) two left feet"* under **FEET**.

Green thumb (n. phr.): A natural talent for gardening

My mother is an avid gardener whose green thumb is considered by family members to be able to coax a stick to grow.

A green thumb can increase the value of your home.

Usage note: I've also seen "*green fingers*"; but "*green thumb*" seems to be more commonly used in the U.S.

Rule of thumb (n. phr.): A basic, general rule; a guideline; a rough measure

Preheating the oven is a basic rule of thumb in baking.

To prevent or cure a hangover, the rule of thumb is to drink six glasses of water for every glass of alcohol. This way, you will keep your body well hydrated.

According to many financial experts, the rule of thumb for savings is that you save ten per cent of your monthly gross income.

Origin: The "*rule of thumb*" was used for measures in many different fields, from brewing to tailoring to money changing to art. The phrase has become associated with wife-beating over more than a century. According to the English Common Law, a man had the right to beat his wife with a stick no thicker than the diameter of his thumb. Some people, especially those advocating for women's liberation/and/or feminism, have dismissed this as a myth. A more likely theory is that it stems from the ancient use of the last joint of the thumb as a measuring device for roughly an inch. There is even a word in Swedish "*tum*" (inch), which originates from the word "*tumme*" (thumb).

Stick out like a sore thumb (v. phr.): To be overly conspicuous, not fit or blend in

If you wear those jeans to the wedding reception, you'll stick out like a sore thumb.

You may think you talk "normal". Maybe normal for around here, but go to where I'm from and you'll stick out like a sore thumb!

Origin: The term refers to an injured thumb that, once bandaged, would be very noticeable. It would also be largely immoveable and would 'stick out' at an unusual angle.

Usage note: Variants: *"to stick out", "to stick out a mile".*

Thumb a ride (v. phr.): To signal with one's thumb for a ride from passing cars

Our car broke down on the highway, so we had to <u>thumb a ride</u> to the repair shop.

Usage notes:

1. The gesture used by people who want a ride while standing at a roadside is to make a fist with the thumb extended upward.
2. Variants: *" thumb a lift", " hitchhike", "hitch a ride"*

Thumb your nose at someone (v. phr.): See under **NOSE**.

Thumb through something (v. phr.): To turn the pages quickly and only read small parts of it

I haven't had a chance to read the whole report yet, but I did <u>thumb through it</u> quickly during my lunch break.

Linda wanted to cook something as a special treat for her family, so she <u>thumbed through some cookbooks</u> looking for ideas.

Thumbs down (n. phr.): An expression of rejection, refusal, or disapproval

The Union people turned <u>thumbs down</u> on our wish to postpone the meeting until tomorrow.

The boss gave our plan the <u>thumbs down</u>.

Thumbs up (n. phr.): An expression of approval

Crossing the legs has gotten a <u>thumbs up</u> from orthopedic experts who say that the posture is "physiologically valuable."

<u>Thumbs up</u> to the athletic director for hiring such a proven head basketball coach.

Origin: The phrase is attributed to the ancient Romans and the Gladiators who fought in the Coliseum. When one Gladiator emerged victorious in a fight, the spectators would get to decide if the loser should live or die. If they felt the loser had fought bravely enough, his life would be spared; otherwise he would be killed. The spectators signaled their vote with a "*thumbs up*" for life and "*thumbs down*" for death.

Usage note: To show greater approval (or greater disapproval), one would say "*two thumbs up*" (or "*two thumbs down*"). This phrase also has a corresponding gesture, using both hands:

Two thumbs up for this great movie.

Twiddle your thumbs (v. phr.): To spend time idly, do nothing

Don't just sit there twiddling your thumb! Help me clean the house!

I wish this doctor would schedule his time better. I always end up in the waiting room, twiddling my thumbs.

Origin: It alludes to the habit of idly turning one's thumbs about one another during a period of inactivity.

Usage notes:

1. This phrase can be used to convey boredom and wasted time.
2. Other phrases used to express the same idea are: *"sit on your thumb"*, *"sit on your hands"*, *"sit on your butt/ass"* and *"sit (back) on your heels"*.

Under someone's thumb (prep. phr.): Subservient to or under the control of someone

After all these years, she's still under her husband's thumb.

After his first 100 PGA Tour events as a professional, Tiger Woods had the golf world under his thumb.

Origin: According to Rogers (1985), the idea of being subservient seems to be emphasized by the "thumb" which is the controlling finger of the controlling hand.

"Thumbs" Bonus

A thumbnail sketch (n. phr.): A brief, concise account of something

Whenever you want to plan an artwork or try out an idea, make a thumbnail sketch.

TOES

In Their Words:

"Parents who are afraid to put their foot down usually have children step on their toes."

Chinese Proverb

"He who tip-toes cannot stand; he who strides cannot walk."

Jean de la Bruyere (1645 – 1696)
French philosopher

English doesn't have the names for the toes as it does for the fingers (except for "the big toe" and "the little toe").

Dip a/your/ toe (v. phr.): To begin to do something new or unfamiliar

Under financial pressure the American Movie Institute dipped a toe into marketing waters that included selling licensed T-shirts and CD ROMs.

After finally dipping her toe in the political stream, the candidate's wife looked like she was starting to enjoy it.

Origin: It alludes to the timid swimmer slowly getting into the water.

Usage note: See also *"get your feet wet"* under **FEET**.

Get /have/ a toehold (v. phr.): To loosely secure a position

As soon as he gets a toehold on how to run this place, I'll let him take over.

New York city is a magnet for immigrants; many will perhaps move elsewhere once they get a toehold in their new country.

Usage notes:

1. To *"get/have/ a foothold"*, on the other hand, means to have a more substantial position.
2. The opposite is *"to get/gain/ a firm footing"*.

Go toe-to-toe (v. phr.): To challenge aggressively, fight hard, stand up to

The players on both teams can go toe-to-toe during the game and then go off patting each other on the back.

On your toes (adj. phr.): Alert, ready to act

The big boss is here. No wonder everybody is on their toes.

"I am happy I have competition. It keeps me on my toes all the while and stops me from becoming complacent. So it works to my advantage."

Amisha Patel (1979-)
Indian actress

Usage note: Very common expression

Step on (someone's) toes (v. phr.): To offend or embarrass someone; to encroach on the feelings of someone

The shy dad stepped on the bride's toes by not participating in the traditional father-daughter dance.

"It is impossible to get anything made or accomplished without stepping on some toes; enemies are inevitable when one is a doer."

Norma Shearer (1900-1983)
American actress

Origin: This metaphoric idiom transfers physical to emotional pain.

Tiptoe around something (v. phr.): To try to avoid something

According to the government reports, many travelers entering the country are ignorant of the law about declaring quarantine produce. Others, however, clearly try to tiptoe around it.

Usage note: Variant: *"to dance around something"*

Toe the line /toe the mark (v. phr.): To adhere to rules conscientiously

John was never one to toe the corporate line. He never saw himself working

in a big law firm. That never felt comfortable to him.

If you join the army, you really have to toe the line. You can't do whatever you want like you're doing right now.

Origin: The term is probably a reference to foot-racing, where the competitors must keep their feet behind a "line" or on a "mark" at the start of a race, as in "on your mark, get set, go!" So the one who "toes" is one who does not allow his foot to stray over the line.

The term could also of military origin: soldiers are expected to put their toes on a line, and submit to the inspection.

Twinkle toes (n. phr.): A dancer; a person who dances with great skill

You should've seen the way he dances. He's a real twinkle toes.

Usage notes:

1. Used in a humorous, silly way
2. The opposite of *"two left feet"*

"Toes" Bonus

Pigeon toed (adj. phr.): Having the toes turned inward (the way a pigeon actually walks); the opposite is "splay footed"

Toe-curling (adj.): British. Making one feel extremely embarrassed and ashamed for someone else (http://dictionary.cambridge.org)

That was the worst comedy show I've ever seen – absolutely toe-curling!

Turn up your toes (v. phr.): To die.

Origin: It alludes to the position of the toes when one lies flat on one's back without moving.

Usage notes:

1. The term may be obsolete.
2. Also, *"curl up your toes and die"* and *"turn up your heels"*

TONGUE

In Their Words:

"The tongue (is) like a sharp knife. (It) kills without drawing blood."
The Buddha

"With the tongue we praise The Lord our Father, and with it we curse men, who have been made in God's likeness."
The Bible, James 3:9

There is no shortage of popular wisdom when it comes to the tongue. The Bible, sayings and proverbs from other sources are full of tongue-content: the power of the tongue, how we misuse it, how we should use it and/or refrain from using it.

A sharp tongue (n. phr.): A tendency to reply sharply or sarcastically

They claimed the candidate had a nasty temper and a sharp tongue; the combination of the two would kill him.

"A tart temper never mellows with age; and a sharp tongue is the only edged tool that grows keener with constant use."
Washington Irving (1783-1859)
American author

Usage notes:

1. Also used in the adj. form *"sharp- tongued*":

   She's as sharp- tongued as ever.

2. Unlike *"a sharp eye"*, *"a sharp wit"* and *"a sharp mind"*, *"a sharp tongue"* is usually not a good quality to have; however, it can sometimes be used in a positive sense, for example:

   He has a sharp tongue and a cutting sense of humor. He loves that back-and-forth repartee with someone – guys bantering and trading good-natured insults.

A slip of the tongue (n. phr.): A word that slips out, a spoken error/ mistake

I don't think she meant to hurt your feelings. It might have been just a slip of the tongue.

You have to watch what you say when you are questioned by the lawyer on the witness stand. One slip of the tongue can get you in big trouble!

Bite your tongue (v. phr.): Has two meanings:

1. Used as an order, meaning, "don't say that or it might happen" (often said humorously), or "shouldn't have said that"

   "I heard there's going to be a real big earthquake sometime this year."
   "Bite your tongue!"

   I started to criticize my brother-in-law and his bad temper when my mom walked in and interrupted, "Bite your tongue!"

2. To stop yourself from saying something even if you would like to say it

   I had to bite my tongue from saying how ridiculous her new hairdo looked!

Cat got your tongue? (expression): Can't talk?, why are you not talking?

Are you in shock or something? Cat got your tongue?

"What's the matter? Cat got your tongue?" John asked Susan when he noticed that she was unusually quiet.

Origin: There are many theories as to the origin of this saying. One theory is that it is used primarily when addressing a child who refuses to answer a parent's questions after some mischief.

Some sources say it can also be used to address a shy child (i.e. you are not speaking maybe because you have no tongue and can't speak. Maybe a cat caught and ate your tongue.)

Another theory is that the expression comes from the English sailing ship days. It refers to the *"cat of nine tails"*, a whip. When the captain told someone something in secrecy, if that person were to tell the others he would *"get the cat"*. If the others wanted to know what had been said they would ask "tell us, or are you afraid?" that is, *"has the cat got your tongue?* (www.phrases.org.uk/bulletinboard/)

Rogers (1985), besides referring to the *"cat-o'-nine-tails"*, also offers other explanations: the *'cat'* might be the medicinal cat (or kat), which acts on the heart and could produce temporary silence as a side effect; or it could simply be that the cat's habit of staring quietly at people suggested an analogy with the suddenly silent person.

Usage notes:

1. This is something you say to someone when you are annoyed because they will not speak. Also, it is sometimes used in a nicer sense as to ask what's wrong or why someone is not talking. It is almost always phrased as a question. The full form is *"Has the cat got your tongue?"* but often shortened to *"Cat got your tongue?"*
2. I was told that this same expression exists in Spanish, but instead of "cat", it's "rats" (or "mice") – *"Te comieron la lengua los ratones?"* ("Has your tongue been eaten by the mice?") (Contributed by Melissa Milburn and Alexandro Kerk)

Hold your tongue (v. phr.): To be or to keep silent

You'd better learn to hold your tongue if you want to keep your job here.

I don't always agree with my stepmother, but I hold my tongue.

"If it's very painful for you to criticize your friends – you're safe in doing it. But if you take the slightest pleasure in it, that's the time to hold your tongue."

Alice Duer Miller (1874-1942)
American writer, poet

Usage note: There's a difference between "*bite your tongue*" and "*hold your tongue*": the former refers to something more immediate, more specific, whereas the latter is about something in general:

I had to bite my tongue to keep from telling him what I had just heard.

I really have to learn how to hold my tongue.

Keep a civil tongue in your head (expression): To keep your speech dignified

Disagree all you want, but keep a civil tongue in your head.

Lose one's tongue (v. phr.): To lose the capacity to speak, as from shock

It's easy to lose your tongue in front of a large audience.

The groom suddenly lost his tongue when he tried to give a thank-you speech to the guests.

Usage note: Compare: "*your mind goes blank*"

Loosen someone's tongue (v. phr.): To make someone speak more freely

The police hope that the $50,000 reward will loosen someone's tongue to come forward with the information about the arson.

He learned long time ago that alcohol was the easiest way to make people loosen their tongue.

Usage note: Don't get *"loosen someone's tongue"* mixed up with *"lose one's tongue"*.

On the tip of your tongue (prep. phr.): On the verge of being recalled or expressed; to be very close to figuring out or remembering something

Oh, there's a word for that. It's right on the tip of my tongue.

I remember that girl. She used to work here a few years ago. Let'see...what's her name? It's right on the tip of my tongue.

Silver-tongued (adj.): Having a convincing and moving way of speaking, very pleasant and persuasive

You've charmed us all, you silver- tongued devil!

It's hard to resist those silver-tongued, charismatic con men.

Usage notes:

1. Used to refer to a person who can get his own way, often in regards to a man who is good with convincing women.

2. It can also be used as a noun:

He has a way with words. He can charm and cajole anyone with his silver tongue.

3. There is also the term "*silver-tongued orator* " which means an eloquent speaker.

Speak with (a) forked tongue (expression): To tell lies or say one thing and mean another

Career politicians often speak with forked tongue so that they might reach out to all.

Did these officials 'speak straight' or did they 'speak with forked tongue'?

Origin: The term alludes to snakes. They have forked tongues and are often portrayed as deceitful in stories. Then there's the Serpent in the Garden of Eden.

In the old cowboy-and-Indian westerns, there's a classic line spoken by a wise Indian chief after some horrible injustice had been done to his people by the whites: *"White man speak with forked tongue"*, meaning *"he's lying."*

The Indians even have their sign language for this expression. It uses the index and middle finger, slightly spread, forked shaped, and the hand is passed over the mouth, to indicate speaking with forked tongue.

Usage notes:

1. I've seen it used both ways – "*speak with forked tongue*" or "*speak with a forked tongue*".
2. There's a Jamaican saying: "*The devil has a serpent's tongue.*" And a Chinese saying: "*He who speaks with forked tongue doesn't need chopsticks.*"
3. There's a difference between *"speak with forked tongue"* and *"speak from both sides of the mouth"*: the key words are "to tell lies" vs. "to say things that are contradictory". It seems to me, however, that people often use them interchangeably.

Tongue in cheek (n. phr., adj. phr., adv. phr.): Teasing while pretending to be serious; in a joking manner; characterized by whimsical exaggeration or irony

The jokes were done for fun and tongue in cheek.

This movie is a tongue-in-cheek story about marrying into money.

The movie producer described himself tongue-in-cheek as "an overnight sensation after 18 years."

Origin: The term probably comes from the way you might put your tongue in your cheek, as you might wink, to show that you are not being serious.

Tongue-lashing (n.): A verbal scolding

Because of his poor performance, the basketball star got a tongue- lashing and benching from his coach.

She gave him a good tongue-lashing for being late.

Usage note: Or, "*to give someone a dressing down*"

Tongue-tied (adj.): Having difficulty expressing yourself because you are nervous

He got tongue-tied when he asked her to the dance.

Tongue twisters (n. phr.): Sentences or phrases that are (sometimes intended to be) difficult to say, especially when repeated quickly and often

'She sells sea shells by the seashore' is a popular tongue twister; most American kids are taught how to say it in school.

According to this website, the most difficult tongue-twister is 'the sixth sick sheik's sixth sheep's sick.'

Tongues wag (v. phr.): People speak in a gossipy manner

If a married woman has too many male friends, tongues will wag.

When the clerk showed up for work in a brand new BMW, tongues wagged.

Usage notes:

1. A few interesting quotes on 'tongue wagging':

"If the tongue wags long enough, it will say something evil sooner or later."

Author Unknown

"The reason a dog has so many friends is that he wags his tail instead of his tongue."

Author Unknown

2. *"Quit wagging your tongue!"* is an American expression meaning "stop talking!" It can be rude, depending on the contexts.

"Tongue" Bonus

Mother tongue (n. phr.): The first language that you learn

Roll off the tongue (v. phr.): To be easy to pronounce

Wow!, what a name! It doesn't exactly roll off the tongue.

Usage notes:

1. Also, *"to get your tongue (around)"*, often used in negatives or with a negative meaning:

   Some TV news people can't even get their tongue around the names of foreign places.

2. See also *"a jawbreaker"* (under **"Jaw" Bonus)** and *"a mouthful"* (under **MOUTH**).

Speak in tongues (expression): The phenomenon of spontaneously speaking in a form of speech not recognizable to anyone, practiced in certain denominations of fundamentalist Christianity

Take the clothespin off your tongue! (expression): American. Someone once said this to me, trying to get me to talk. I found out later that it's an old expression - something parents might use with their (young) children.

MISCELLANEOUS

In His Words:

"Take up one idea. Make that one idea your life-think of it, dream of it, live on idea. Let the brain, muscles, nerves, every part of your body, be full of that idea, and just leave every other idea alone. This is the way to success."
Swami Vivekananda (1863-1902)
Indian spiritual leader of the Hindu religion

The list is by no means complete.

A kick in the shins (n. phr.): An insult; a set back

For the candidate, it was a sharp kick in the shins by the people in Iowa.

NASA got yet another hard kick in the shins from the Columbia space shuttle disaster. What a sad flashback from the Challenger disaster a decade ago!

Origin: You literally give someone such "a kick" when you're trying to show your anger at (or disapproval of) someone's actions or words. It can be quite chastening and humiliating for the person who receives it, though. Such an idea provides the basis for its figurative meaning.

A slap on the wrist (n. phr.): A mild rebuke

A sentence of 50 hours community service given to the state attorney for failing to file annual sales tax return was a mere slap on the wrist.

Usage note: Contrast: *"a slap on the face"*. See under **FACE**.

At the top of your lungs (adv. phr.): As loud as you possibly can

Don't you hate it when you're in a movie theater and someone talks on their cell phone at the top of their lungs?

Battle of the bulge (n. phr.): The constant struggle to keep slim

According to these findings, the battle of the bulge affects almost every aspect of a woman's life.

Origin: A bulge means a curved shape sticking out from the surface of something. This battle to lose the bulge (i.e. to lose weight) is the play on the original Battle of the Bulge that occurred in 1944 when German forces broke through Allied lines into Belgium, forming a "bulge" in the defending lines.

Be at your wits' end (v. phr.): To be very worried and upset because you've tried every possible way to solve a problem but can't do it

I've tried everything to make my baby eat but nothing seems to work; I'm at my wits' end.

Bosom buddy (n. phr.): An extremely close friend

Origin: From the Bible --Saint John is portrayed as the bosom friend of Jesus.

Usage note: Variants: *"bosom pals", "close pals"* or *" the best of friends"*

Bowler's wrist (n. phr.): A condition or problem one develops in your wrist, usually from such sports as bowling or tennis

Don't get your bowels in an uproar! (old expression): Calm down!

Usage note: Similar to *"don't get your panties in a knot!"* or *"don't get your knickers in a twist!*

Don't pop a vein! (expression): American. Calm down! Don't get so angry! (Thanks to Gloria Gomez for this.)

Flap your gums (v. phr.): To keep talking nonstop

Instead of just flapping his gums, the Mayor should actually do something for his city.

Usage notes:

1. It's usually used in the negative sense.
2. Same as *"flap your jaw"*; see under **JAW.**
3. The person who does it is "*a gum flapper*":

Follow in someone's footsteps (v. phr.): To follow the same activity or career that someone else has done

Why don't you follow in my mother's footsteps and become a lawyer?

Go out of your skull (v. phr.): To be overcome with emotions, become nervous, excited

The crowd went out of their skulls when the actor grabbed the mike and started to sing.

Usage note: Also, *"to be bored out of your skull":*

Being forced to sit in a stuffy room, the kids were bored out of their skulls.

Have a good/healthy/ pair of lungs (expression): Something you say when a baby cries loudly

Usage note: I was told that it's more commonly used as slang to refer to a woman's breasts.

Highbrow (adj., n.): A person who has superior intellectual or cultural interests and tastes
Lowbrow (adj., n.): A person with little interests in matters of intellect or culture
Middlebrow (adj., n.): A person of conventional tastes and interests (www.randomhouse.com/wotd/index.pperl?date+20000425)

Shakespeare's audience consisted of a wide variety of people of all intellectual levels –highbrows, lowbrows, and in between brows. When he wrote, he might have intended to be understood by all of them.

The reviewer showed an admirable job of treating highbrow, lowbrow and middlebrow films on their merits.

Origin: The term *"highbrow"* came into the language about 100 years ago. It refers to a high brow, or forehead, leaving plenty of room for a large brain. *"Lowbrow"* might have come in later to be contrasted to *"highbrow"*. *"Middlebrow"* is the latest of the three terms.

Usage notes:

1. In American context, *"highbrow"* could sometimes be used derogatory or humorously.
2. "*Nobrows*", the newest term of them all, are people who have made (intelligent) compromises with commercial culture/pop culture subjects; for them, commercial culture is a source of status. (www.kcet.org/lifeandtimes/archieves/200003/2000315.php)

Lily-livered (adj.): Used to describe a coward or weakling

Some lawmakers were lily-livered not to stand up to the President's rush to war.

We're taking a lily-livered attitude to the whole matter of enforcement of the laws.

Origin: The liver was believed to be the seat of human passions. A liver that was 'as white as a lily' lacked real blood, which is synonymous with courage, making 'lily-livered', a synonym for weak and cowardly

Liver spots (n. phr.): Brown large freckles on the back of the hands and on the arm and face, often associated with aging or sun exposure.

Usage note: Also known as "age spots", "brown spots" or "sun spots"

Love handles n. phr.): Extra flesh around your waist

Though I walk daily, I've developed some pretty noticeable love handles.

Origin: The name comes from the fact that this extra fat sometimes forms 'handles' or 'grips' that a lover could grab or hold onto.

Usage notes:

1. Also known as *"spare tire"* (n. phr., usually singular).
2. The opposite is "*to have a six-pack*"-to have a firm, toned abdominal muscles (referring to the six ribs, three rows on each side). Used for both men and women:

   I've never had a six-pack. I never wanted one, to be honest; it seems like too much hard work.

   She almost fainted with delight when she saw his six-pack.

Make a clean breast of something (v. phr.): To make a full confession

He decided to go to the police and made a clean breast of his involvement in the bank robbery.

Middle-age spread (n. phr.): Tendency to gain weight and lose you ideal figure as you get older

Want to avoid middle-age spread? Keep the pounds at bay? Eat your fruits and veggies.

Over my dead body (!) (expression): Informal. There's no way I'll allow you to do that, to let that happen

"I want to marry your daughter."
"Over my dead body!"

Over my dead body will they make me go back there!

Usage notes:

1. Used when you resist or oppose something strongly
3. Sometimes used humorously

Raise eyebrows (v. phr.): To show disapproval or surprise

The assemblyman's proposal to legalize prostitution raised eyebrows from his constituents.

Whenever one does something radically different, it raises eyebrows.

Risk life and limb (v. phr.): To risk death or serious injury

A firefighter must be willing to risk life and limb on the job.

You would risk life and limb if you went white-water rafting in a rainstorm.

Skeleton in the closet/in the cupboard (n. phr.): A shameful and shocking secret that people try to keep hidden

He's not telling us everything. I bet he has a skeleton or two in the closet.

Smooth as a baby's bottom (expression): Very smooth

Stick to your ribs/stick to (by) the ribs (v. phr.): Informal. To keep you from getting hungry again too quickly

My mother used to cook us a real hearty stew with a lot of meat and potatoes and heavy sauce. It stuck to our ribs the whole day.

Usage note: It is often used to convey the idea that you're enjoying what you're eating –it's filling and/or nourishing food.

Vent your spleen (v. phr.): To air your anger or opinion

Many people think that Town Hall meetings are a good place for them to vent their spleen.

I never can understand why some people feel free to vent their spleen and their deepest secrets to total strangers.

Origin: The term alludes to the fact that the spleen was once thought to be the source of the hot temper; so by venting (used in the sense of "airing") the spleen you would be letting loose your anger.

Usage note: You can just say *"(I needed) to vent."*

SOURCES CONSULTED

The sources I've used are often cited throughout the book. The following are the ones I've relied heavily on:

Ammer, Christine. *The American Heritage Dictionary of Idioms.* Houghton Mifflin Company 1997

Fairbanks, George. *Ass Idioms.* www.groupedia.com/node/view

http://dictionary.cambridge.org

Rogers, James. *The Dictionary of Clichés.* New York: Wings Books, 1985

INDEX

ARMS

"Arms" Bonus

ASS

"Ass" Bonus

BACK

"Back" Bonus

BELLY

"Belly" Bonus

BLOOD

"Blood" Bonus

BONES

"Bones" Bonus

BRAIN

"Brain " Bonus

BREATH

"Breath" Bonus

BUTT (& CO.)

"Butt" Bonus

CHEEKS

"Cheeks" Bonus

CHEST

CHIN

"Chin" Bonus

EARS

"Ears" Bonus

ELBOWS

"Elbows" Bonus

EYES

"Eyes" Bonus

FACE

"Face" Bonus

FEET

"Feet" Bonus

FINGERS

"Fingers" Bonus

FISTS

"Fists" Bonus

FLESH

"Flesh" Bonus

GUT

"Gut" Bonus

HAIR

"Hair" Bonus

HANDS

"Hands" Bonus

HEAD

"Head" Bonus

HEART

"Heart" Bonus

HEELS

"Heels" Bonus

HIPS

LEGS

"Legs" Bonus

LIPS

"Lips" Bonus

MIND

"Mind" Bonus

MOUTH

"Neck" Bonus

NERVES

"Nerves" Bonus

NOSE

"Nose" Bonus

PALM

"Palm" Bonus

SHOULDERS

"Shoulders" Bonus

SKIN

"Skin" Bonus

SOUL

"Soul" Bonus

SPINE

"Spine" Bonus

STOMACH

"Stomach" Bonus

SWEAT

"Sweat" Bonus

TEETH

"Teeth" Bonus

THROAT

"Throat" Bonus

THUMBS

"Thumbs" Bonus

TOES

"Toes" Bonus

TONGUE

"Tongue" Bonus

MISCELLANEOUS